PRAISE FOR
THE PURPOSEFUL GROWTH REVOLUTION

"Mark Mears is the perfect champion for *The Purposeful Growth Revolution*. Over the last three decades, he has elevated the companies and teams he led by leveraging the lessons in this very book."

— Joan Ray, Executive Vice President, The Elliot Group

"*The Purposeful Growth Revolution* is a playbook for personal change. Mark beautifully architected every detail of the reading experience to inspire readers to take action with provoking questions, anecdotes, stories, and mental models for how to pursue your life's purpose. It's not just a book. It's a legacy he's cultivated over a lifetime of experience from the front-line to the C-Suite, academia and beyond."

— Jacqueline Mueller, CCXP, Director Personal Services Sales, Smartsheet

"*The Purposeful Growth Revolution* is masterful at crossing the chasm from individual growth to team growth to organizational growth, all in one book. Mark Mears lays out the questions and shared experiences on how to navigate these skill-sets while not having to wait around to experience them yourself. What an opportunity to short-circuit the learning process."

— Adam Chandler, COO & Co-Founder Eulerity

"This book is for anyone who has faced adversity and pondered their life purpose. In *The Purposeful Growth Revolution*, Mark Mears beautifully combines his experiences as a business executive and his spiritual insights to show how we can grow through pain, fulfill our life potential, and leave this world a better place."

— Susan Lintonsmith, Former CEO, Quiznos, Board Member, Author

"Mark Mears is really onto something in his powerful book, *The Purposeful Growth Revolution*. What better time than the "Great Resignation" to take stock in what your individual, team, and organizational purpose really is, and plant the right seeds to fuel sustainable growth that will leave everyone more fulfilled! Hats off to Mark for leading this revolution!"

— Brad Taylor, Founder/CMO, Taylor Built Brands and former Senior Vice President, Marketing and Sales, National Accounts at The Coca-Cola Company

"Mark Mears has clearly found his purpose: in *The Purposeful Growth Revolution*, he shares the lessons he's learned as a leader and brings them to life in a way that educates, engages, inspires and entertains. I have had the pleasure to work closely with Mark and can attest to the impact his 4 LEAF Growth model can have in building more purposeful individuals, teams, organizations and the communities we serve."

— Jean Boland, Chief People Officer, WOWorks

"I've read a lot of books on leadership, and *The Purposeful Growth Revolution* has become one of my favorites as it examines the importance of paying it backward to leave a living legacy. Mark's thesis is very well organized, and the use of personal stories really helps drive home his key points in ways that stick."

— Christopher Chadick, Senior Vice-President, Morgan Stanley Wealth Management

"*The Purposeful Growth Revolution* is one of the most insightful, uniquely crafted and powerful reads I've come across on topic of personal and professional leadership growth and development—applicable to all who want more out of life and work in every season of life."

— Gil Hanson, Global Brand Strategist, Design + Personal Brand and Host of *Be Your Best Podcast*

"Mark Mears has long embraced the mantra of 'doing good is good for business.' So easy to say, but how it unfolds in the business world is not easy. In his new book, *The Purposeful Growth Revolution*, Mark shares a wealth of insights from his remarkable career journey that should inspire us all."

— Diana Hovey, Senior Vice President, Corporate Partnerships, No Kid Hungry Campaign

"Many of the brands you love you fell in love with because of Mark Mears. Mark helped you see their value. Now, thankfully he is doing that for us! Mark uses his years of expertise, wisdom, and observations to help you leverage your true value as a leader to build a living legacy in helping others along their growth journeys."

— Rusty George, Pastor, Author and Host of the *Leading Simple Podcast*

"Mark Mears' *The Purposeful Growth Revolution* is a must-read for leaders who want more from their own lives and the teams they inspire, so together they can reach ever higher. This message could not have come at a better time for me both personally and professionally as I navigate the changing seasons of my own life."

— James Beasley, Senior National Business Development Manager, PepsiCo

"As an owner of a virtual, work from anywhere digital ad agency, we constantly challenge ourselves to maintain a strong sense of purpose across our team. Mark Mears seems to have cracked this code. Throughout his career, he has consistently demonstrated success inspiring organizations with his refreshing 4 LEAF Growth model. And reading Mears' book, *The Purposeful Growth Revolution*, has inspired me with my own refreshed sense of purpose."

— Tom Cole, Executive Chairman, Tandem Theory

"As a global business strategist who specializes in corporate and personal branding, *The Purposeful Growth Revolution* translates very well across all cultures. Mark Mears shares his C-level insights and "insider" stories that bring his unique 4 LEAF Growth model to life in ways we can all understand and apply to help fulfill our own lives and careers."

— Brigitte Bojkowszky, PhD, Founder/Owner, Bridget Brands and Host of *Brands Talk Podcast*

"Filled with both personal anecdotes and practical advice, *The Purposeful Growth Revolution* will resonate with anyone seeking more fulfillment in their life and work. Finding one's purpose is profound subject matter that is often difficult to grapple with. Mark's engaging and empathetic style makes you want to share the journey with him."

— Wendy Cohen, President, WCSMS

"I've always been a fan of Mark's LEAF metaphor for finding and fulfilling one's true growth potential. *The Purposeful Growth Revolution* is a powerful guidebook packed with personal stories and growth lessons that come straight from Mark's life experiences."

— Jan Talamo, Chief Creative Officer, VSBLTY

"Wow! More than a self-help book, *The Purposeful Growth Revolution* is the new mantra for leading the life you not only want but deserve. Bravo Mark! Bravo!"

— Janice Miller, Managing Partner at Miller Haga Law Group, LLP

"In a changing world, sustained growth comes from a clear focus on purpose. In *The Purposeful Growth Revolution*, Mark Mears shares his experience of big growth wins. The secret sauce of business success shared by a true winner.

— Arjun Sen, Founder & CEO ZenMango

"This book is a leadership guide, a self-help book and a memoir layered with practical advice for anyone at any point in their career."

— Jen Kern, Chief Marketing Officer, Qu and Hostess of *Restaurants Reinvented Podcast*

"I enjoyed the creative use of LEAF as a metaphor for growth and rebirth in *The Purposeful Growth Revolution*. Mark Mears has built a wealth of business and leadership experiences that clearly resonate throughout. Anyone looking to enhance their personal growth or professional expertise will clearly benefit from his instructive storytelling."

— Jim Rassmussen, Former Chief Information Officer, The Cheesecake Factory

"Today, discovering and fulfilling one's purpose is essential for individuals, brands and businesses. Mark's book could not have come at a better time."

— John Ellett, Author of *The CMO Manifesto*

"Mark's Purposeful Growth Revolution is a more organic way to view business; organizations are not static organisms, but constantly changing and dynamic, as seen through the lens of nature. Mark Mears believes that teamwork is most successful when it is purposeful, intentional, and regenerative; and great ideas are formed, fostered, and flourish when there is a proper balance within an organization."

— Ken Calwell, Chief Marketing Officer,
Compassion International

"I have known Mark Mears for several years and I've enjoyed watching every company grow and progress under his thoughtful leadership. *The Purposeful Growth Revolution* represents his future vision on how the world is changing and how do we as individuals, leaders and citizens respond in our own transformation for personal and professional growth."

— Wallace Doolin, Co-Founder, Investor, Advisor,
and Board Member, Black Box Intelligence

"Who would have thought an ordinary leaf, taken for granted can be a metaphor for a richer meaning and outlook on life?"

— Dennis Patton, Johnson County K-State Research and
Extension Horticulture Agent

"In *The Purposeful Growth Revolution*, Mark Mears has provided the reader with a clear path forward to next-level leadership and growth. Now it's time for you to put it to work."

— Sean Gleason, former marketing leader at
Pizza Hut, Dr Pepper Snapple Group and Dave & Buster's

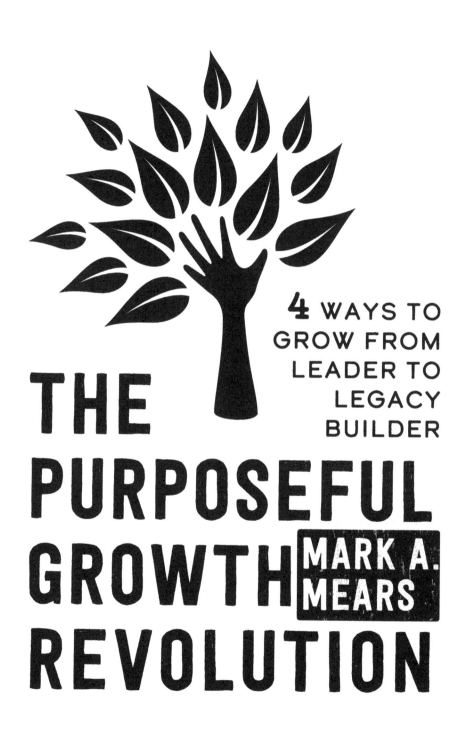

4 WAYS TO GROW FROM LEADER TO LEGACY BUILDER

THE PURPOSEFUL GROWTH REVOLUTION

MARK A. MEARS

THE PURPOSEFUL GROWTH REVOLUTION
4 Ways to Grow from Leader to Legacy Builder

Copyright ©2022 by Mark A. Mears. All rights reserved.

Published by:
Aviva Publishing
Lake Placid, NY
(518) 523-1320
www.AvivaPubs.com

All Rights Reserved. No part of this book may be used or reproduced in any manner whatsoever without the expressed written permission of the author.

Address all inquiries to:
Mark A. Mears
www.MarkAMears.com

Hardcover ISBN: 978-1-63618-212-4
Paperback ISBN: 978-1-63618-213-1
Library of Congress Control Number: 2022910690

Editors: Tyler Tichelaar and Larry Alexander,
Superior Book Productions
Cover Design & Interior Book Layout: Fusion Creative Works
Author Photo: Holly Linden
Video Credit: Chad Diamond Dann, Grindstone Films

Every attempt has been made to properly source all quotes.

Printed in the United States of America

First Edition

2 4 6 8 10 12

DEDICATION

To my mother, Shirley, who lived her life in service to others.

To Susan,

Thanks so much for your "Be-LEAF" in me and support of my Speaker journey.

Keep on GROWING!

(Rock chalk!)

— Mark

CONTENTS

Preface	15
Trees	25
Introduction	27
Part I: Cultivating Your Field for Purposeful Growth	**37**
Chapter 1: *GROWTH* Matters	39
Chapter 2: The Power of Purpose	55
Chapter 3: May the 4s Be with You!	73
Chapter 4: You Say You Want a Revolution?	83
Part II: Planting Your Seeds for Purposeful Self	**91**
Chapter 5: Growth 4 Every Season	93
Chapter 6: What's Your Gen(i)us?	103
Chapter 7: Serving Your Purpose	113
Chapter 8: Who Are You?	133
Chapter 9: Who is Brand *You?*	157
Chapter 10: Get the FUDD Out!	179
Chapter 11: Are You Ready to TURN Over a New LEAF?	189
Part III: Growing You 4-Ward for Purposeful Work	**209**
The Purposeful Leadership Revolution:	
A Season for Planting Growth	211

Chapter 12: Leadership Revolves Around Growth 'C'eeds   213

Chapter 13: Leading with Clarity
>from Purpose to Priorities   221

Chapter 14: Leading with Connection
>from Priorities to Plans   241

Chapter 15: Leading through Communication
>from Plans to People   249

Chapter 16: Leading with Commitment
>from People to Performance   255

The Purposeful Engagement Revolution:

A Season for Transforming Growth   **261**

Chapter 17: Engagement Revolves Around
>*GROWTH* Savia   263

Chapter 18: Engaging Your Heart
>from Purpose to Motivation   271

Chapter 19: Engaging Your Head
>from Motivation to Mindset   283

Chapter 20: Engaging Your Hands
>from Mindset to Development   295

Chapter 21: Engaging Your Habits
>from Development to Mastery   305

The Purposeful Accountability Revolution:

A Season for Harvesting Growth   **321**

Chapter 22: Accountability Revolves Around
>*GROWTH* Offshoots   323

Chapter 23: Accounting for Outcomes
    from Purpose to Measurement   327

Chapter 24: Accounting for Obstacles
    from Measurement to Adaptability   337

Chapter 25: Accounting for Outliers
    from Adaptability to Excellence   347

Chapter 26: Accounting for Obsolescence
    from Excellence to Innovation   361

The Purposeful Fulfillment Revolution:

A Season for Nurturing Growth   **373**

Chapter 27: Fulfillment Revolves Around
    GROWTH Ecosystems   375

Chapter 28: Cultivating Fulfilling People
    from Purpose to Principles   383

Chapter 29: Cultivating Fulfilling Places
    from Principles to Playgrounds   401

Chapter 30: Cultivating Fulfilling Processes
    from Playgrounds to Productivity   417

Chapter 31: Cultivating Fulfilling Performances
    from Productivity to Profitability   435

Part IV: Scattering Your Seeds for Purposeful Life   **445**

Chapter 32: Moving From *Me-Go* to *We-Growth!*   447

Acknowledgments   455

About the Author   461

Grow with Mark A. Mears   463

PREFACE

Most of us live a fast-paced, hectic lifestyle that includes making and keeping commitments that influence both our personal and work lives. We rarely take time out to pause and consider how interconnected we are—to each other, the teams we play on, or the world we share. Within our daily swirl of activities, we might say sometimes it can be difficult to "see the forest through the trees."

My epiphany came in one of my darkest hours—literally and figuratively—when I woke with a jolt one February morning at dawn the day after a significant life event. I stumbled out of bed, rubbed the sleep from my weary eyes, opened the back door to let the dog out, and there—just beginning to take shape on the tip of a branch of our once-dormant fig tree…

I SAW A LEAF!

Now, I admit that observation doesn't seem very profound since the world is filled with leaves of all shapes, sizes, textures, and colors growing from a wide variety of trees, plants, and flowers. But that lone leaf, which had been a bud only a few days earlier and now glistened with dew in the dim glow of daybreak, was evidence that winter would soon give way to spring. Ahh...nature!

Who knew this simple, natural, transformative growth process could have such a huge effect on my life—and, hopefully, your life as well?

You see, a leaf is a natural symbol of organic growth—like its source of life, a leaf "revolves" around the sun through a cycle of 4 seasons: *spring*—a time for planting seeds and establishing roots; *summer*—a time for growth and development; *fall*—a time for transformation and harvest; and *winter*—a time for rest, pruning, and regeneration in preparation for the "revolutionary" rebirth that follows once again...in spring!

Each season of life represents an opportunity for growth through development, transformation, harvest, and regeneration.

Life in any form goes through its seasons. And make no mistake, we humans are not so different from a tree with roots, a trunk, branches, a system of nourishment, and life-giving leaves. A tree needs to be planted in fertile soil and given the right balance of water, sunshine, oxygen, and carbon dioxide for photosynthesis to occur, all while being carefully pruned and nurtured by a loving hand to bear the ripest fruit, and thus, fulfill its growth potential.

Similarly, we humans all go through many different seasons and experience the very same growth dynamics exhibited in nature—intertwined within God's creation—as we seek to find and serve his purpose for our lives.

As I studied that leaf a bit closer, this beautiful metaphor for organic *growth* and rebirth also made me realize LEAF could be an acronym for Leadership, Engagement, Accountability, and Fulfillment, each reflecting 4 very simple, yet powerful and tightly integrated growth processes.

When woven together in support of a powerful purpose, I could clearly envision each component as part of 4 "revolutionary" processes for organically growing *individuals, teams, and organizations*—helping each to find their unique purpose to fulfill their growth potential. And by doing so, enriching the *world*—including the desired outcome for what each process is *"ment"* to accomplish:

LEAF

Leadership (Seed and Root System) = *Growth Alignment*

- *Clarity* around your purposeful Vision, Mission, and Values; *Connection* between organizational priorities and business plans; inspiring internal/external *Communications*; aligned personal and team *Commitments* to provide a solid foundation that can support future growth.

Engagement (Trunk and Branches) = *Growth Empowerment*

- A purposeful commitment of one's *Heart* to know why, *Head* to know what, *Hands* to know how, and *Habits* to know when; living out your Mission every day by creating a reliable source of nourishment that empowers organic growth.

Accountability (Leaf and Fruit) = *Growth Achievement*

- A path to purpose that measures the *Outcomes* that matter most; factoring in the importance of adaptability to overcome unexpected *Obstacles*; leveraging the demonstrated Best Practices of *Outliers*; creating a spirit of continuous improvement and innovation to harvest both current and future growth potential to avoid *Obsolescence* and thrive.

Fulfillment (Care and Feeding) = *Growth Environment*

- A cultural environment where a diverse team of *People* can grow into their purpose; a *Place* that nurtures the unique and special talents of everyone; the establishment of *Processes* that turn big ideas into productive actions; all resulting in achieving desired *Performance* goals and a deep sense of personal and professional growth fulfillment.

As a visionary business leader, I've been told one of my gifts is the ability to see patterns and possibilities many cannot. This includes connecting dots that others may not even see to form a vividly clear picture out of complexity and chaos—representing ideas and innovations that help maximize growth potential.

Speaking of vision, in junior high I had difficulty reading the blackboard. To see better, I preferred to sit in the front row while most of my friends were content to occupy seats in the back. Still, I found myself squinting so badly it caused me to have headaches. So, I asked my mother to take me to an eye doctor. As it turned out, I was extremely near-sighted, meaning I could see images up close, but I had difficulty discerning images from a distance.

When I got glasses, I was blown away by my ability to see the precise outline and vivid colors of leaves on a tree where previously all I had seen were clumps of green or brown. Wow, what a huge difference!

As I got older, my vision changed with the help of Lasik eye surgery. Today, I can see things far away with little problem; however, due to the aging process, I must rely heavily on "cheaters" to see things up close.

I find it amazing that I can have the same set of eyes, but in different seasons of my life require assistance to see things as they truly exist compared to how I perceive them based upon my current physical abilities or previous memories. I believe the same logic holds true not only for those who possess visionary leadership capabilities, but also for those who need help to "see" how they can *grow* into their unique and special purpose.

During my more than thirty-five-year business career, I have been blessed to have worked for or with some of the world's most iconic and well-respected companies such as PepsiCo/Pizza Hut, McDonald's, Frito-Lay, JCPenney, NBCUniversal, and The Cheesecake Factory. In addition, I gained tremendous experience working on the agency side with Bozell, Leo Burnett, DDB Promotions, EuroRSCG Retail, Promotional Partners Worldwide, and TIC TOC, a division of Omnicom.

Within those organizations, I have held positions ranging from assistant account executive to president and chief executive officer—including account executive, associate manager, manager, director, group account director, vice president, senior vice president, executive vice president, chief strategy officer, chief concept officer, chief marketing officer, and chief growth officer.

During my career, I have been blessed on twenty occasions to hear either:

"Congratulations, Mark! The search committee has selected you for…"

"Congratulations, Mark! We've decided it's time to promote you to…"

In addition to growing my strategic marketing and executive management skills, I have had the benefit of obtaining exposure to some dynamic leaders, caring mentors, and loyal friends—all of whom have helped shape and mold the whole person I've (tried to) become.

Before that, my academic foundation was built as an undergrad studying journalism and mass communications at the University of Kansas and later earning a master's degree in what is now called Integrated Marketing Communication at Northwestern University. In both academic settings, my life was positively impacted by two brilliant and extremely dynamic professors who inspired me to pursue the career path I chose.

Despite the breadth and depth of my experiences and the helpful advice and counsel of my mentors, friends, and family, my life journey is far from complete. While I have certainly been endowed with many tremendous gifts, like a leaf in its transformative season of growth, I am still (very much) a work in progress with a lifelong goal of fulfilling the size, shape, texture, and color God made me to be.

As I mentioned, I have been blessed to learn from many great mentors who have helped me progress along my career path to become not only a better, more effective team member and business leader, but a stronger, deeper, and more outward-directed human.

But to be honest, at several points on my journey, I encountered significant bumps in the path that shook my faith and tested my resolve. In some cases, I became so distraught, depressed, and defeated that I feared for my future.

You see, in addition to those new job offers and internal promotions, there have also been a few—well, let's just say *not* so congratulatory conversations:

"Mark, unfortunately, we have selected another candidate."

"Mark, we've decided to move in a different direction."

But God had other plans...a unique and special purpose for me I could not (yet) "see."

And the dark hour I mentioned? Several years ago, I was unceremoniously removed from a corporate leadership position. It happened the morning after the official sale of our company to a new owner who, after months of courtship and detailed planning, decided to "move in a different direction" by bringing in their own team.

It's nothing personal, just business, right?

Wrong!

It was extremely personal to me since my team and I had sacrificed so much to help turn around that company's fortunes. In addition to overcoming double-digit sales losses, my role as president and chief concept officer was to lead the strategic vision, multi-faceted development, and highly successful test of an exciting new concept that would profitably extend and enhance the company's offerings and brand recognition. At the same time, I was sworn to secrecy after our board decided to leverage the progress we had begun by investigating "strategic opportunities" for the brand.

All the hours spent in our support center, visiting restaurants, and traveling—working side by side with my executive team, our thousands of dedicated, hard-working restaurant-level team members, loyal suppliers, and agency partners—would (finally) pay off. It would be a turnaround story for the ages! Um, not so fast....

"Sorry, Mark, but we'll take it from here."

While certainly devastating in the moment, this event forced me into a season of rebirth as I prayed for God's direction—that God's will be done, not mine. Over time, I was carefully pruned by God's loving hands to reveal growth opportunities where I could become even more productive professionally and fulfilled personally. In fact, during this dark time of soul searching and self-reflection I found my life's purpose.

Or did my purpose find me?

> *"I am thankful for my struggle because without it I wouldn't have stumbled across my strength."*
>
> — Alex Elle

As a result, I've been blessed with these thoughts that—after more than thirty-five years of high-level marketing and executive leadership experience and a few more spent in deeply satisfying consulting and teaching roles—I have now put into both words and actions.

As you will see, this book is not a scholarly, scientific tome—although I will cite relevant information from scholars and scientists. Rather, it is more of a memoir—representing a collection of my personal experiences and observations of others I admire along with key lessons from several subject matter experts who are more educated, talented, and notable than me.

May the fruits of my experiences, observations, and lessons—including my many triumphs and (many more) travails—provide seeds of mentorship that may sprout new growth to help you transform your life and career through your own seasons. Instead of "The Great Resignation," I prefer to call this era "The Great Repurposing"—an opportunity for each of us to reexamine how we can find purpose in fulfilling our life's work, become better leaders, and build a *living* legacy.

- If you are just starting out in your career and looking for a path to personal and professional growth in fulfilling your goals, this book is for *you*.

- If you are farther along in your career yet feeling "stuck in a rut" where you are merely surviving instead of thriving, this book is for *you*.

- If you are already an executive but want to learn (or unlearn) behaviors that will improve your team, your organization, yourself, and the world, this book is for *you*.

- If you are getting ready for your "second act" and want to ensure it is even more fulfilling than your first, this book is for *you*.

Whichever season you may be in, I am humbled and honored to assist you on your purposeful growth journey. Together, we can change the world.

Let's get *GROWING!*

TREES

by Joyce Kilmer

I think that I shall never see
A poem lovely as a tree.

A tree whose hungry mouth is prest
Against the earth's sweet flowing breast;

A tree that looks at God all day,
And lifts her leafy arms to pray;

A tree that may in summer wear
A nest of robins in her hair;

Upon whose bosom snow has lain;
Who intimately lives with rain.

Poems are made by fools like me,
But only God can make a tree.

INTRODUCTION

I must confess I am a *growth* junkie. I have an unquenchable passion for growth in all forms—personal, professional, relational, and spiritual. I love to learn about growth but in equal measure, I love serving others on their growth journeys.

I also love Starbucks coffee. A few days a week, I drive about fifteen minutes from home to fetch my grande dark roast at the Starbucks' drive-thru before heading back home to enjoy it. On most occasions, I pay for the car just behind me—blessing them with a free drink or two. With this small gesture of kindness, I'm letting them know they matter to someone else—even though I am a total stranger.

I have no idea what the people in the car behind me are thinking about or going through, but I believe my intentional (not random) act of kindness probably makes them do a double-take and feel blessed as they drive away. Most of the time, I suspect this single act of goodwill turns into a chain reaction of gestures down the row of cars as the benefactor of my kindness often feels led to do likewise for the car behind them. And so on, and so forth....

I'm sure you've heard the term, "paying it forward." However, I think my simple gesture is more accurately "paying it backward."

Similarly, in writing this book, I am digging deep into my memories, thinking back on a vast collection of personal experiences, observations, and key lessons from others whom I have admired along my personal and professional growth journey. I am also going to share some candid and brutally honest feedback I've received from those who cared enough to make a difference in my life. It is important we use this information in our individual quest to become better leaders; however, I believe it is equally important that we share our insights with others to leave behind a *living* legacy to benefit both current and future generations.

I want to share these words in the sincere hope of helping you on your own growth journey—asking myself this one important question at each step along the way: "What if I knew then, what I know now?"

What would I tell a young Mark Mears if I had an opportunity to mentor him? How would my personal growth have changed if I had been mentored by an older me? What about my interpersonal relationships, career path, and/or my life?

> *"You can't connect the dots looking forward; you can only connect them looking backward. So you have to trust that the dots will somehow connect in your future. You have to trust in something—your gut, destiny, life, karma, whatever. This approach has never let me down, and it has made all the difference in my life."*
>
> — Steve Jobs

After the company where I worked was sold and my subsequent exit, as I mentioned in the preface, I had some time on my hands. I reached out to a few friends and business acquaintances for advice as

I contemplated my next move. During one of these calls, my friend and former business colleague Tom Millweard told me about a book he had read that might be relevant.

The subtitle of Bob Buford's *Halftime* really resonated with me: *Moving from Success to Significance*.

Brilliant!

According to the book's description, "Bob Buford believes the second half of your life can be better than your first. Much better. In *Halftime*, Buford focuses on this important time of transition—the time when, as he says, a person moves beyond the first half of the game of life. It's halftime, a time of revitalization and for catching a new vision for living the second half, the half where life can be lived at its most rewarding. As Buford explains, 'My passion is to multiply all that God has given me and, in the process, give it back.'"

Me too, Bob—me too!

Since this concept resonated with me, I began to work on a personal brand plan within the context of my revolutionary 4 LEAF *GROWTH* model, guided by my purpose statement: "I don't want to just make money and retire; I want to make a difference and inspire."

This purpose statement features two important and related distinctions:

- *Make a difference* by enriching the lives of others
- *Inspire* others to do likewise

My goal is to create a virtuous cycle of reciprocity that will leave a *living* legacy by positively influencing individuals, teams, organizations, and yes, even the world at-large.

I then developed a series of objectives, strategies, and tactics to bring my purpose statement to life. Essentially, I broke this plan up into the areas where I believed I could best use my gifts and resources to help others find their purpose and fulfill their true growth potential.

- **Time**—Teaching, Speaking, Mentoring, Coaching, and Consulting
- **Talents**—Leadership, Executive Management, and Communications
- **Treasures**—Financial Investments and Charitable Contributions
- **Triumphs/Travails**—Personal and Professional Experiences

In fact, this book is a microcosm of the growth journey I have been working on for the last several years. At first, it was kind of a cathartic hobby to keep me occupied while I got back on the corporate executive track. Today, it serves as the foundation for a much bigger goal—to *pay it backward* by growing into my unique purpose while helping others do likewise.

You may be asking: "Why, Mark?" Well, me too! Seriously, I believe I am following God's purpose for me in using my leadership experience, talents and servant's heart to support others in the various seasons of their growth journeys. Not only helping people become stronger, more purposeful leaders, but legacy builders who feel led to *pay it backward*.

And while I have enjoyed a very satisfying and rewarding career, I am in no way famous or particularly noteworthy. But as we learn in the Bible, God has a long and successful track record of selecting ordinary people to accomplish extraordinary things that have changed the world in profound ways. Here is how God repurposed the lives of just a few people in the Bible:

- **Moses:** From a hiding murderer to a vocal leader.
- **Nehemiah:** From a comfortable food taster to a revolutionary renovator.
- **Mary:** From an unwed, pregnant teen to the mother of God.
- **Simon Peter:** From a foul-mouthed fisherman to the foundation of the church.
- **Abraham and Sarah:** From shopping for Depends to shopping for Pampers.
- **Noah:** From AARP to ark.
- **David:** From a lowly shepherd boy to a mighty king.
- **Esther:** From a slave to a savior.
- **Paul:** From a persecutor to a pastor.
- **Jesus:** From a meek, mild baby to the risen savior.

And finally, as my good friend, Pastor Brandon Beard often said, "If God can use an ass to deliver His message (Numbers 22:22-34), He can certainly use me!"

Amen, Brandon—me too!

I am very proud of the many relationships I have gained, observations I have made, and lessons I have learned throughout the course of my thirty-five-year professional career; all the ups and downs and in-betweens have shaped me both personally and professionally. And I'll admit, I have been extremely blessed and honored to enjoy some uber-cool experiences along the way.

While I have certainly had more than my share of "pinch me" moments, I have also suffered through some devastating "gut punches"—some inflicted on me very cruelly and deliberately by others and several more I unwittingly stepped into. But like a deeply rooted tree, I was able to weather the storms and continue my growth journey—learning from each event to become wiser, stronger, and more resilient. This is what *growth* is all about. In fact, isn't this what *life* is all about?

We are a collection of our life experiences, which build our character, resilience, and grit as we progress along our journey. However, each new day represents an opportunity for personal and professional growth in every season so we can persevere and, ultimately, fulfill our life's purpose.

Although I will be sharing many personal examples, I assure you my reasons for writing this book are not about me. My purpose is to use my experiences (the good, the bad, and the ugly), observations of those I admire, and key lessons from influencers, subject matter experts, and thought leaders to help inform, educate, instruct, and inspire you in each season of your growth journey.

My goal is not just to relate my personal experiences, observations, and knowledge in a one-way, top-down monologue, but to serve as a catalyst for sparking a two-way, interactive dialogue where I can continue to progress along my growth journey by listening to and learning from you.

Admittedly, this book contains a lot to digest since it is difficult to package thirty-five years of experiences, observations, and nuggets of wisdom into a single book. In fact, several of the concepts I will share with you could (and probably should) be explored much deeper in separate books. Please forgive me for merely hitting the highlights of some important topics. Hopefully, what I include will pique your curiosity enough for you to investigate them further.

I want this book to be memorable, personally engaging, and highly interactive to help you retain and, hopefully, apply what you learn. Plus, retention will make it easier for you to *pay it backward* by sharing what you learn to help others in their growth journey. As a result, I see this as much more than a static, two-dimensional book; I hope it will be a dynamic, three-dimensional resource. Like our solar calendar, it is important to remember that these revolutionary 4 LEAF *GROWTH* processes remain consistent no matter what season you may be in.

GRAB ON TO SOME "MIND HANDLES" (AND HOLD ON TIGHT!)

To help establish and/or reinforce the most important concepts supporting my revolutionary 4 LEAF *GROWTH* processes, I will use "Mind Handle" techniques.

I first heard the term mind handle from Ken Womack, the creative director of a marketing agency I worked for several years ago in Dallas. I latched onto the term because it captured the essence of what all brand marketers strive to achieve—to have their brand occupy valuable space that is clear, memorable, relevant, and actionable in the minds of their target audience. The goal is for the target audience to immediately think of, try, repurchase, and advocate for your brand when thinking of what they need, want, or desire.

As we see in the Bible, Jesus used parables to communicate his message so his audience could best understand it. I will borrow a few of my personal favorite parables to help convey some *growth*-relevant messages.

First, I will establish the foundation by introducing the critically important number 4, which is linked to a simple but powerful visual—a 4-circle Venn diagram—to give dimension to the interwoven nature of the 4 LEAF *GROWTH* process. On top of that foundation, I will add in a few grammatical techniques to make it easier to learn, retain, and share this information. Next, I will employ a "from X to Y" framework—building upon a popular reframing technique with what I prefer to call repurposing—so you can follow along as I connect the dots in unpacking the key tenets of each revolutionary 4 LEAF *GROWTH* process.

From…Reframing

A conscious process of choosing to redefine our beliefs and attitudes.

To…Repurposing

According to Webster's Dictionary, this means "to give a new purpose or use to." A process by which an object with one use value is transformed or redeployed as an object with an alternative use value toward one's ability to grow into their unique purpose.

Again, each of these foundational elements is included to help you make steady progress on your journey in every season as you grow from leader to legacy builder.

As you know, a good doctor will ask a series of questions and then often more probing questions after they've heard your initial answers. They want to find out exactly where your pain is, what may have caused it, and how they can help relieve it. Based on this information, the doctor can provide the proper diagnosis and personalized treatment for your specific ailment.

Likewise, I will provide a "Purposeful Growth Self-Assessment" at www.MarkAMears.com featuring a list of questions designed to help you think deeply and critically about how you can grow as an *individual*, a member of a *team*, and part of a broader *organization*, while helping to improve the *world* around you. Your answers to these questions will show us objectively where your specific growth opportunities lie.

I can only cover so much content to keep this book a manageable length, but I will share some excellent resources that have inspired me along my journey so you can dig deeper into the thoughts that most intrigue you. I am confident you will also find tremendous value in exploring them as you continue your lifelong pursuit of personal and professional growth.

I certainly understand this entire journey can seem a bit overwhelming, but don't be discouraged by the number, breadth, and depth of available resources. Instead, start by reading this book to get an overview of The Purposeful Growth Revolution broken down into 4 key growth processes we find in nature:

- Cultivating Your Field for **Purposeful Growth**
- Planting Your Seeds for **Purposeful Self**
- Growing You 4-ward for **Purposeful Work**
- Scattering Your Seeds for **Purposeful Life**

Remember that to be successful in any endeavor, you must be open-minded, intellectually curious, and an intentional lifelong learner with a voracious appetite for continuous growth.

Before we get too far into the weeds, let me take a few steps back to prep the soil and establish fertile ground for this revolutionary 4 LEAF *GROWTH* plan(t) to take root, grow and flourish.

PART I

CULTIVATING YOUR FIELD FOR PURPOSEFUL GROWTH

*"Look deep into nature,
and then you will understand everything better."*

— Albert Einstein

CHAPTER 1

GROWTH MATTERS

"Life is growth. You grow or you die."

— Phil Knight

Let me start by asking a question: Do you want to *grow*?

Of course, *you* do. We *all* do. You see, without growth, like any living organism, we would simply wither and die over time—sometimes very quickly, but other times very slowly and, in some cases, quite painfully. With steady, sustainable growth, we can thrive with purpose, passion, and a sense of accomplishment that will, no doubt, fuel our desire for even more growth.

Our innate yearning for growth tends to accompany each stage of human development: from sitting up and crawling to standing and walking; from the breast or bottle to soft then solid food; from sounds and gibberish to the formation of words and sentences; from weakness and dependency to strength and autonomy; from questions and learning to intellect and wisdom.

When I was growing up in the 1960s and '70s, my father had an interesting habit of writing phone numbers on the wallpaper in pencil next to our telephone. These phone numbers were the ones he and my mother called most often, so I guess that method came in handy when it was time to dial a friend, doctor, or family member.

Not far from those phone numbers, and adjacent to the wooden door frame, were the familiar tic marks representing the year-by-year height of each child in our family. We had tic marks for my older sister Julie, my older brother David, and my younger brother Terry—and, of course, tic marks for me. This was a way for our parents to keep track of how much we had grown and a special source of pride for each of us.

Each tic mark represented visible progress, eliciting comments of pride and validation from Mom and Dad like, "Wow, just look at how much you've grown?" or "My, what a big girl/boy you are growing up to be!"

And closely related to these annual height measurements was usually the question, "What do you want to be when you grow up?" This would elicit an aspirational response: "I want to be an astronaut!" or "…a doctor!" or "…a firefighter!" or some such noble and exciting vocation. But I believe the better question is, "*Who* do you want to be when you grow up?" This conjures up a much more complex and introspective examination of ourselves than we are typically ready for until we are much older.

In either case, we all know growth doesn't happen overnight, at least not visibly. Like the fig tree in our backyard, measurable growth takes many seasons as evidenced by its rings. And each ring represents a unique year of the tree's life—an annual revolution that consists of a series of events and experiences—possibly serving as a metaphor for our own life.

The best type of growth is *purposeful growth*.

As humans, each ring in our trunk represents not only a memory of our experiences, but an opportunity to learn things we can take on our journey to help improve and enrich our lives. In fact, our experiences matter little if we don't internalize the lessons they teach us, which leads to true growth.

At its core, growth is really a dynamic, *revolutionary* process that has a beginning, a middle, but virtually no end—until, of course, "The End." Even then, much like a leaf to a tree, we can "leave" a legacy that can live on in the lives of others long after we have physically left the earth. Pretty cool, huh?

At our core, we are all endowed with a unique purpose. Our purpose is first manifested as who we are as *individuals*, then often as a member of a *team*, and then for many of us, we may play a role as part of a collection of individuals and teams called an *organization*. Finally, the measure of true worth for every individual, team, and organization lies in its collective influence on the lives of others, representing an opportunity—indeed a responsibility—to make a positive and lasting difference in the *world*.

Let me start by asking you a few probing questions to get you thinking both internally (about yourself) and externally (about others) within each of these 4 integrated growth areas:

- **INDIVIDUAL GROWTH**

As humans, we all have a desire for growth. In fact, personal growth and development (or self-help) is a multi-billion-dollar industry, including books, conferences, seminars, webinars, coaching, blogs, vlogs, podcasts, and social media.

- When did you feel you were the *best* version of yourself?
- What were the circumstances?
- How did that time and circumstance make you feel alive?
- Who has been your most inspirational or greatest influence? Why?
- Whom do you consider to be among the greatest individuals in history?
- What did they do and how did it change the world?
- How do you think they were able to do what they did?

Individual growth is a big part of what this book is designed to help you accomplish. We're going to spend the first part focused on *you*—helping you find your unique purpose and establishing a solid foundation for building both your personal brand and professional growth plan.

Then we will apply your purpose in ways that align with your team or organization to attain career growth. But the coolest part is you'll learn how to fulfill your true growth potential—personally and professionally—while also helping to make the *world* better for others by leaving behind a *living* legacy.

FROM INDIVIDUAL TO TEAM GROWTH

"If you want to go fast, go alone. If you want to go far, go together."

— African Proverb

- **TEAM GROWTH**

We've all seen inspirational posters—you know, the ones that say, "TEAM = Together Everyone Achieves More" or "Teamwork makes the dream work!" While those statements may sound corny or clichéd, they happen to be true on many levels. Whether you are part of a sports team, a school project team, a cross-functional business team, or even a coparenting team raising a family, I'm sure you can easily relate to the necessity and importance of teamwork, right?

- Which team have you been part of (sports, business, organization, etc.) that worked closely to accomplish a goal?
- What were the circumstances?
- What role did you play to add value to the team?
- How did you overcome any personality or ideology conflicts that arose?
- Which sports teams do you admire as having the ability to work together as a team to accomplish noteworthy performances?
- Which characteristics are common among those teams?
- Why do you consider them extraordinary?

Legendary McDonald's leader Ray Kroc had a saying, "None of us is greater than *all* of us."

As Dr. Rick Perea, former NFL linebacker and now sports psychologist for the Denver Broncos and Colorado Rockies, likes to point out, "A collection of individuals on a street corner is called a group, whereas a group of individuals working together toward a shared objective is called a team."

I attended the 1996 Summer Olympics in Atlanta with a close group of friends. Our group became closer because we stayed together on a houseboat floating on Lake Lanier since we couldn't find a hotel room anywhere near Atlanta. In retrospect, it was a great opportunity to combine a vacation and the Olympics into one highly memorable trip. We got to hang out on the lake during the hot, humid summer days and then drive into Atlanta to see the events we had tickets for at night. On days we didn't have tickets, we grilled out on the lower deck and watched the Olympics on a TV we brought on board with us. Pretty sweet!

One day, we attended a rowing event not far from where we were staying. Watching the eight-person teams with coxswain performing together up close on such tiny, ultra-thin shells was truly a marvel. Each team member possessed different physical attributes, strengths, and skills, yet they worked together to row in unison based on the coxswain's cadence. With all the oars in the water and rowing at the same time and intensity, the boats were able to slice through the water with precise alignment and great speed. Any minor fluctuation from either side of the boat would cause it to rock or sway and slow down, allowing a competitor to take the lead.

Clearly, it takes strength, stamina, technique, and discipline to be a successful rower. In fact, every team that qualified for the Olympics no doubt consisted of physically strong, well-trained, highly skilled, and deeply committed participants. However, the teams who were the most synchronized as a *team* reached the finish line first. I learned this is called "The Swing".

> *"If you could get all the people in the organization rowing in the same direction, you could dominate any industry, in any market, against any competition, at any time."*
>
> — Patrick Lencioni

In all cases, the goal is to *grow* together to create a well-functioning, high-performing *team*, one that can communicate clearly, openly, and honestly with one another, use a diverse set of experiences, skills, and thoughts, one that can work together to overcome obstacles to achieve specific and measurable milestones along the path to a shared objective, and, ultimately, one that can fulfill their true growth potential—together.

FROM TEAM TO ORGANIZATIONAL GROWTH

• ORGANIZATIONAL GROWTH

Organizations come in all shapes, sizes, and industries. Whether large or small, public or private, non-profit or entrepreneurial, an organization is essentially an integrated web of a few to sometimes many different teams that must work in synch to achieve a collective goal.

- Which company or business have you been part of that followed a specific action plan and accomplished its goals?
- What were the circumstances?
- What role did you play and how did you add value to the organization?
- Which great brands or companies helped revolutionize the world in some way?
- How did they change the way we think, live, work, or play?
- Why do you think they were able to do so?

For those who have worked in a corporate environment for many years or are those just starting out, navigating a much broader collection of individuals and teams to achieve organizational growth can be tricky. In fact, many factors influence our ability to sustain growth from year to year (e.g., macro- and micro-economics, heightened competition, government regulation, disruptive innovation, demographic shifts, availability/cost of labor, cost of goods, weather patterns, supply chain variability, etc.). As a result, we must seek step function change growth opportunities. If we continue to do what we've always done, we don't just run in place—we may even go backward.

At Pizza Hut back in the late 1980s and early 1990s, we viewed the rollout of delivery as a step function change growth opportunity. Taking "America's favorite pizza" and creating a new channel of distribution beyond our dine-in and carryout model was a game-changer for the brand. In fact, delivery service ushered in a new era of convenience for our guests—creating a ripple effect that is felt to this day.

More than just business growth, we enjoyed a unique and special culture that started at the top with outstanding senior leaders. In addition to our executive team, we boasted a marketing team of the best and brightest from top graduate schools like Harvard, Northwestern, Stanford, Virginia, Michigan, Indiana, and BYU that reads like a who's who list of marketing professionals. Many of my peers went on to become successful CEOs, presidents, or C-level executives at other organizations.

What an incredible wealth of talent—indeed an embarrassment of riches—all working together at the same time as a unified *team* to pursue an aspirational quest for greatness. In fact, the brand tagline that drove us to be great was, *"Pizza Hut… Makin' it great!"*

As the saying goes, "Iron sharpens iron," so I will admit we were a very competitive bunch. Our intramural basketball league, impromptu football games, early morning "Wallyball" matches, and individual feats of speed, strength, stamina, and skill inside and outside of our workout facility were legendary. (I'm looking at you, Ken Calwell!) The Pizza Hut culture could be seen as, "Work hard. Play harder!"

Yet we were extremely collaborative and collegial when it came time to make decisions and execute programs to achieve our shared goals. In fact, David Novak, our senior vice president of marketing and one of the best leaders I've ever been blessed to work for, had a saying that resonated deeply with all of us, "When it's great, there's no debate!" And David nearly always had a keen eye for what great looked like.

Long before Pizza Hut was originally spun off as part of Tri-Con and now YUM!, it was owned by PepsiCo. Our chairman and CEO then was Wayne Calloway. When asked about his human resource strategy, this extraordinary leader said, "At PepsiCo, we are looking for eagles who can fly in formation." What an incredibly powerful visual, right?

Therein lies the recipe for greatness within a supremely motivated, well-aligned, fiercely competitive, and, ultimately, incredibly successful, high-performance *team!*

> *"Coming together is the beginning. Keeping together is progress. Working together is success."*
>
> — Henry Ford

FROM ORGANIZATIONAL TO WORLD GROWTH

• WORLD GROWTH

With more than 7.7 billion inhabitants, the world is getting more and more complex, with challenges on many levels. Despite the rise in populism or nationalism among some major global powers, we are still more interconnected than at any point in history based upon increasing information sharing, digitalization, data/analytics, and, of course, the amplification of social media.

According to a recent study by the Paris-based Global Inequality Lab, as reported by Bloomberg, about 2,750 billionaires control 3.5 percent of the world's wealth. This is up from 1 percent in 1995, with the fastest gains coming since the pandemic hit. The poorest half of the planet's population owns about 2 percent of its riches.

Unfortunately, the chasm between the "haves" and "have nots" continues to widen at an alarming rate. Clearly not everyone has benefitted equally since the Great Recession began in 2007—or rode the wave back up after the COVID-19 dip and resurgence. The old adage, "The rich get richer," is certainly true in this case.

In a 2019 article written for the Associated Press, Christopher Rugaber said:

> Household wealth—the value of homes, stock portfolios and bank accounts, minus mortgage and credit card debt and other loans—jumped 80 percent in the last decade. More than one-third of that gain—$16.2 trillion in riches—went to the wealthiest 1 percent, figures from the Federal Reserve show. Just 25 percent of it went to middle-to-upper-middle class households. The bottom half of the population gained just 2 percent.

But this is not merely an American phenomenon—and certainly not a recent one. In what is aptly described as the "Champagne Glass Distribution of Wealth" chart,[1] we learn the top 1 percent hold more than 50 percent of the entire world's wealth. For perspective, that is more than the total net worth of 4 billion people at the bottom of the scale. Indeed, the bottom 20 percent hold just 1.4 percent of the world's wealth, eking out a living and barely able to survive from day-to-day.

According to *Fox Business*, the latest census figures show that wealth inequality has reached its highest level in fifty years.

---

1 UNDP Human Development Report 1992. New York: Oxford University Press, 1992.

While you may not be among the top 1 percent, my guess is everyone reading this book enjoys the privilege of having their basic needs met, allowing them to strive for greater personal and professional growth. On the other side of the ledger, we must all be aware that much of the world's population lives in poverty, stunted by illiteracy, embroiled in civil war, or living in fear and injustice of some kind. In fact, for literally billions of people, the task of satisfying their daily needs and merely surviving for another day is all they *have* to look forward to.

You likely have heard of Abraham Maslow's Hierarchy of Needs, usually depicted as a pyramid. At the bottom of the pyramid are what Maslow categorized as *Deficiency Needs*—the essential needs for basic survival:

- **Biological and Physiological Needs**
  - Food, Water, Sleep, Shelter, Sex
- **Safety Needs**
  - Discipline, Order
- **Belongingness and Love Needs**
  - Emotionally Deeper Interpersonal Relationships
- **Esteem Needs**
  - Honor, Recognition, Self-Respect

The next grouping is categorized as *Growth Needs*—those needs providing us with a sense of purpose and fulfillment.

- **Cognitive Needs**
  - Intelligence, Knowledge, Understanding

- **Aesthetic Needs**
  - Beauty, Nature, Artistic Imagery
- **Self-Actualization**
  - Achieving One's Full Potential
- **Transcendence/Spiritual Needs**
  - Purpose Fulfillment

While those who have reached the top half of this pyramid should absolutely continue to strive upward, these needs and the attainment of most of them sets up the need for *individuals, teams,* and *organizations* to help provide support for those who remain at the pyramid's bottom half.

Every human deserves dignity and an opportunity to pursue growth, regardless of who they are, where they are from, or which season of life they may be in.

You see, the people I am referring to do not have the luxury of attempting to attain the top of the pyramid within Maslow's Hierarchy of Needs; they need help to move up from the very bottom, right?

"There, but for the grace of God, go I."

— John Bradford

You probably know the story of the Good Samaritan from the Bible. Today, this story represents anyone who goes out of their way to help someone in need—whoever they may be.

One example of this mentality centers around a homeless man in the Kansas City area called "Dave," who lives in his Chevy Suburban due to some difficulties that befell him. On Sunday, January 20,

2019, the AFC championship between the hometown Kansas City Chiefs and the New England Patriots was being held at Arrowhead Stadium. A huge snowstorm enveloped the area overnight, and ice beneath the snow made streets very difficult to navigate. Many cars slid off the road or got stuck in snowdrifts.

Given the size and stability of his truck, Dave decided to drive around and look for people he could help get unstuck. After a while, he came upon a car stuck in a ditch and proceeded to engage the driver, helping him find a solution. Dave soon realized the guy he was helping was a Kansas City Chiefs player named Jeff Allen whose car had careened off the road on his way to the stadium.

Of course, this is but one of many stories where one human reached out to help another. Countless other stories exist of individuals voluntarily giving of their resources to help people in need—donations of money, food, clothing, blood, expertise, etc. *Helping people get unstuck.*

One thing I look back on with great satisfaction in my career was the opportunity to work for several organizations that truly lived out our shared values. These great companies used their abundance of resources, assets, and equities (i.e., time, money, team members, guests, supplier partners, media, etc.) to help support others in need. This included the mobilization of individuals who cared about other humans, their communities, and those in need across the country and around the world.

In each case, the awareness generated and the financial and/or product contributions were significant. And when combined with the actual lives touched (both externally among those in need and internally among those who participated) by corporate social responsibility (CSR) initiatives, partnering with these organizations provided a growth opportunity that cannot be measured on a balance sheet or profit and loss statement.

I love the name given to this practice because it emphasizes the word "responsibility." Linking this powerful word with an authentic commitment and the coordinated actions of individuals, teams, and organizations for the collective good adds immeasurable value for all stakeholders.

Simply put, I believe we are all placed on earth to be part of something much bigger than to live, die, and pay taxes in between. And for those of us privileged to be able to do so, I feel we have a responsibility to extend our gifts to enrich, extend, brighten, and/or save the lives of others and endeavor to make our world a better place.

We are all threads in the tapestry of life—woven together from many sizes, shapes, and colors—to create a masterful work of art founded in love and support for one another.

"An invisible thread connects those who are destined to meet, regardless of time, place, or circumstance. The thread may stretch or tangle, but it will never break."

— Ancient Chinese Belief

CHAPTER 2

THE POWER OF PURPOSE

"When I chased after money, I never had enough. When I got my life on purpose and focused on giving of myself and everything that arrived into my life, then I was prosperous."

— Dr. Wayne W. Dyer

While it's been there all along (possibly hidden in plain sight), the concept of purpose has been gaining a lot of traction recently. From spiritual teaching to scholarly research and changing demographic trends along with the increasing reliance on digital devices for social interaction, there is solid evidence that connecting individuals to their higher purposes helps increase job satisfaction, productivity, longevity/loyalty, and outer directedness that benefits others.

Researchers Aaron Hurst, Brandon Peele, Tim Kelley, Zach Mercurio, and their team at The Science of Purpose (www.scienceofpurpose.org) have discovered statistics supporting the power of purpose in our lives. The following represents a high-level summary of ways in which purpose influences work both individually and collectively as organizations.

Individuals with a connection to their purpose experience:

- 63 percent increase in income, wealth, and leadership effectiveness
- 64 percent increase in fulfillment
- Learn twice as much
- Are 4 times more engaged
- And are 175 percent more productive

Companies with a connection to their purpose experience:

- Higher margins as purpose-driven firms are 30 percent more innovative
- 73 percent of customers will switch to higher purpose brands
- 55 percent of customers will pay more for higher purpose brands
- 47 percent higher Net Promoter scores and related length of tenure
- 54 percent more fulfilling work relationships

Particularly now as we recover from the effects of COVID-19—and face dire prognostications on climate change and other life-threatening obstacles—the concept of purpose has risen much higher in our consciousness. There simply *has to be* more to life than just going through the daily motions of eating, sleeping, breathing, working, retiring, and dying, right?

We all go through various seasons, and most of us are desperately searching for our specific purpose in the fleeting time we are given to dance here on earth. Even before the Great Resignation, trends were moving in this direction, but with the COVID-related reset, there's an increasing movement to question what is *expected of us* and relate it to what really *matters to us*. In fact, probably the most profound questions we all share are, "Who am I?" and "What am I here for?"

> *"The two most important days of your life are the day you were born and the day you find out why."*
>
> — Mark Twain

Since the dawn of human consciousness, most of us have wrestled with the question, "What is the meaning of *life*?" But, for me, that comes across a bit too passive and generalized. I believe in repurposing this question to be more active and personalized—"What does life mean to *you*?"

> *"The meaning of life is to find your gift.*
> *The purpose of life is to give it away."*
>
> — Pablo Picasso

Before we dive headlong into the search for our own individual purpose, I would first like to establish the awesome power of purpose as a broader, multi-dimensional concept.

- **INDIVIDUAL PURPOSE**

Back in 2002, Rick Warren wrote *The Purpose Driven Life,* which has sold more than 50 million copies in eighty-five languages and had a positive influence on many more lives because his Bible-based thesis has become a standard-bearer for the Christian community.

While I grew up in the church and was baptized at age ten, I confess there were times when I strayed from my beliefs and walked far away from God. Some of those times can be chalked up to immaturity and the weakness of our human condition or sinful impulses. Other times, I walked away out of impatience with God for not hearing (or granting) my prayers.

During these times, my relationship with God was like a car with misaligned wheels and, sometimes, it even skidded out of control. Like some sort of celestial ATM, we pray to God for what we need (or want). But I learned early in *The Purpose Driven Life* how wrong I was:

"It's not about you."

Wait…. What? Really?

Pastor Warren says:

> The purpose of your life is far greater than your own personal fulfillment, your peace of mind, or even your happiness. It's far greater than your family, your career, or even your wildest dreams and ambitions. If you want to know why you were placed on this planet, you must begin with God. You were born by his purpose and for his purpose.

Wow, mind…blown!

Warren's thesis is there is not one purpose for your life; there are actually five integrated purposes that meld into the one (and only) *you*.

> **Purpose #1:** *You* Were Planned for God's Pleasure
> **Purpose #2:** *You* Were Formed for God's Family
> **Purpose #3:** *You* Were Created to Become Like Christ
> **Purpose #4:** *You* Were Shaped for Serving God
> **Purpose #5:** *You* Were Made for a Mission

Philosophers have pondered life's purpose for centuries. Some are well-known such as Socrates, Plato, Aristotle, Kant, Nietzsche, and Kierkegaard; others have emerged in recent times to offer their personal view on this topic.

No doubt, there are widely divergent philosophical, theological, scientific, and metaphysical positions. But despite different perspectives on *where* our life's purpose may come from, I think we can all agree that *having one* plays a vital role in the joy and sense of fulfillment we experience—both by giving and receiving—during our time on earth. Research collected by the Science of Purpose cited previously supports the power of purpose in ways that enhance our lives and relationships. This includes better health, memory, cognition, executive function, mood, and contentment as well as stronger cells and DNA—all leading to longer, more productive, and more fulfilling lives.

Let's take a few moments to ponder these questions:

- Do you believe your life has a specific purpose?
- If so, do you have any idea what it is/could be?
- Might your purpose change within a given season of life?

- What special activities or events feel purposeful to you?
- When did you feel you were truly living on purpose?
- How did those times make you feel more vital and alive?
- How might your purpose benefit others?

• TEAM PURPOSE

I have been blessed to have served on many types of teams—sports, school, business, advisory boards, fraternity, church, parenting, philanthropic, community service, etc. In all cases, the unifying purpose of each team was to work together to achieve our shared purpose.

Some people are more individualistic and take great pride in their personal achievements. I, however, have always loved the camaraderie of a team environment where we get to merge our individual gifts into a shared *purpose* that leads to growth, learning, and achievement—*together*.

In my many team experiences, the trials, tribulations, and yes, even some blood, sweat, and tears, provided opportunities to bond in pursuit of our desired outcome. In fact, the sweet taste of victory (however you define it) is even more satisfying after persevering through temporary setbacks or periods of adversity.

Stephen Strasburg, the perennial all-star pitcher who was named MVP of the Washington Nationals improbable run to the 2019 World Series championship, said it very well:

> I would like to think baseball is a lot like life—I would think that's what draws a lot of people to the game. It's a game based upon failure. I think this team has proved that if you

believe in one another and keep fighting, you can achieve things that most people thought were impossible.

Even legendary golfer Tiger Woods, one of the most decorated individual champions the game has ever seen, believes in the importance of teamwork on a higher level. In the late fall of 2019, Woods served as both captain and player for the US President's Cup team—a biannual tournament played by the very best golfers in the United States against the best international players in the world.

After leading the comeback victory for the US team over the International team at Royal Melbourne on the tournament's final day, Woods was visibly emotional. Despite his eighty-two PGA tournament victories—including fifteen majors—and millions (and millions) of dollars in prize winnings and endorsement deals, Woods truly values the importance of team accomplishment. During his post-tournament interview, Woods said, "Any time you have moments where you're able to do something that is bigger than us as an individual, it's so much more meaningful and so much more special."

Think back to some teams you may have played on:

- What central passion or purpose did you share?
- What obstacles did you face along the way?
- How did you work together to overcome them?
- How did that make you feel?
- When you get together with your teammates, what stories do you recount in reminiscing about your experiences?

Ah yes, it is indeed our *stories* that tend to bind us together. You know how it is when you attend a reunion. Once the stories start flowing, it seems almost as if time stands still thinking back nostalgically on the special memories you share.

When I served as senior vice president and chief marketing officer for The Cheesecake Factory, it was always so interesting for me to hear about the company's tremendous lore. Not only the unique circumstances of when, where, and how it started, but what I found most poignant were the individual stories of its team members. I recall listening to vivid reflections of what life was like when a given team member joined the organization, their experiences from the restaurant(s) they worked in, and most importantly, the person(s) who trained or positively influenced them in some way. At the end of the day, it always comes down to *people*.

While I never had the honor to serve in the military, I have always held immense respect for those who put their lives on the line to protect our country and the freedoms we all enjoy. Each branch of service is vitally important in the specific role it plays. However, as a brand marketing executive, I have always admired the positioning line of the Marines. "The Few. The Proud. The Marines." It gives me chills just thinking about it.

But what struck me as particularly relevant in supporting purpose within a team is their motto: "*Semper Fidelis*" (always faithful). *Semper Fi* represents the tremendous level of commitment, dedication, pride, and loyalty each soldier has to the corps and, of course, to each other. And the phrase, "Once a Marine, always a Marine," suggests the shared values and related leadership disciplines are not just reserved for their time in service, but woven into the fabric of their civilian lives forever.

Whether you play on a sports team, serve in the military, or participate on a team at work, a deep sense of passion and optimistic resiliency behind an aligned purpose can bond teammates closer together. And that bonding almost always helps them overcome obstacles and/or achieve a higher level of success than they could have independently.

- **ORGANIZATIONAL PURPOSE**

As mentioned previously, an organization is primarily made up of a wide variety of individuals and teams working collaboratively together to help achieve a shared vision, mission, values, and desired goals. Several research studies and inspired critical analyses demonstrate the importance of aligning an organization around a unique purpose.

Therese Caruso, The Zeno Group's managing director of Global Strategy + Planning, unveiled select US results from its "Strength of Purpose" study—a survey of 8,000 people across eight countries and three continents. The study probes the key attributes of purposeful companies to understand if there are differences between companies that are viewed to have a valued purpose and those that do not.

Zeno's insights included:

- **When companies and brands get purpose right, they are rewarded.**

    Seventy-eight percent of Zeno's US respondents said they either started buying from a brand or encouraged others to support it, or publicly shared their positive views about it when they found they believed in a company or brand's purpose.

- **When brands and companies get purpose wrong, they face the "cancel culture."**

    Seventy-three percent of those Zeno surveyed in the US either permanently stopped buying from a brand, actively discouraged others from buying it, or turned to a competing brand, if they disagreed with an action that a company or brand had taken.

- **With strong purpose comes reputation insurance.**

    Ninety percent of Zeno's US survey respondents said they are more likely to continue to support a brand or a company after it has made a misstep if it has a strong purpose.

Zeno said the findings reflected a strong influence of younger generations; they place greater value on how companies treat employees, often using that lens to judge a company's mission. For example, 39 percent of Gen Z respondents in the US said they are more likely to seek employment with companies that have a purpose they agree with versus 26 percent for all other generations.

According to Robert E. Quinn and Anjan V. Thakor in their 2018 *Harvard Business Review* article "Creating a Purpose-Driven Organization—How to get employees to bring their smarts and energies to work," purposeful organizations perform at a much higher level when the purpose is authentic and communicated with clarity. Their thesis is based upon consulting work with hundreds of organizations and extensive interviews with dozens of leaders. As a result, they developed a theoretical model to draw an important conclusion:

> When an authentic purpose permeates business strategy and decision making, the personal good and the collective good become one. Positive peer pressure kicks in, and employees are reenergized. Collaboration increases, learning accelerates, and performance climbs.

Here is a high-level overview of the theoretical model they created to help organizations find and fulfill their unique purpose for the growth of all stakeholders:

1. Envision an inspired workforce
2. Discover the purpose
3. Recognize the need for authenticity
4. Turn the authentic message into a constant message
5. Stimulate individual learning
6. Turn mid-level managers into purpose-driven leaders
7. Connect the people to the purpose
8. Unleash the positive energizers

The authors summarize their thesis:

> So, purpose is not just a lofty ideal; it has practical implications for your company's financial health and competitiveness. People who find meaning in their work don't hoard their energy and dedication. They give them freely, defying conventional economic assumptions about

self-interest. They grow rather than stagnate. They do more—and they do it better. By tapping into that power, you can transform an entire organization.

I recently read a blog post by Christopher Wellise, chief sustainability officer for Hewlett Packard Enterprises, which demonstrates the awesome power of purpose in achieving growth goals that benefit not only the organization, its customers, and shareholders, but the world at-large. What was most interesting to me about this example was not that it was some recent revelation or new-fangled, whiz-bang, flavor-of-the-month gimmick; it was a commitment made by HP's co-founders…more than sixty years ago!

> *"Why are we here? I think many people assume, wrongly, that a company exists solely to make money.… We have to go deeper and find the real reason for our being."*
>
> — Dave Packard, 1960

Mr. Wellise wrote:

> From the start, Bill Hewlett and Dave Packard baked a commitment to corporate citizenship into the DNA of our company—a commitment which has guided our strategy over the decades to the benefit of our company, our customers, and society at large. It's one of the reasons I chose to work for Hewlett Packard, and now Hewlett Packard Enterprise (HPE).
>
> Under the leadership of our CEO, Antonio Neri, HPE has reaffirmed these roots and sparked a cultural transformation that will lead us into the future as a purpose-driven company. Today, my pride in HPE is heightened as HPE is recognized

as the industry leader on the prestigious Dow Jones Sustainability Index (DJSI).

It's a privilege to work for a company committed to applying technological innovation to advance the way people live and work.

Aligning individual, team, and organizational purpose is indeed an incredibly powerful blueprint for revolutionary growth on many levels. But it's clearly not a new idea.

Where does purpose (really) come from?

With more than 10 million views, Simon Sinek's TED Talk "Start with Why" has reawakened the concept of purpose for almost every organization. Sinek's thesis is very simple, yet profound. He calls it his "Golden Circle" which features three concentric circles—the *what*, the *how*, and the *why*—described as follows:

The What—Every organization on the planet knows *what* they do. These are the products they sell or the services they offer.

The How—Some organizations know *how* they do it. These are the things that make them special or set them apart from the competition.

The Why—Very few organizations know *why* they do what they do. *Why* is not about making money. That is a result. The *why* is a purpose, cause, or belief. It is the very reason your organization exists.

But Sinek's insight of using reverse logic to very clearly assert why it is so important to start with the *why*—as opposed to the *how* or the *what*—is both highly illuminating and incredibly powerful. Think of the image of his "Golden Circle" as an archery target—he argues that everything must emanate outward from the middle of that bullseye—*the why*.

> "He who has a why to live can bear almost any how."
>
> — Friedrich Nietzsche

And just like the previous example of a team, an organization of any size—aligned behind an inspiring purposeful mission—can provide significant benefits across all stakeholders.

Think back to an organization you may have worked for:

- Did the organization have a stated purpose?
- If so, how broadly and deeply was it communicated?
- Was it integrated into every aspect of the business?
- Did you see yourself as personally invested in it?
- How did that make you feel?

- **GLOBAL PURPOSE**

In addition to understanding how the *power of purpose* can enrich our lives, the teams we play on, and the organizations we belong to, I believe we have a responsibility to extend our purpose to enrich the lives of others.

I was recently invited to become a member of the Senior Leader Network within an outstanding organization called Conscious Capitalism. It is based on a book written by Whole Foods co-CEO, John Mackey and Conscious Capitalism, Inc. co-founder, Raj

Sisodia. Their thesis is that both business and capitalism are inherently good, and that following 4 specific tenets—*higher purpose, stakeholder integration, conscious leadership*, and *conscious culture and management*—can help build strong businesses, move capitalism closer to its highest potential, and foster a more positive environment for all of us. Its mission really resonated with me and fits my personal brand:

ELEVATING HUMANITY THROUGH BUSINESS

Based upon Plato's philosophy on human purpose, which stems from three ideals—the Good, the True, and the Beautiful—the founders of Conscious Capitalism agree, but have added a fourth ideal, the Heroic, that links each of them to a purposeful business enterprise:

The Good: Service to others—improving health, education, communication, and quality of life

The True: Discovering and furthering human knowledge

The Beautiful: Excellence and the creation of beauty

The Heroic: Courage to do what is right to change and improve the world

Conscious Capitalism is a way of thinking about capitalism and business that better reflects where we are in the human journey, the state of our world today, and the potential of business to make the world a better place for all. Companies that practice conscious capitalism perform ten times better than the S&P 500. Conscious capitalism is now rightfully becoming both a force for good and a key competitive advantage for companies.

Here are a few key stats that demonstrate the importance of this outlook and the fact that organizations can do well by doing good:

- ✓ Among Americans, 92 percent agree it's important for large companies to promote an economy that serves all Americans.

- ✓ Only 50 percent of Americans believe that companies are currently a positive force in the world.

- ✓ Companies with a highly engaged workforce outperform their peers by 147 percent in earnings per share.

And beyond US borders, a separate study indicated that 88 percent of Millennials believe their companies should play a role in helping to solve major problems in the world. Global purpose matters!

The 2020 Deloitte global survey revealed that the top concerns for younger generations are climate change and protecting the environment. And they support corporate brands that reflect their values. This is likely to be the reason for the 50 percent increase in conscious consumerism in the last 18-24 months.

While numerous organizations tout sustainability as part of their purposeful approach to doing business, many actually "put their money where their mouth is." One such company is Patagonia, whose purpose is extremely inspirational and aspirational, yet it says nothing about any type of product superiority, market share, or profit goals:

WE'RE IN BUSINESS TO SAVE OUR HOME PLANET.

Wow, very powerful indeed! And Patagonia lives out its purpose every day in multiple ways that provide its stakeholders—both internal and external—with a deeper level of engagement than what you find in most organizations. The "Patagonia Purpose" can be seen in several ways.

- **Supportable:** Patagonia donates 1 percent of sales to help support grassroots organizations all over the world.

- **Measurable:** Patagonia Action Works helps to connect individuals with a passion to get involved with those grassroots organizations in ways that truly make a difference on a local/regional level.

- **Sustainable:** *Patagonia Provisions* supports sustainable food growing and supply chain techniques that are environmentally safe.

- **Recyclable:** Patagonia *Worn Wear* is an initiative that helps repair damaged products and accepts trade-ins for store credit instead of having customers discard them in a landfill.

Purposeful organizations are not just a bunch of namby-pamby, tree-huggers, baby seal-lovers, or do-gooders; they are also among the most *profitable* companies. Here's a list of companies doing well by doing good taken from an article written by Catherine Brock for *The Motley Fool*:

- Salesforce
- Nvidia
- Microsoft
- Best Buy
- Pool
- Idexx Laboratories
- Adobe
- Intuit
- Cadence
- Lam Research

Brock wrote:

> By employing a combination of purposeful endeavors including community activism, charitable contributions, employee diversity, inclusion and enrichment, sustainability, social welfare, and global outreach, these companies are committed to making the world a better place while generating healthy returns for shareholders.

And, in addition to self-fulfillment, our individual purpose can be melded together with the alignment, strength, and commitment of others to make our collective teams and organizations achieve a much bigger, broader purpose. Given that labor cost is traditionally the biggest line item of a company's profit and loss sheet—not just salaries and benefits, but also factoring in the cost of recruiting, hiring, training, recognition, and rewards—alignment behind one's purpose can optimize productivity and lengthen an individual's tenure. This leads directly to improved profitability—the goal of any business enterprise.

"Always remember, your focus determines your reality."

— George Lucas

Think about the connection between a company and global issues such as climate change, sustainability, disaster relief efforts, and human rights.

- Do you feel a personal connection to these issues?
- Do you feel like companies have a responsibility to help?
- What brands do a great job of "doing well by doing good"?
- How does that effect your perception of those companies?
- Would you personally like to work for one of them?

CHAPTER 3

MAY THE 4S BE WITH YOU!

"Balance is the key to everything. What we do, think, say, eat, feel, they all require awareness, and through this awareness we can grow."

— Koi Fresco

Those who know me best understand I am big on symbolism, symmetry, and balance—I love it when a plan comes together with a strong beginning, middle, and end that tells a powerful story, one that inspires me emotionally, intellectually, physically, or spiritually in some way. It doesn't matter whether it is a song, book, poem, play, painting, sermon, workout, movie, game, or yes, even a business plan (I'm such a geek!).

The well-known concept *The Rule of 3s* outlines the symmetry of a particular thesis in three parts. Let's see…there is the three-ring circus, the Three Musketeers, the Three Stooges, the Three Amigos, a successful TED Talk format—so I'm told. I even saw a TV commercial for Dodge Ram trucks recently that specifically cited this concept, so I guess it is officially "a thing." And I'm sure there are many more examples than those I've cited.

However, as much as I used to subscribe to *The Rule of 3s*, I now firmly believe in a "Higher Power"—*The Higher Power of 4s!*

You see, I had an epiphany when I served as president and chief concept officer for Mimi's Cafe, a 145-location casual dining restaurant chain based in California. My job was to lead the brand through a massive turnaround and establish a reimagined concept the parent company could invest in to support its future growth. I felt we could accomplish our ambitious growth objectives via a maniacal focus on three key tenets:

- ✓ **Leadership**
- ✓ **Engagement**
- ✓ **Accountability**

Sound familiar? Each week, these three tenets became my mantra as I sent out recorded voicemails and weekly emails featuring results from some of our top performers to our leaders and their teams to reinforce this approach with living examples.

I am happy to report that through a variety of guest-centric, on-brand sales-driving strategies and tactics, we began to slowly turn our business fortunes around—going from double-digit negative revenue trends to positive revenue in a relatively short time.

At the same time, we were developing, prototyping, and testing a multi-dimensional restaurant model to extend and enhance the Mimi's brand essence called Mimi's Bakery, Cafe & Bistro. It was based on a more contemporary and experiential brand positioning: "A neighborhood bistro, inspired by France." This unique approach was born out of extensive research, industry trends, competitor mapping, and concept testing. The new and improved Mimi's reflected an innovative "store-within-a-store" concept featuring a French bakery that served French roast hot or cold coffee drinks, boulangerie-quality breads, and patisserie-style baked goods and treats, including croissants, tarts, and macarons among many other goodies.

Guests could enjoy items from this new French bakery kiosk as either grab-and-go or via café seating in addition to our full-service restaurant dining experience.

Updated bistro menus featured innovative, French-inspired breakfast, brunch, lunch, and dinner items, including a bistro bar stocked with a full array of beers, spirits, and a new wine program featuring wine and sparkling wine flights. In addition to both restaurant design and new menu offerings, we rolled out new bistro-style uniforms and chef togs in concert with an extensive hospitality training program. We even had every team member reinterview for their job to ensure we put the right people in the right places to consistently bring this exciting new experience to life for our guests.

We opened the new Mimi's Bakery, Cafe & Bistro with great fanfare in Valencia, California—a Los Angeles suburb. A festive ribbon cutting ceremony featured local dignitaries, celebrities, and members of the chamber of commerce and was covered by the media. Soon, people were lined up out the door as we served satisfied guests who marveled at the extreme makeover of "their Mimi's" and the quality of inventive new menu items and legendary hospitality.

Sales skyrocketed, and we shed tears of joy, hugged, and high-fived everyone directly (or indirectly) related to this tremendous accomplishment. It was indeed a total team effort! Based on our sales and profit trajectory, we were on track to achieve our *pro forma* return on invested capital (ROIC) well before originally projected.

However, while our team was physically exhausted from the months of long days (and late nights and weekends) planning, training, and executing this vision, it appeared we were also spent emotionally.

The gas gauge was sitting close to empty and falling....

I suddenly realized performance for the sake of performance was only satisfying to a point. We were chasing numbers for the sake of numbers, and living and dying based on our daily/weekly sales, profits, guest satisfaction scores, and other relevant performance metrics.

WASH. RINSE. REPEAT.

Now, don't get this twisted. To achieve our stated growth goals in all aspects of our business, we absolutely needed outstanding *leadership* and a greater breadth and depth of emotional *engagement* emphasizing personal and team *accountability*.

That said, something was glaringly missing in the equation. I found it personally unsatisfying, and my team felt likewise as the pursuit of our stated financial goals was just not...well, er, fulfilling... until I discovered what is now my *fourth* organic growth process: *Fulfillment*.

Like the Rule of 3s, the Higher Power of 4s is symmetrical, but even more balanced. A three-legged stool will still stand up and carry weight, but simply not as well as a 4-legged stool. And if you look closely, you might even see a fourth tenet hidden within the Rule of 3s to enhance the Higher Power of 4s—making it even more relevant to growth.

For example, the 4-leaf clover is a rare variation of the common three-leaf clover. According to Irish tradition, those who find a 4-leaf clover are destined for good luck, for each leaf in the clover symbolizes one of 4 good omens: faith, hope, love, and luck for the finder.

In addition to these 4 omens, there are 4 key characteristics of a 4-leaf clover we can apply to ourselves—we are all:

✓ Rare

✓ Unique

✓ Special

✓ Valuable

Now, let's look at several ways the number 4 effects each of our lives—pay close attention to the ones that symbolize the power of organic growth processes. Can you find them?

4 seasons (spring, summer, fall, winter)

4 directions (north, east, west, south)

4 chambers in the human heart (right and left atrium, right and left ventricle)

4 valves in the human heart (mitral, tricuspid, aortic, pulmonary)

4 particles of the atom (nucleus, protons, neutrons, electrons)

4 main elements of life (carbon, oxygen, hydrogen, nitrogen)

4 states of matter (solid, liquid, gas, and plasma)

4 fundamental forces (electromagnetism, gravity, weak nuclear force, strong nuclear force)

4 stages of metamorphosis (embryo, larva, pupa, imago)

4 Gospels of Christ (Matthew, Mark, Luke, and John)

4 types of love (storge, philios, eros, agape)

4 Greek classical elements (air, earth, fire, water)

4 cardinal virtues (justice, fortitude, temperance, prudence)

4 suits in a deck of cards (hearts, spades, clubs, diamonds)

4 limbs to the human body (right and left arm, right and left leg)

4 parts of musical harmony (bass, alto, tenor, soprano)

4 sections of an orchestra (strings, woodwinds, brass, percussion)

4 humors (black bile/melancholic; yellow bile/choleric; phlegm/phlegmatic; blood/sanguine)

4 Beatles (John Lennon, Paul McCartney, George Harrison, Ringo Starr)

And, of course, 4 letters in the word four.

Whew! Okay, that's enough "4-play"—I hope I've made my point!

But for some added perspective, let's turn this argument around to ask: What if only three elements were listed in each example? We'd still have symmetry, but not the same balance and harmonious interrelationships leading to the outcomes we all need for organic growth.

You've heard the term "third wheel," right? Nobody wants to be *that*. It's awkward, uncomfortable, and out of balance. Likewise, imagine only three directions, three seasons, three parts of music, or three elements. Which one would you leave out? I know what some of you northerners are thinking—winter. But, as you will see later, that would be a huge mistake because winter plays a very important role in nurturing the growth process, setting the stage for rebirth each spring. We simply can't have any one without the other three.

Now that we have established the *Higher Power of 4s*, let's look at how we can use this device to break down the fundamental components of the 4 LEAF *GROWTH* processes in greater detail within a "mind handle" I call the 4 x 4 Approach.

THE 4 X 4 APPROACH

Several of the top-selling vehicles on the road today are trucks and sport utility vehicles (SUVs). These types of vehicles are an absolute necessity for those who live up in the mountains, on farms, and in remote areas with uneven terrain or areas that receive heavy rains, sleet, or snow. They are also good for the sheer utility value of hauling "stuff."

But that isn't the reason I feel trucks and SUVs are so popular. In addition to their rugged looks and versatility, I believe it is because many come with a 4-wheel drive option. In fact, the 4 x 4 provides several benefits for driving enthusiasts living within even the most benign suburbs. Other than just looking cool, the functional purpose of a 4 x 4 vehicle is to provide traction, optimal performance, productivity, and value.

Based upon this 4 x 4 approach, I will unpack the purposeful 4 LEAF *GROWTH* model—Leadership, Engagement, Accountability, and Fulfillment—with 4 key support points designed to bring each revolutionary process to life.

In addition to coining the LEAF acronym, I have found a way to anchor each of the 4 key support points with the same first letter—using an alliteration technique to make it easier to understand, retain, apply, and share this information.

The "4 x 4 Approach" is the *4* major themes with *4* key support points all starting with the same first letter. Get it? Got it. Good!

Finally, and most importantly, I will give the Higher Power of 4s dimension using a classic Venn diagram featuring 4 interlocking circles. Remember the example of the 4-leaf clover I mentioned previously? This is very much the same image I would like to "plant" in your mind as you consider the integrated "nature" of the revolutionary 4 LEAF *GROWTH* processes we will review a bit later—all revolving around a unique purpose.

I am not suggesting each circle is *always* the same size—or possibly *ever* the same size. I am saying just the opposite since each circle represents a dynamic process where, based on a given season of life, it will likely grow larger or smaller relative to the other circles. *But they always overlap and revolve around a purpose for growth to occur.*

Picture the example of the 4 seasons. We know that while there are specific dates on the calendar signaling the official beginning of each new season, the actual length of a given season is shorter or longer in various parts of the country. And certainly, this gets flipped on its head when you consider the difference between the northern and southern hemispheres.

The important point is the interconnectedness of this diagram—representing the symbolism, symmetry, and balance of the *Higher Power of 4s* concept—in breaking down the key elements of each 4 LEAF *GROWTH* process to help fulfill one's unique purpose.

Make sense?

CHAPTER 4

YOU SAY YOU WANT A REVOLUTION?

"The Revolution introduced me to art, and in turn, art introduced me to the Revolution!"

— Albert Einstein

As a journalism major and longtime marketing executive, I love a good play on words—alliteration, double-entendres, acronyms, metaphors, colloquialisms, idioms, puns, and the like. I believe they help keep language alive by creating a deeper, more colorful, and emotionally evocative meaning beyond the mere black-and-white definition of a specific word in isolation.

I'm sure you will pick up some of my other little grammar and punctuation idiosyncrasies as you continue reading. Please do not blame my editors. It's ironic that I have twin daughters who both recently graduated from college—one studied journalism (she *hates* this!) and the other studied linguistics (she *loves* this!). Go figure.

My goal is simply to communicate *with* you as opposed to *at* you.

Growing up in Kansas and living for many years in Texas, you tend to hear some…well, let's just say…interesting phrasing you probably don't hear most other places.

For example, when people ask me, "How are you?" I tend to respond a bit more creatively. Sometimes, on a particularly hectic day, I reply, "I'm busier than a blind dog in a meat house." That image in their mind gets my point across in a fun, unique way.

On other occasions, I might say, "You know, I couldn't be better unless I were twins!" Now, as a father of twin girls, there were certainly times when they were growing up when that response may not have come across so positively. (Sorry, girls.)

And still other times, I might reply, "Well, not as good as you, but every day I get up and try my best!" That always disarms folks and leaves them feeling good with a little chuckle or smile on their face. Is that so terrible?

I used to say, "Better than I deserve," until I learned the well-known and beloved personal finance coach Dave Ramsey uses that as his catch phrase when replying to people who call-in to his radio show. Looks like I need to be a bit more creative and come up with some fresh new replies.

In fact, I believe words matter in many ways that are relevant for stimulating growth in our daily lives. Taking us *from* where we are *to* where we would like to go.

- "Thank you" can lead to…"You're welcome." Polite, courteous words can help build trusting, respectful relationships.
- "I love you!" can lead to… "I DO!" Expressions of love (in both word and deed) can lead to a union of two people.

- "I'm sorry" can lead to… "I forgive you." The humility of an apology (both requested and granted) can help rebuild trust, leading to long-term healing that can create an even stronger bond.

- "Yes, Dear" can lead to… "Let's do it!" Subservience in putting our partner's needs above our own can (sometimes) get us where we want to go.

All kidding aside, there is one word that I find extremely powerful and multidimensional in both its definition and connotation—its deeper philosophical meaning—in cultivating growth. In fact, this word serves as the foundation from which each of the purposeful 4 LEAF *GROWTH* processes are brought to life.

I'm talking about the word *revolution*.

Of course, we find slightly different variations in how *revolution* is defined according to various dictionaries. However, the three I found most relevant to the validation and application of my 4 LEAF *GROWTH* processes are:

Rev-uh-loo-shuhn (n)

1. **An uprising of the people:**

    History shows us that when people feel oppressed and lack growth opportunities, they revolt against authority. In fact, "an uprising of the people" spawned revolutions that led to the formation of new forms of government, policies, ideologies, or movements (e.g., the American Revolution, French Revolution, Arab Spring, #MeToo, Black Lives Matter, etc.).

Today, given the significant impact of COVID-19 on both our personal lives and related workplace dynamics, many people are using this opportunity to pause and reflect upon what (and who) matters most in their lives. Leaving unsatisfying jobs and/or toxic work environments that no longer suit them—creating a flexible Gig Economy that has resulted in labor shortages across many industries causing management to revolutionize their approach to optimize human resource practices in a new era of work.

2. A dramatic change in the status quo:

This is a reference to the spirit of innovation in revolutionizing the world and how we live, work, and play (e.g., electricity, telephone, trains, cars, planes, computers, smart phones, artificial intelligence, augmented reality, etc.).

In today's dynamic and increasingly competitive business environment, we cannot grow by maintaining the *status quo* or settling for creeping incrementalism. On the contrary, we must employ a *step function change* mentality to overcome strong headwinds and maximize our growth opportunities.

3. A circular orbit around an object:

Our unique purpose is the epicenter of our universe—everything we do must revolve around it for us to fulfill our growth potential.

But, in the process of doing so, we have an opportunity—indeed a responsibility—to help others along their journey. This perpetuates a virtuous cycle of reciprocity that helps to make the world go 'round. It's a transition from *me-go* to *we-growth*.

While the first two definitions of revolution are pertinent to my thesis regarding the importance of change, the third, "A circular orbit around an object," struck me as foundational in helping us truly unlock the 4 interwoven, purposeful growth processes.

In fact, by looking at 4 historic major growth examples, a familiar and consistent theme emerges—a circular orbit around an object.

- The earth revolving around the sun = life/existence
- The wheel revolving around an axle = movement/productivity
- The compass hand revolving around points = direction/guidance
- The clock's hands revolving around hours in a day = time/rhythm

The universe has a natural and undeniable rhythm "revolving" in/around most living things—people, animals, and yes, even plants.

According to my research, circadian rhythms are physical, mental, and behavioral changes that follow a roughly twenty-four-hour cycle, responding primarily to light and darkness in an organism's environment. The study of circadian rhythms is called chronobiology. (Chrono in Greek means "related to time.")

A circadian clock, or circadian oscillator, is a biochemical oscillator that oscillates with a stable phase relationship to solar time. The in vivo period, averaged over an earth year, for such a clock is necessarily almost exactly twenty-four hours (the earth's current solar day).

As you can see, my decision to inject the word *revolutionary* in front of growth is so much more than mere hyperbole or word craft. In fact, it represents the actual dynamics of how each of the interrelated processes of my 4 LEAF *GROWTH* model are always moving forward and "revolving" around one's unique purpose throughout every season of life, resulting in the potentially significant difference it could make in you as an *individual*, as part of a *team*, or broader *organization*, and yes, even within your *world*.

And as I learned from my friend Rebecca Blust, when you examine the word r-***evol***-ution a bit closer, you can see the word *love* is right in there written backward—hidden in plain sight.

Hmm... "Pay it backward!" Coincidence? I think not.

All three definitions of the word revolution are important in supporting my thesis regarding the vitally important process of "change"—something everyone wants, but not everyone wants to *do* for a variety of reasons.

To that point, *do* is another word I love because, for only having two letters, it is extremely powerful and complex. If you studied the computer programming language Fortran in college, you know the reference to revolution is called a *do* loop. According to Merriam-Webster, *do* has twenty-two different meanings as a transitive verb, another nine as an intransitive verb, and still more as an auxiliary verb. Plus, in different contexts, the word *do* can also be used as a noun. Now that's one hard-working, two-letter word, right?

Whew! That sounds exhausting...let's *do* lunch.

While *do* has many different meanings, the two I favor most and will amplify in this context are: 1) to put forth: exert, and 2) to bring to pass: carry out. Built upon what I refer to as a "repurposing" technique (as opposed to reframing) as mentioned previously, it means to move *from* a thought, idea, or feeling *to doing* something. For example, we might have an idea and feel compelled to take specific action leading to a desired growth outcome.

I believe Nike's historic "Just Do It" campaign was brilliant on many levels and featured one of the most powerful, strategically focused, and enduring lines of all time. Not only does the brand stand for excellence in athletic performance (rational benefit), but it created a call to action to the athlete in all of us (emotional benefit).

Again, the word *do* is vitally important here because it reminds us that we have the power to take control of our lives, find our passion, and fulfill our purpose if we have the courage to get off the couch and take the first step (preferably in fashionable Nike shoes and workout apparel, of course).

Just *do* it!

I still get a chuckle when I remember an old boss of mine at Pizza Hut years ago who was big on creating daily to-do lists. Like many of our contemporaries back in the day, "Will" carried around a Franklin-Covey planner—a notebook binder in which he took copious notes during various meetings along with a detailed list of action items for follow-up, most of which he directed me to take care of by saying, "Mark, this is my to-do list for today—now, make it go away!"

One morning, Will summoned me into his office and asked for a progress report on X, Y, and Z tasks. Trying to speak his language, I proudly pointed to my own Franklin-Covey planner and said, "Will, they are on my to-do list." The tone of his response made it clear he was not impressed nor amused: "Well, get them from 'to do' to 'to done'!"

Just *do* it!

Up to this point, we have established the importance of organic growth within a framework that includes the following 4 components—all interrelated and building upon the other:

- **The Number** = Replacing the Rule of 3s with the Higher Power of 4 to unpack the purposeful 4 LEAF *GROWTH* model.

- **The Model** = Using a Venn diagram of 4 interlocking circles representing integration with a *From… To…* growth repurposing technique.

- **The Goal** = Finding and focusing your unique, life-fulfilling purpose as the central theme for each of the 4 LEAF *GROWTH* processes.

- **The Process** = Employing a "4 x 4" Approach—*revolving* around purposeful growth—to maximize your growth opportunities while helping others *do* likewise.

Now that we have cultivated the field, let's turn the spotlight on *you* so you can start to plant the seeds necessary for your growth journey.

PART II

PLANTING YOUR SEEDS FOR PURPOSEFUL SELF

"You were designed for accomplishment, engineered for success, and endowed with the seeds of greatness."

— Zig Ziglar

CHAPTER 5

GROWTH 4 EVERY SEASON

"Every season is one of becoming, but not always one of blooming. Be gracious with your ever-evolving self."

— B. Oakman

Like the seasons we experience on the earth, we go through various seasons in our lives—encompassing both personal and professional events:

1. **Spring** = Planting

2. **Summer** = Transformation

3. **Fall** = Harvest

4. **Winter** = Rejuvenation

The 4 seasons are founded on the earth's exposure and tilt while revolving around the sun throughout the course of its annual orbit cycle. The beginning of each season centers around the summer and winter solstices and vernal and autumnal equinoxes.

Seasons have specific dates, but none really start or end on a specific schedule; rather, depending upon where we live, there is overlap in the transition from one season to another:

1. **Spring:** "March roars in like a lion and goes out like a lamb," or "April showers bring May flowers," so the sayings go; however, the Rocky Mountains can get a lot of snow in April, and May can be one of the wettest months in some states.

2. **Summer:** Traditionally, the hottest months of the year, but not everywhere and not always. According to a quote attributed to Mark Twain, "The coldest winter I ever saw was the summer I spent in San Francisco." In fact, I can remember when the traditional Fourth of July Fireworks show on Aspen Mountain in Colorado was cancelled one year due to snow!

3. **Fall:** In Minnesota, Halloween costumes are planned around whatever coat, hat, and gloves kids must wear to keep warm while out "trick-or-treating" in the early frost that traditionally envelops that region at the end of October.

4. **Winter:** The concept of a mid-winter warmup giving us a false sense of hope that spring is on the way is represented by Groundhog Day with Punxsutawney Phil seeing or not seeing his shadow, which determines how many more weeks of winter we must endure before spring arrives. I'm sure his shadow means something in some places, but not everywhere.

Okay, you get the point. In our own lives, we also go through seasons that, in many cases, overlap. The same can be said for the teams on which we participate or the organizations to which we belong, and certainly the world in which we live. It's a dynamic and revolutionary process that never ends.

> *"A man that views the world at fifty as he did at twenty has wasted thirty years of his life."*
>
> — Muhammad Ali

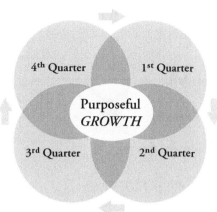

THE SEASONS OF LIFE

For those fortunate to live long enough to experience them all, I believe a variety of seasons comprise our lifespan which can be broken down into 4 quarters.

✓ **1st Quarter (Spring): Adolescent Youth—Planting**

- Learning
- Growing
- Achieving
- Exploring
- Discovering

✓ **2nd Quarter (Summer): Young Adult—Transformation**

- First Job
- Early Career
- Newly Married
- First House
- Young Family

✓ **3rd Quarter (Fall): Mature Adult—Harvest**

- Job Progression
- Soccer Mom/Dad
- Striving for "Success"
- College/Retirement Saving
- Divorce/New Family Dynamics

✓ **4th Quarter (Winter): Wise Adult—Regeneration**

- Job Transition (Career Change/Second Act)
- Empty Nest
- Married Children/Grandkids
- Retirement/Bucket List
- Health/Family Issues

These are just some familiar—or possibly stereotypical—types of seasons we may experience during various stages of life. As opposed to linear, I view our seasons as integrated and overlapping across each quarter like the 4-circle Venn diagram. We often see elements of different seasons overlapping, and some people experience a given season at a radically different age than others.

For instance, it is not uncommon for people to change jobs within the mature or wise adult stage, seeking a new career or "second act" once they've found their unique purpose. Or people may suffer from health/family issues much earlier, prompting them to reevaluate or delay their personal and professional growth plans. And, of course, we should never stop exercising the growth-minded elements of the first quarter—adolescent youth that keep us vital and alive through every season.

In addition to individuals, teams also have seasons (e.g., Tuckman's model of forming, storming, norming, performing), organizations (e.g., introduction, growth, maturity, decline), or entrepreneurial businesses (e.g., entry, growth, crucible, cruise). Seasons clearly influence us as individuals, teams, and organizations, so I don't in any way want to diminish their importance. But for now, let's just focus on *you*.

In my research, I ran across a model developed by Frederic Hudson aptly named Hudson's Renewal Cycle. Much like I view the changing of seasons, he describes our lives as chapters featuring 4 different, but interrelated stages. I've added my brief summation of each one.

- **Heroic or "Go for It"**
  We're living the dream—on top of the world!

- **Disillusioned or "Stuck in the Doldrums"**
  We're feeling a bit stale in our daily routine.

- **Reflective or "Looking Inward"**
  We're taking a mental health break to get refocused.

- **Revitalized or "Taking On/Moving Forward"**
  We're jumping (back) in with both feet!

And the cycle of renewal continues. But to be clear, we can experience different seasons from several angles. Our relationships, job satisfaction, outside interests/hobbies, and of course, spiritual/mental/physical health and wellbeing. In fact, it would be rare for us to be in the same stage across each area of our life regardless of season.

And that's okay.

Throughout history, major step function change growth opportunities traditionally occur as a result of some type of catalytic event (e.g., war, weather, famine, technology, innovation, science, research, discovery, etc.). I think it is safe to say the scourge of COVID-19 (and its variants) has touched us all. For many, it has led to questioning what (and who) really matters most to us.

According to some pundits, we are in the midst of "The Great Resignation," as people are leaving the workforce *en masse* for a variety of reasons. Some have been touched by the pandemic directly—some getting sick themselves or losing family or friends to COVID, while many others have been touched indirectly—by long periods of isolation and/or the loss of connection with those they love, the things they enjoy doing, or putting plans on hold. All these factors would certainly be just cause for self-reflection. But I believe one reason has risen above the others—we are all asking, "Is this all there is to life?"

Said another way, many of us are using this opportunity to question our life's purpose—and that's not a bad thing at all. "Am I living to work, or working to live?" Or possibly, "Am I actively thriving, or merely surviving?" And maybe an even deeper introspection as we discussed earlier, "Why am I here, and what is God's plan for me?"

These reflective questions got me thinking about how we might transition to a new and even more powerful starting point from which to build regardless of which season we are in.

COVID-19 has caused many to leave their unsatisfying, ill-fitting jobs to pursue more meaningful and fulfilling opportunities. This has caused a tremendous shortage of labor in many industries. I maintain we are all in the "people" business and COVID-19 has merely made it easier for people to opt-out of an oppressive system they have tolerated for years.

A January 11, 2022, *MIT Sloan Management Review* article by Donald Sull, Charles Sull, and Ben Zweig about a massive research study in which 34 million people from a wide variety of industries were interviewed suggests a much bigger issue. While the results varied by industry and even among companies within the same industry, one important piece of data cannot be ignored. In 2021, "toxic culture" was cited ten-plus times more often than the second leading reason for resigning. And compensation was way down at number sixteen on the list!

I don't care for the term "The Great Resignation" because it suggests two potential outcomes based upon its definition. Either we have decided to give up and resign from the workforce, quitting altogether: "That's it—I am so *done*!" Or possibly worse, we may have resigned ourselves to an unsatisfying *status quo* and decided to quit… and stay. Just soldier on like our fathers and mothers did before us and obey the rules of engagement—"Toughen up, Buttercup; work hard and keep your nose to the ol' grindstone." I think we can agree neither of those outcomes are "great."

Why does it have to be either/or? It doesn't!

As such, "The Great Resignation" should serve as a wake-up call for organizations to become more purposeful and people-centric as opposed to merely dutiful and profit-focused. So, what if companies—and their teams—use this era as an opportunity to repurpose the *status quo*?

To that end, I prefer to view this season as "The Great Repurposing"—helping to shift the paradigm to a more humanistic balance that benefits the *who* we collectively serve. In doing so, I believe it all starts with purpose. And when we lose our way or face change along life's journey, it is a time to "repurpose" ourselves in preparation for our next great adventure. We have been given a golden opportunity to reevaluate what (and who) is most important—and fulfill our unique purpose(s).

The good news is we do not have to merely conform to a worn-out, outdated model for work/life balance; rather, we can use this opportunity to transform ourselves in ways that accomplish both…while allowing us to grow into our purpose and fulfill our life's work.

No matter what season you are in, *now* is the perfect time to seek out your unique purpose, a foundation you can build upon to help achieve your full growth potential. Make finding your purpose number one on your personal to-do list.

To achieve fulfillment, however you measure it, *now* is the time to *repurpose*, not *resign*.

Regardless of where you are in your personal life, the team you play on, or the organization you belong to, one common denominator leads to growth: Change!

> "Change is the law of life and those who look only to the past or present are certain to miss the future."
>
> — John F. Kennedy

What season(s) are you in, and even more importantly, where do you want to *grow*? What has to change to get there? Are you ready to sacrifice or take risks to achieve your dreams? Or are you comfortable in the warm, cozy, familiar comfort of your unsatisfying status quo?

Do you have a person or—better yet—a team of people who can help you on your growth journey in whatever season you find yourself? Are you prepared to play a similar role to help support others in their seasons of growth?

"A friend is one that knows you as you are,
understands where you have been,
accepts what you have become and still gently allows you to grow."

— Author Unknown

To that point, there is a very beautiful poem that claims, "people are put in your life for a *season*, a *reason*, or a *lifetime*." Many have probably heard the title phrase, yet may not be familiar with the entire poem. I thought this excerpt was particularly relevant to our discussion of the importance of navigating life's seasons.

Reason, Season, or Lifetime

People come into your life for a reason, a season, or a lifetime.
When you figure out which one it is,
you will know what to do for each person.

The point is we are better *together* than we are alone. We need help to progress in our growth journey. I specifically appreciate the section of the poem devoted to *seasons* as I feel it is particularly relevant to my 4 LEAF *GROWTH* process: "Some people come into your life for a *season* because your turn has come to share, grow, or learn."

Regardless of which season(s) you may find yourself in, you can grow into your unique purpose and attain a higher level of personal and professional fulfillment when you takes steps to change.

"A journey of a thousand miles starts with one step."

— Lao Tzu, *The Tao Te Ching*

CHAPTER 6

WHAT'S YOUR GEN(I)US?

"Be yourself; everyone else is already taken."

— Oscar Wilde

What's your gen(i)us? Wow, that's a provocative question, isn't it? Let's start by breaking this concept down into two different, but very interrelated components. In botanical terms, the question would be: What's your *genus*?

Genus is a class of animals or plants with similar traits, qualities, or features. An example of a genus is all the species of mushrooms that are part of the Amanita family.

All plants are members of a particular plant family, and these, in turn, are divided into genera, which vary greatly in number, some containing a single species, others a few thousand. The scientific names of many plants, particularly wild plants, consist of two words; the first part of the name, the genus, gives the genus the plant belongs to. The first letter of this first part of the name is always capitalized.

For example, the genus name for species of oak is *Quercus*.

The Plant List is a working list of all known plant species. It aims to be comprehensive for species of Vascular plant (flowering plants, conifers, ferns, and their allies) and of Bryophytes (mosses and liverworts).

Collaboration between the Royal Botanic Gardens, Kew, and Missouri Botanical Garden enabled the creation of The Plant List by combining multiple data sets held by these institutions and other collaborators.

The Plant List includes 1,064,035 scientific plant names of species rank. Of these 350,699 are accepted species names. It also contains 642 plant families and 17,020 plant genera.

When I think back to places I have lived or visited, it is no coincidence a specific type of tree or plant plays a key role in my memory. And, of course, I can't "leave" out the fig tree in my backyard in Valencia, California that provided the original epiphany leading to this book.

Trees and plants of all types, shapes, sizes, and characteristics serve many functions—providing oxygen, shelter, shade, fruit, fire, building materials, paper products, and more. It is no wonder that God created a garden for Adam and Eve to live in.

What's your "genus"? To oversimplify things a bit, let's pick just 4 familiar types of trees that—like many personality assessments—might describe you based upon their known characteristics:

1. **Oak**—Strong, sturdy, and fruitful. (Provides a bountiful source of food, but also seeds of new growth opportunities.)

2. **Maple**—Showy leaves, influential, and needy. (Soaks up a lot of water, but creates outstanding beauty.)

3. **Aspen**—Connector, consistent, and versatile. (Features an interconnected root system, but appears as a unique living organism above ground.)

4. **Palm**—Flexible, resilient, and multi-purposed. (Bends in a storm, but provides shade and bears fruit.)

These trees require different types of soil, climate, and nourishment to fulfill their true potential. We'll cover this in more detail within *The Purposeful Fulfillment Revolution* section later in this book. For now, let's move the discussion from plant form (Genus) to human form (Genius).

"What's your genius?"

If the first part of this concept is based upon key characteristics and personality traits linked to our genus, then the second component—based upon the definition of genius—links to our unique purpose and related gifts.

We have many notable examples of genius—extraordinary musicians (Mozart, Beethoven), artists (Michelangelo, Van Gogh), philosophers (Plato, Socrates), astronomers (Galileo, Copernicus), physicists (Newton, Curie), inventors (Edison, Bell), leaders (Franklin, Lincoln), or possibly the most recognizable example, Albert Einstein.

But then, aren't we *all* "geniuses" in our own right? I believe we are. Let me explain what I mean.

In ancient Rome, the *genius* was the guiding spirit or tutelary deity of a person, family (*gens*), or place (*genius loci*). The noun is related to the Latin verb *genui, genitus*, "to bring into being, create, produce," and the Greek word for birth. Because the achievements of exceptional individuals seemed to indicate the presence of a particularly powerful *genius*, by the time of Augustus, the word acquired its secondary meaning of "inspiration, talent."

The term *genius* acquired its modern sense in the eighteenth century and is a conflation of two Latin terms: *genius* and *ingenium*, a related noun referring to our innate dispositions, talents, and inborn nature.

Given there is only one *you*—indeed *you* are (by definition) the "genius" of *you!*

> *"A genius is one who is most like himself."*
>
> — Thelonious Monk, Jazz Musician

Another take on this concept comes from Dr. Craig Wright, who teaches a course on genius at Yale. Wright has spent decades studying the phenomenon and published his findings in a book called *The Hidden Habits of Genius: Beyond Talent, IQ, and Grit—Unlocking the Secrets of Greatness*.

According to an interview posted on Jessi Hempel's "Hello Monday" blog on October 19, 2020, Wright "Challenges what we have come to believe about truly exceptional people. He takes issue with IQ tests, and he will make you rethink your definition of intelligence. He can tell us a lot about what genius really is, and how we can cultivate it—in ourselves and others."

On what it means to be smart, Wright says:

> I think IQ is overrated because it's a standardized test that you take. It's such a small part of the human experience that it's not particularly relevant. I tend to think of this in

terms of what Howard Gardner called multiple intelligence. What the heck does it mean to be smart? There are all kinds of smart in this world and people such as Martin Luther King or Mahatma Gandhi, I have no idea what they would have scored on an IQ test, but they certainly had particular kinds of skills that could never have been measured on the standardized IQ test.

Wright's genius equation: "In an odd way, it can be reduced down to a simple mathematical equation: Genius equals significance times number of people influenced times duration."

While I am certainly no math genius, I can get behind that equation—can *you*?

uBu

uBu is the shorthand version of "you be you" that encourages individuality and the freedom to be yourself and tell the world who you are. What would happen if we decided it would be easier, less risky, or more comfortable to put on a mask and hide our genius? What would be the harm in that? Or even worse, what if we surrounded ourselves with friends, family, and loved ones who knowingly (or unknowingly) kept us from fulfilling our true genius?

I don't know—maybe we wouldn't have obtained the tremendous benefit of some of the world's most innovative and creative minds, their skills and accomplishments. Here's just a few examples of what I mean:

Walt Whitman originally released *Leaves of Grass* in 1855 as a collection of twelve unnamed poems; however, Walt continued to work on his *magnum opus*, and on his deathbed in 1892, he rereleased the book with 383 poems.

Initially, Whitman's work was universally panned (quite an understatement) by literary critics, government leaders, church officers, and society folk of the day. Today—more than 150 years later—we revere *Leaves of Grass* and place it among the most important collections of poems in American literature. In fact, several schools across the country are named in Whitman's honor and his work was featured in the award-winning movie *Dead Poets Society* starring Robin Williams.

Other notable "geniuses" who were scoffed at by critics in their time include:

- **Copernicus:** He developed the heliocentric view that earth and all planets revolve around the sun and that earth itself rotates each day.

- **Galileo:** He died in 1642 after being put under house arrest for heresy because he used science and mathematics to disprove Aristotle's theory that earth was the center of the universe, which the Catholic Church had adopted as biblical truth. In 1758—more than 100 years later—the Catholic Church lifted its ban on Copernican theory. Finally, in 1835, it dropped its opposition to heliocentrism altogether.

- **Alexander Graham Bell:** He invented the telephone—originally called the "speaking telegraph"—and offered to sell the patent to Western Union for $100,000. They refused.

- **Thomas Edison:** He had to be home-schooled because he was deemed "too difficult" as a child. He went on to own a record

1,093 patents, created the telegraph, universal stock ticker, the phonograph, the incandescent electric light bulb, alkaline storage batteries, and the kinetograph motion picture camera. He merged Edison Illumination Company with General Electric, which later became one of the biggest companies in the world.

- **Jeff Bezos:** He started Amazon as an online bookstore from his garage. Since its humble beginnings, Amazon has expanded to a variety of products and services, including video and audio streaming. It is currently the world's largest online sales company and the world's largest provider of cloud infrastructure services via its Amazon Web Services arm. The first centi-billionaire on the *Forbes* wealth index, Bezos' net worth was estimated at $193.3 billion in 2021.

- **Elon Musk:** He invented Tesla, SpaceX, SolarCity, and PayPal. In addition to his primary business pursuits, Musk has envisioned a high-speed transportation system known as the Hyperloop and has proposed a vertical takeoff and landing supersonic jet electric aircraft with electric fan propulsion, known as the Musk electric jet. Musk has stated the goals of SpaceX, Tesla, and SolarCity revolve around his vision to change the world and humanity. Elon Musk had a net worth estimated at more than $255.2 billion in 2021.

- **Lady Gaga:** She had a unique look and created outlandish costumes to support her musical art. Originally singled out as untalented, hyperbolic, and just plain weird, Lady Gaga is now viewed as one of the most gifted and beloved musical artists alive today, performing during halftime at the Super

Bowl in front of 118 million people. She has sold more than 63 million albums and has a net worth estimated at $300 million. Her talents have been honored with nine Grammy Awards, and as a film star, she has won both a Golden Globe and an Academy Award.

Many artists' work—Beethoven, Monet, Picasso, Van Gogh, etc.—was criticized or mocked in their own time.

Your true *genius* lies in the ability to fully align your purpose—a combination of your natural gifts and internal passions—with your vocation so you are truly able to achieve a fulfilling "life-work" balance during each season of life. Rather than as a means to an end, think of your life's work as a masterpiece—one that lives on and grows in value even after you are gone.

I have been a huge fan of Patrick Lencioni for a long time. His many books on leadership, teamwork, culture, and execution—including *The 5 Dysfunctions of a Team*—have helped me and countless others raise our performance to new and higher levels. Recently, I ran across a fairly new concept he and the members of his The Table Group organization developed that I felt fit my "Genius" model on a very real and practical level. He calls it *The 6 Types of Working Genius*, which includes:

1. **The Genius of Wonder:** The natural gift of pondering the possibility of greater potential and opportunity in a given situation.

2. **The Genius of Invention:** The natural gift of creating original and novel ideas and solutions.

3. **The Genius of Discernment:** The natural gift of intuitively and instinctively evaluating ideas and situations.

4. **The Genius of Galvanizing:** The natural gift of rallying, inspiring, and organizing others to take action.

5. **The Genius of Enablement:** The natural gift of providing encouragement and assistance for an idea or project.

6. **The Genius of Tenacity:** The natural gift of pushing projects or tasks to completion to achieve results.

If you take the Working Genius Assessment (available from www.WorkingGenius.com), the tool will break down your results into three key categories:

- **Working Genius:** Two of those six types come naturally to you, meaning that you are good at them and that they give you energy and joy.

- **Working Competency:** Two types fall in between; you can do them fairly well, maybe even very well, but you don't derive great joy or energy from them.

- **Working Frustration:** Two of them are neither natural nor energizing for you, and most likely, you aren't particularly good at doing them.

This information will help you identify your areas of Working Genius, Competency, and Frustration, and allow you to make adjustments in your life that increase your work satisfaction, raise your level of effectiveness, and increase the likelihood of sustainable success.

Key Message: uBu. Make no mistake—you *will* have critics, but don't let them distract you from realizing your true genius because it is essential in finding and fulfilling your unique purpose. Remember, revolutionary thinking is almost never understood or fully appreciated when originally presented. Challenging the status quo and/or speaking truth to power is very difficult—as is the case when attempting to influence all forms of change. It takes a ton of courage to put yourself out there on a limb, knowing that at any moment it could be lopped off. But the courage of your conviction may be exactly what your team or organization needs from you to fulfill your shared growth objectives.

But before we attempt to lead change among others, we must first look to make positive changes within ourselves.

> *"Here's to the crazy ones. The misfits. The rebels. The troublemakers. The round pegs in the square holes. The ones who see things differently. They're not fond of rules. And they have no respect for the status quo. You can quote them, disagree with them, glorify or vilify them. About the only thing you can't do is ignore them. Because they change things. They push the human race forward. And while some may see them as the crazy ones, we see genius. Because the people who are crazy enough to think they can change the world, are the ones who do."*
>
> — Rob Siltanen (Apple "Think Different")

CHAPTER 7

SERVING YOUR PURPOSE

"There is no passion to be found playing small—in settling for a life that is less than the one you are capable of living."

— Nelson Mandela

Earlier we explored the power of purpose from an individual, team, organizational, and global perspective. Let's now put the focus on *you* and me. But before we can *serve* our purpose, we must first *find* our unique purpose. As I've learned on my own purpose-finding journey, this isn't as easy as it sounds; it requires deep introspection and diligent work. It is much like what Curly, the crusty old trail boss played by Jack Palance in the movie *City Slickers*, said was the secret to life: "It's the one thing." The question is: What is your one thing?

After several years of contemplating the question myself, I have come up with my own high-level answer: Your *passion* is your *purpose*! Or...Your *purpose* is your *passion*!

I had heard this phrase before, but I began to finally think, feel, and act this way after being inspired by an astute observation from my friend and former colleague, Nowell Upham. He said, "Mark, it appears to me you are most inspired and truly at your best when you are fighting for a cause you passionately believe in."

Nowell was spot on! In fact, his observation gave me the epiphany that led me to think differently about my career trajectory. That inspired me to serve the heck out of the great brands I had the honor and privilege of representing, my teammates, and the communities we served who needed our help. In the process of serving these three primary stakeholders, I was better able to serve myself.

> *"If you can't figure out your purpose, figure out your passion. For your passion will lead you right into your purpose."*
>
> — Bishop T. D. Jakes

When I wrote down what Nowell said, 4 powerful "root" words seemed to jump off the page:

- Inspired
- Cause-Fighter
- Passionate
- Believer

You may recall the phrase I shared that serves as the purpose statement for my personal brand and incorporates the essence of these words: "I don't want to just make money and retire; I want to make a difference and inspire."

Again, this statement has two different, but interrelated areas of focus:

1. *Make a difference* in helping to enrich the lives of others.

2. *Inspire* others to do likewise.

Reduced to just 4 words, my personal brand statement is:

I INSPIRE *PURPOSEFUL GROWTH.*

Some people call this an "elevator story." It concisely explains the essence of who you are and what you do quickly, like during an elevator ride. The idea is to intrigue with the big picture of your uniqueness and leave listeners wanting to know more.

Ding! "*Grow*-ing *up*, please!"

Inspiring others is a cause worth fighting for. It gets me fired up every morning and serves as a beacon guiding me through each day—cutting through even the foggiest, stormiest weather I may encounter.

At the end of each day, I take a moment to reflect by asking myself this question: "Did I do everything I could do today to grow into my purpose?" If my answer is yes, then it was a productive day; if my answer is no, I recommit myself to ensure I can give a different answer at the end of the next day. You will have good days and bad days, so you must not confuse purpose with a fleeting passion; rather, it must come from deep inside your heart.

> *"Your work is going to fill a large part of your life, and the only way to be truly satisfied is to do what you believe is great work. And the only way to do great work is to love what you do."*
>
> — Steve Jobs

As you'll learn throughout this book, I believe it is equally important for *individuals,* *teams,* and *organizations* to understand exactly *why* they believe in becoming involved in something much bigger than themselves to make a positive difference in the *world*. We're all desperately yearning to find our unique purpose—*why* we are here.

But as much as I agree with and admire Simon Sinek's original thesis based upon the interrelationship of his three circles—the *why*, the *how*, and the *what*—I believe a fourth element should be added and even moved up to the first position.

I believe we should start with *who*.

When we have crystal-clear focus, indeed a specific mental image, of *who* we serve, it becomes extremely personal and allows our *why*, *how*, and *what* to be relevant, purposeful, and fulfilling. I purposefully emphasize the word "serve." In my experience, "servant leaders" are the best leaders—they positively affect business, home, and community relationships while making the world a better place.

Service is also biblically supported in the form of arguably the greatest leader ever.

> *"For even the Son of Man did not come to be served, but to serve, and to give His life as a ransom for many."*
>
> — Mark 10:45 (NIV)

To that point, I recall having a great discussion with Susan Lintonsmith, a bright, young Indiana MBA graduate who was interviewing for a marketing position at Pizza Hut years ago. When I asked her what type of management style she preferred in a leader, she said, "Instead of just someone with a stopwatch on the bleachers barking out split-times, I prefer a coach who actually runs with the team." I thought that analogy was extremely insightful and powerful.

But unlike Sinek's concentric "Golden Circle" model, which suggests a path of progression from the inside out, I look at this *Purposeful Growth Revolution* model as a 4-circle Venn diagram featuring one's unique purpose in the center—with 4 different, yet interrelated and dynamic categories—all revolving around it.

Again, I believe in the *Higher Power of 4s* over the old, outdated *Rule of 3s*.

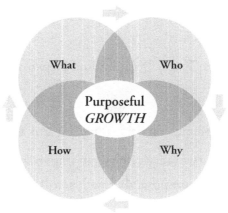

Throughout my brand-building career, I was taught to focus on identifying and satisfying our target audience's wants, needs, and desires. In sales, the target audience is referred to as a "persona" or "ideal customer avatar." Within a corporate organization, I believe the *who* we serve includes both our internal brand and external brand stakeholders—again, integrated and revolving around the purposeful vision, mission, and shared values of:

- Team Members
- Guests/Customers
- Business Partners
- Communities

The *who* we serve always comes first.

As individuals, I define our *who* as 4 different, but interrelated and dynamic categories of service:

1. Spiritual

✓ God, Religious Deity, Higher Power, Belief System

2. Relational

✓ Spouse/Partner, Family, Friends, Neighbors, Community

3. Professional

✓ Customers, Team, Organization, Network

4. Personal

✓ Physical/Mental/Emotional Health and Wellbeing

Again, each category of service plays an important role in establishing a foundation for purposeful growth across all 4 dimensions.

For example, it may sound noble to put the spiritual first, but what happens if we don't take care of our personal needs? We may end up unhealthy or worse, and then we're no good to anyone. Or what if we put our professional pursuits ahead of our relational commitments? We might lose our family and/or friends. On the flip side, what if we invest too much in our relational commitments at the expense of our professional pursuits? We may lose our job and the ability to provide for those we love.

The point is that these 4 categories of service—our *who*—are not linear, nor sequentially numbered; rather, they are integrated, with each one playing an important role within the others. For example, those who are spiritually inclined may put God first in every category as opposed to merely the spiritual realm. Each must be carefully nurtured and balanced over time, knowing there will be seasons of specific focus or heightened emphasis along life's journey.

Having a specific target of exactly *who you serve* can ensure a deeper level of alignment that makes your story very personal. Attaching a human face to your purpose helps make it even more powerful. And the importance of the word *serve* simply cannot be overstated. When you establish a mindset of being "of service" to another being, it opens a whole new world of possibilities by balancing both your inner-directed and outer-directed self in ways that can help you fulfill your unique purpose.

Again, do you have a visual in your mind of *who* you serve?

I was reminded of this concept when I read an article in the *Kansas City Star* in early 2021 highlighting Sarah Kiehl, a registered nurse who works in the ICU at Truman Medical Centers/University Health. Kiehl was selected to be the first healthcare worker in Kansas City to receive the Pfizer-BioNTech vaccine against COVID-19. I thought her reaction was extremely poignant and heartfelt: "I just keep imagining all the patients I've watched die in this time, all the patients who I've FaceTimed with their families on their deathbeds. I could see their faces in my mind and just think this might be how we finally get out of this really tragic, heavy time."

Kiehl went on to reinforce this point: "It's exhausting, yes. But the whole reason I got into nursing is to serve the population we serve at Truman. They deserve excellent care in the midst of this."

It is clear Sarah Kiehl knows *who she serves*, which helps her grow into her unique purpose—her *why*. And while we may not all be healthcare professionals serving on the front lines of a global pandemic like Kiehl, we can still practice the same visualization technique in whatever role we play. "Seeing" the faces of those we serve is a very powerful and motivating concept on many levels.

For as long as I can remember, I've wanted to be great in some way. But not in some "Hey, look at *me*!" narcissistic way; rather, I wanted to simply give my very best in all endeavors, leaving everything I had on the field with no regrets afterwards. We're only given one life, right?

I felt that approach—squeezing the very most out of my God-given abilities—was my path to greatness. I knew I may not have more size, strength, talent, or intellect than others, but I was determined to do my level best with what I *did* have by caring more, outworking those around me, and saying yes to opportunities others may have found too challenging or risky. That sounds pretty great to me.

But then I got to thinking, how do others measure greatness?

> *"The greatest among you must be a servant. But those who exalt themselves will be humbled, and those who humble themselves will be exalted."*
>
> — Matthew 23:11-12 (NLT)

> *"Everyone can be great…because everyone can serve."*
>
> — Martin Luther King, Jr.

> *"Humility is not thinking less of yourself. It's simply thinking of yourself less often."*
>
> — C. S. Lewis

Simply put, true greatness is measured by service and humility.

Again, we must first start with *who* we serve even before the *why* we *do* what we do and well before the *how* and *what* we *do* matters.

I *do* need to get the very most out of my God-given talents by being focused, industrious, and productive; however, I must do so with a heart of service and humility to ensure others' interests are put before (or at least equal to) my own. Got it!

> *"As we lose ourselves in the service of others, we discover our own lives and our own happiness."*
>
> — Dieter F. Uchtdorf

Who do *you* serve?

From a business perspective, the development of personas—bringing a target customer "to life" with specific details of *who* we serve—has been around in marketing and sales for some time. When I served as director of sales planning and promotion at JCPenney, we always left a chair in our board room empty. We did so to represent our female target customer. During various debates on potential ideas or proposed actions under consideration, we would often look over and ask, "What would *she* have to say about this?"

Let me give you another example of how this approach aligns with a commercial brand when I served as executive vice president and chief marketing officer for Noodles & Company—an innovative fast casual dining chain based in a suburb of Denver. I had long admired this brand because they serve a wide variety of fresh, made-to-order pasta dishes with flavor profiles inspired by different parts of Asia, the Mediterranean, and the Americas.

During my first week, I found myself attending a high-level meeting in a conference room that featured writing painted along the top of a wall near the ceiling. It said, "To always Nourish and Inspire every team member, guest, and community we serve."

I leaned over to the person sitting next to me and whispered, "Is that our mission statement?" They said, "I think it used to be, but we don't use that anymore." I leaned over to the person sitting on the other side of me and asked the same question. They said, "No, I believe that was our original founder's mission statement, but our current CEO has us using another one."

Wow! Other than switching the first word from "to" to "we," I thought this might be one of the most powerful and purposeful mission statements I had ever seen.

As a chief marketing officer, my job is always to look after the whole brand, not just the *external* brand featuring our menu strategy, marketing plan, and advertising campaign, but also our *internal* brand. This includes working with human resources, training, and operations to ensure we have 100 percent alignment between our brand's promise and its consistent delivery by the people tasked with executing it in our restaurants with every guest. I began to socialize some of my thoughts with others (I called this "planting seeds"—go figure) to see if it would be possible to go back to the original mission statement.

I used the Simon Sinek *Start with Why* philosophy featuring his Golden Circle model to build my case, but I also added an important fourth element—the *who*, which was based on our agency's research—to make it feel more personal.

- **Our *Who*: Millennial Families**
    - Dual-income Millennial moms with kids ten and under
    - The "live fast, eat slow" crowd
    - Food-forward, but health-conscious
    - Desire a (safe) culinary "adventure"
- **Our *Why*: Make a Difference**
    - To always *Nourish* and *Inspire* every team member, guest, and community we serve.
        - We *Nourish* our Guests and their Millennial family relationships, both physically and emotionally.
        - We *Inspire* our team members, guests, business partners, and communities to "use your noodle" to make a difference and leave a positive and lasting impression on your world.
- **Our *How*: Made. Different.**
    - *Real* Food, *Real* Cooking, *Real* Flavors, Culinary Platform
    - Highest Quality, Clean Ingredients
    - Artisan Sauces and Global Flavors
    - Freshly Prepared and Customized to Order
    - Hand-Crafted and Sautéed with a Sense of Theater
- **Our *What*: World Kitchen**
    - "A World of Flavors Made Just for You"
    - Globally Inspired Recipes and Ingredients

- *The* "Noodle Authority!"

- Multicultural Appeal and Adoption

Not only did our new "Made. Different." language resonate with our target audience, but it served as the foundation for our internal brand values and related team engagement and community service principles. Our agency shot a powerful and inspiring video that captured the essence of *who* we serve that led to our *why* and then our *how* and *what*. Our CEO at the time, Kevin Reddy, used to say about gatherings over a family meal, "Life happens over a bowl of noodles." I still get chills when I recall the line, "In a world intent on tearing us apart, noodles…bring us together."

In fact, "nourish and inspire" became the theme for our biannual convention in Scottsdale, Arizona, that year, which included representatives from the Noodles & Company support center, our restaurant management teams, and our many business partners. It also included representatives from Share Our Strength's *No Kid Hungry* program, with whom we announced a multi-year partnership to give back by nourishing and inspiring those in need within our communities.

Once again, *who* do *you* serve?

Whether it is spiritual, relational, professional, or personal—or likely some combination of each—you must first focus on exactly *who* you serve. This will allow you to persevere when obstacles appear in your way, help recharge your batteries when you feel tired, and provide a North Star when you get lost along the journey. Again, I believe those who are servant leaders are the best leaders; they instill a deep level of trust and confidence that results in higher individual, team, and organizational performance.

Sorry, Simon, but I personally prefer to start with *who*.

> *"You cannot teach a man anything;*
> *you can only help him find it within himself."*
>
> — Galileo

Chip Conley, former Airbnb executive and founder of the Modern Elder Academy, has these insightful words to say about the distinction between purpose and purposeful.

> You can't have the noun if you don't do the verb. As a noun, purpose is something you possess—a valued asset in your grasp that you can show to others. But, as a verb, it's a deliberate and conscious way of being: to be purposeful. In this approach, you don't have to obtain or clutch your purpose as an object that might slip through your fingers. You show up being purposeful, and, magically, you become a magnet for the possibility that your purpose may come to you rather than having to track it down. It's like happiness: always better when it arrives organically and on its own time, rather than as something being pursued. In fact, acting purposefully may be more important than discovering your purpose.

I agree with Mr. Conley's assessment because my thesis is all about growing into one's purpose, which is a lifelong pursuit based upon taking purposeful actions to help get "there."

As every journalist knows, there are some fundamental questions involved in reporting any news story. Likewise, I believe there is wisdom in using key elements of this technique to help us identify our unique purpose or passions in telling our life story.

To that end, I have developed a series of questions I believe are useful in sorting through several different, but related areas in identifying your unique purpose. From this foundation, we can grow into becoming more purposeful and, ultimately, fulfill our true growth potential.

- **OUR *WHO***

—Who *do* you serve?

Let's start with *who* you "serve"—*who* do you count on and *who* counts on you? Remember, *do* is an action word. Write down a list of answers relevant to *you* and make a mental image in your mind of the specific faces you see in these 4 areas:

1. **Spiritual**
   - ✓ God, Religious Deity, Higher Power, Belief System
2. **Relational**
   - ✓ Spouse/Partner, Family, Friends, Neighbors, Community
3. **Professional**
   - ✓ Customers, Team, Organization, Network
4. **Personal**
   - ✓ Physical/Mental/Emotional Health and Wellbeing

The point of this exercise is to really understand on a deep, emotional level *who* we serve because it will provide the foundation for helping us grow into our unique purpose.

> *"Discover your uniqueness and learn to exploit it in the service of others, and you are guaranteed success, happiness, and prosperity."*
>
> — Larry Winget

- ## OUR *WHY*

   —**Why *do* you exist?**

Next, let's examine your *why* by reflecting on the things you are *most* passionate about. These 4 areas are based loosely on the Japanese concept of *Ikigai* (ee-key-guy). "Iki" means life; "gai" means value or worth. It is the Japanese version of one's "reason for being"—essentially, how to live a purposeful life:

1. **What you *love***

   - What do you love to do/study most?

2. **What you are *good at***

   - What are you best/most skilled at?

3. **What the world *needs***

   - What value can you add to others' lives?

4. **What you can get *paid for***

   - What can you make a living doing?

I've found that passion is the distinguishing factor between the things we think we should do (possibly out of obligation such as guilt, peer pressure, parents' expectations, family business, etc.) as opposed to those our hearts desire (and thoroughly enjoy doing because we're not only good at them, but we feel personally fulfilled in the process). This is an opportunity to be honest and vulnerable with yourself. Unpacking what makes you authentically *you* as opposed to who others expect you to be.

Unfortunately, most of us do not think (or dream) big enough, so we tend to suppress our true passion and end up settling for a somewhat safe and practical life, which is not as deeply fulfilling as it could be.

Let me ask you: Personally and/or professionally, are you thriving or merely surviving?

Based on the introspective work you've done, are there 4 key words that seem to bubble to the surface? As I mentioned previously, the 4 key words for me are: *I inspire purposeful growth.*

Looking back on my career, those words were always there; however, I didn't recognize them as such. But today, I am much more intentional about growing into my purpose—recognizing the *who* I serve in helping me live out my *why*.

What is your *why*?

"When you live your life doing the things that turn you on. That you're good at. That bring you joy.... You walk around so lit up that you shoot sunbeams out your eyeballs. Which is precisely why you're here; to shine your big-ass ball of fire onto this world of ours. A world that literally depends on your light to survive."

— Jen Sincero, *You Are a Badass*

- ## OUR *HOW*

—How *do* you invest your resources?

Once we have identified *who* we serve along with *why* we do so, we can begin to turn our attention toward building our *how*—the specific ways we invest in bringing our *why* to life in practical ways. And like any investment, it is reasonable to expect a return, right? I'm sure you can think of several people who made similar investments that made a positive difference in your life. How will you *pay it backward?*

As I outlined earlier in the development of my own personal brand plan, we can break this out based on where we invest our resources in both ourselves and others across 4 categories:

1. **Time**—Personal and Professional Mentoring

2. **Talents**—Interests, Skills, and Abilities

3. **Treasures**—Financial and Charitable Contributions

4. **Triumphs/Travails**—Life Experiences (both good and bad)

How will you invest your resources in pursuit of your *why* for the enrichment of *who* you serve?

> "You cannot get through a single day without impacting the world around you. What you do makes a difference, and you have to decide what kind of difference you want to make."
>
> — Jane Goodall

• OUR *WHAT*

—What do *you* (plan to) *do* for a living?

Our unique purpose is not usually brought to light in our youth. In fact, we must grow into it, understanding it may "revolve" over time—depending upon what season we are in. For example, I did not have my personal epiphany when I was a teenager or a fresh-faced college grad; I had it well into my career as a mature(ing) adult. However, I believe I saw tell-tale signs of some of my central themes revolving around my core purpose many years earlier.

Upon reflection, my love of leading by serving and inspiring others to do likewise may have led me to pursue a career in retail, restaurants, entertainment, and hospitality. Would I have found my way into these related fields otherwise? Perhaps. But I personally don't believe in coincidences since the seeds of my purpose were planted early on but took many years to take root, grow, and shape me. I believe the same holds true for you, so don't stress over it. Remain curious and open-minded to help you discern your own tell-tale signs.

Phil Petrilli, our executive vice president of operations at Noodles & Company, summed things up eloquently and passionately: "Hospitality—the act (art?) of one human being serving another—is among the most important and noble professions in history."

Well said, Phil and, for me, it was spot on!

> *"Don't make money your goal.*
> *Instead, pursue the things you love doing,*
> *and then do them so well people cannot take their eyes off you."*
>
> — Maya Angelou

Finally, there must be a tight fit between *your* purpose and your company's purpose; otherwise, you may find yourself stuck in a miserable situation merely existing, punching a clock, and chasing a paycheck, which is not a very fulfilling experience for anyone.

What's the good news? It doesn't have to be this way. But the onus is on *you* to take the time for honest introspection (who am *I*?) and take the necessary *actions* to fulfill your life's work (what's *my* purpose?) in ways that benefit the people you care about most and likely others you may never know.

What type of job or vocation (really) lights *you* up?

> *"Allow your passion to become your purpose,*
> *and it will one day become your profession."*
>
> —Gabrielle Bernstein

CHAPTER 8

WHO ARE YOU?

"Once you know who you really are being is enough. You feel neither superior to anyone nor inferior to anyone and you have no need for approval because you've awakened to your own infinite worth."

— Deepak Chopra

I've given you a glimpse into who I am, what I stand for, where I've come from, and where I want to go—so what about you? Before you begin to answer that question, let me start you off with 4 things I already know about you, even though I may have never met you. Like a 4-leaf clover:

1. You are **rare**.
2. You are **unique**.
3. You are **special**.
4. You are **valuable**.

"It doesn't matter if you work at a fast-food joint or if you are the CEO of a Fortune 500 company. Your job title does not define your purpose. The size of your paycheck does not make you worthy. What makes you valuable is your contribution to the world and the legacy that you

leave behind. Stop defining yourself by what you do and start defining yourself by who you are!"

— John Geiger, *The Angel Effect*

In my experience, there are 4 dimensions that provide a holistic, 360-degree view of who *you* are:

- Who you *think* you are
- Who you *actually* are
- Who others *see* you being
- Who you *desire* to become

THE 4 DIMENSIONS OF YOU

The first step in the journey to achieving your full growth potential is to start with an honest, candid assessment of who you really are—not necessarily who you think you are—incorporating feedback from others representing the various ways they see you behaving.

"*He who knows others is learned. He who knows himself is wise.*"

— Lao Tse

Finally, the essence of this book is to help you grow into the ideal version of you, who you were meant to be. An honest assessment of these 4 dimensions will help to provide a well-rounded, revolutionary view of what exactly makes you authentically you.

Dr. Stephen Joseph, author of *Authenticity*, discusses the topic in a blog post at *Psychology Today*'s website.[1]

---

[1] https://www.psychologytoday.com/blog/what-doesnt-kill-us/201304/thine-own-self-be-true.

Philosophers throughout history have held the idea of authenticity in high esteem, but few psychologists have taken it seriously until recently when positive psychologists turned to understanding human flourishing.

First, there is our outer authenticity—how well what we say and do matches what is really going on inside us.

Second, there is our inner authenticity—how well we actually know ourselves and are aware of our inner states.

Not surprisingly, surveys show that, on average, people who scored higher on tests for authenticity are more satisfied with life, have higher self-esteem and are generally happier.

I agree with Dr. Joseph because I've had times when I felt the need to wear a metaphorical mask to conform to a situation. In each case, I had to ask myself whether I was being true to my personal brand or merely taking the path of least resistance to get through the moment. Just nod, smile, and keep moving forward—survive and advance, right? But who did that mask really fool? Only myself because the other people involved may not notice or care, or they may even be wearing masks themselves.

> *"Happiness is when what you think, what you say, and what you do are in harmony."*
>
> — Mohandas Gandhi

You see, we must first understand who we are so we can grow into the best possible version of ourselves. I do not believe this is a random evolutionary process, but an intentional *revolutionary* process where improvement can and should be continuous like the growth of a tree—day after day, month after month, and year after year.

And make no mistake, if you want to lead and manage others, you must first be able to lead and manage yourself.

To that end, you must strive to be authentically you every day; however, that does not mean in a static sense. You have a purpose and the power to grow in each season to become the best possible version of the you God intended. But to be clear, who you are is not defined by what you do—the title on your business card is merely a title, and no doubt a temporary one. It does not reflect the true essence of who you are across every dimension.

To obtain a holistic, 360-degree assessment, let's break down the 4 Dimensions of You within each segment.

DIMENSION 1: WHO YOU THINK YOU ARE

Let's start here because the ability to gain self-awareness can be a challenge for some of the following reasons:

- **Physical/Mental:** For some, mental and/or physical health conditions may affect how they come across to others.

- **Blinders:** Some people may have a false or inflated view of themselves. They may not be aware of their "blind spots."

- **Coping:** Those who suffer from selective retention tend to remember exclusively flattering or positive comments about their personality while writing off other comments/thoughts.

- **Ambivalence:** Some are self-absorbed and don't necessarily care how they come across to others.

No matter where you fall in this spectrum, we must all understand the importance of building *emotional intelligence* (referenced as either EI or EQ) to help us become more effective leaders or valued members of a high-performance team.

> *"What lies behind us and what lies before us are tiny matters compared to what lies within us."*
>
> — Ralph Waldo Emerson

I recognize the importance of EQ in building healthy, diversified, high-performance teams, so I will defer to the expert who pioneered this concept—Daniel Goleman, author of *Emotional Intelligence*.

> I would say that IQ is the strongest predictor of which field you can get into and hold a job in, whether you can be an accountant, lawyer, or nurse, for example.

But once you are in that field, emotional intelligence emerges as a much stronger predictor of who will be most successful, because it is how we handle ourselves in our relationships that determines how well we do once we are in a given job.

Goleman's thesis is there are 4 dimensions of emotional intelligence that can be broken down into 4 different, but related categories—*perception* and *behavior* in relation to both *self* and *others*.

THE 4 DIMENSIONS OF EMOTIONAL INTELLIGENCE

1. **Self-Awareness:** The depth to which I know myself, my intentions, and feelings

2. **Social Awareness:** The depth to which I know the intents and feelings of others

3. **Self-Management:** The skills I have in managing my own emotions

4. **Relationship Management:** My ability and willingness to work well with others

> *"In a high-IQ job pool, soft skills such as discipline, drive, and empathy mark those who emerge as outstanding."*
>
> — Daniel Goleman

To find out how emotionally intelligent you are, you can take the Global Leadership Foundation's free online emotional intelligence test https://globalleadershipfoundation.com/. I recommend doing this as a starting point to determine how you can improve your emotional intelligence. Doing so will benefit you in all areas of your life.

Lee Stuart, leadership programs manager at the University of Kansas Edwards Campus in Overland Park, Kansas, stresses the importance of EQ on the job:

> Leaders with high EQ receive feedback from subordinates, colleagues, and customers that they are authentic, transparent, place relationships before tasks and have a collaborative orientation.
>
> That means leaders who make it a priority to understand their emotions and pay attention to the emotions that motivate others' behaviors are better at connecting with their teammates and employees, as well as successfully working together with others.
>
> EQ can be developed through self-assessment, reflection, and introspection, one-on-one coaching, and through a rewards or incentive system that places a premium on cooperation rather than on individual achievement.

Unlike IQ, which doesn't change significantly over the course of your life, Stuart believes EQ can actually increase as you learn to use it, and self-awareness and a constructive work environment also help its development.

Research shows that managers who undergo EQ training deliver twice the profits of the general management population, and employee engagement scores increase four times in emotionally intelligent work environments.

To help solve today's increasingly complex business challenges, technical competency is simply not enough. I have found step function change growth requires a *team* of intelligent and competent individuals working *together* and finding creative solutions.

Business leaders say the most important competencies among incoming workers are:

- Self-motivation/discipline
- Effective communication
- Learning agility
- Self-awareness
- Adaptability/versatility

As recently as twenty years ago, the most important competency was technical mastery, but today, it doesn't even make the top five.

"The soft skills are the hard skills."

— Amy Edmondson, Harvard Business School

In fact, the ability to work in a team environment is critically important to success, promotability, and longevity within an organization. According to the Center for Creative Leadership, 75 percent of careers are derailed due to a lack of these emotional competencies:

- An inability to handle interpersonal problems
- Unsatisfactory team leadership during times of difficulty
- An inability to adapt to change or elicit trust

To overcome these obstacles, I believe every leader must master 4 important EQ skills regardless of industry or job title:

1. Conflict
2. Composure
3. Change
4. Confidence

Let's look at each in more detail.

- **CONFLICT**

—Empathy and resolution over "I win/you lose!"

The ability to put yourself in someone else's position and see an issue the way they see it is vitally important to successful resolutions. I often start off quite passionate about my position, only to change it once I've taken the time to truly listen to and empathize with another person's perspective.

For example, when I was at Noodles & Company, we were in the process of going back to our original mission statement as I mentioned previously. (To always nourish and inspire every team member, guest, and community we serve.) I had been taught the *guest* always comes first. However, Sue Petersen, our human resources leader, felt equally passionate about having *team members* come first. In her role, this certainly shouldn't come as any surprise. This could have become an emotional issue with both of us making strong points and digging in our heels to defend them.

But as I listened to her perspective, I remembered my broader role as CMO was not only to look after marketing, but to represent the whole brand. This encompasses our *internal* brand, which is every bit as important as our *external* brand, if not more so. Upon reflection, I quickly reversed my position before it ever became public. In fact, the re-rollout of this mission statement served as the foundation for making the culture stronger and more accountable than ever. She was absolutely right, and I was dead wrong! As we concluded our dialogue on this issue, I thanked her for reminding me of something I've never forgotten since: Our *people* should *always* come *first*!

- **COMPOSURE**

—Calm and courageous under fire instead of "Hair on fire!"
We all know leaders who have a kind of "Dr. Jekyll and Mr. Hyde" personality, right? One day, they are very calm, cool, and full of personality, but when the heat is turned up and the stress level rises, they can turn into stark raving lunatics.

We hear stories of heroes who demonstrate courage in life-and-death situations, like Captain Chesley "Sully" Sullenberger landing a commercial airliner on the Hudson River when both engines failed in 2009.

> *"The facts tell us what to do and how to do it, but it is our humanity which tells us that we must do something and why we must do it."*
>
> — Chesley "Sully" Sullenberger

Obviously, we are not all expertly trained, highly experienced airline pilots, or brain surgeons, or nuclear physicists, etc. But we *can* work at remaining calm, cool, and collected under stress.

Now, this "hair on fire" mentality can sometimes spur a team to action and a higher level of performance in the short-term, but it tends to erode trust and respect. If you grew up playing sports, you can probably relate to a coach (or two) who falls into this category. I know some very talented athletes (and coworkers) who quit for this very reason. It is a well-worn adage that bears repeating: People don't leave bad organizations; they leave bad leaders.

- **CHANGE**

   —Adaptable and flexible instead of "My way or the highway!"
As we've discussed, change is difficult—whether or not we want to admit it. Oh, we all *want* change, and we realize it is inevitable. We just don't want all the potentially negative consequences that might go along with it, right?

On a team or an organization, the leader must maintain a delicate balance between establishing a vision along with an ability to empower the team to help create and execute a plan to bring it to fruition.

As a business leader who believes in the power of step function change growth, I know this balance is not always easy to attain. But I love it when a person or team takes an idea and makes it even better than what I originally envisioned. That's when you know you have established a deep sense of ownership and empowerment as opposed to merely a dutiful, yet surface-level sense of obligation.

One technique I have found to work very well in accomplishing this objective was made famous by the improv comedians at *The Second City* in Chicago. They call it "Yes, and…." The goal is to build upon a core idea and extend it in creative new ways. People who feel they have a hand in creating an idea feel a greater sense of ownership. The more input the team has, the more ownership the team feels. This owner mentality translates to a deeper commitment that ensures the idea gets executed fully in a high-quality manner.

Today, we refer to it as co-creation or crowdsourcing, but regardless of nomenclature, it's a fun, rewarding process where everyone participates and wins…*together!*

- **CONFIDENCE**

   —Results and trust in we instead of "It's all about me!"
   Arguably, the most important aspect of EQ for leaders is the ability to instill confidence in the team or organization. Confidence in others is highly attractive because their vibe naturally makes us want to follow them and, ultimately, trust them to do right by us.

   Once again, a leader must be able to manage a delicate balance between confidence and over-confidence. A *confident* leader earns the trust of their team over time by demonstrating the ability to use team-generated information, advice, and guidance to help decide the best way forward. On the other hand, an *over-confident* leader may demonstrate a false sense of bravado by attempting to go it alone—ignoring input that could keep the team out of harm's way.

   Confidence must not turn into cockiness or condescension since both are ego-driven approaches that show you care more about "me" than "we." This is a sure way of losing the team's respect, which will limit your further leadership opportunities. Demonstrating a mixture of service, humility, and vulnerability will build confidence and trust in your ability to lead the team, which is the only way to achieve shared goals.

EMOTIONAL INTELLIGENCE VS. RESULTS INTELLIGENCE

As important as *emotional intelligence* is (how *you* work with others), I came upon an excellent corollary to this concept called *results intelligence* (how *you* get things done).

Dean Stamoulis, who leads the Center for Leadership Insight at Russell Reynolds Associates based in Atlanta, defines results intelligence (RI) as:

> Different from classic intelligence, or how much someone knows. Instead, it's the ability to beat the right path to the finish line, regardless of obstacles that may emerge. People with higher levels of RI can envision ways to accomplish large, complex goals that are not obvious to others, and they stick with them past the point when others would quit. By building a leadership team with high RI, companies can innovate more efficiently and effectively. They can focus on what matters, discard what doesn't, and easily pivot to take on new priorities.
>
> RI can be considered a complement to Emotional Intelligence (EI), which is the ability to manage emotions in relating to other people. In the most effective executives, RI and EI balance each other out. If someone is too focused on results, without paying attention to how they make people feel, morale will suffer. Conversely, if someone is too focused on emotions, without thinking about results, productivity will suffer. Together, RI and EI can help leaders make progress without alienating those around them.

In Kansas City, a consortium of business, civic, educational, and vocational leaders assembled to create an organization called KC Rising. A special task force was created (KC Rising Human Capital Common Sectors Competencies Task Force) to develop a blueprint of workplace competencies across multiple industries within the Kansas City area.

The goal is to prepare current and prospective employees to succeed in the workplace of the future. This will create a highly skilled, motivated, and productive labor pipeline for existing companies while also attracting new employers to the Kansas City area.

According to their collaborative studies, the task force found the following competencies—which happen to integrate both emotional *and* results intelligence—to be the most valuable:

- Customer Focus
- Drive Results
- Collaboration
- Instill Trust
- Plan and Align
- Read for Information
- Applied Mathematics

Truly gifted leaders know how to get along with teams and how to skillfully influence behavior and maximize resources to get things done. Again, a harmonious yin-yang balance must be struck to inspire confidence, build trust, influence behavior, and achieve mutually desired results.

Now that we've looked at several ways to understand ourselves, I can ask, are you really who you *think* you are?

Let's move on to learn more about who we *actually* are as we peel back even more layers to reveal our authentic selves.

DIMENSION 2: WHO YOU ACTUALLY ARE

While coming to grips with *who you think you are* can be a bit subjective, I have good news—the ability to obtain quantitative data to substantiate *who you actually are* is readily available. This information comes from a variety of well researched and documented sources and is based on data from millions of personality tests administered over several years. In essence, the results of these assessments can help us answer two important questions:

- *Who are you* in relation to others on your team?
  Everyone has different gifts, backgrounds, experiences, interests, aptitudes, personality types, learning traits, communication styles, work dynamics, etc. In a strengths-based environment, different is good.

- How might *you* use this information to be a better teammate?
  Like different positions within a sports team, the key is to integrate our gifts in ways that complement the rest of the team, giving everyone the opportunity to win together.

As we'll discuss later, diversity is extremely important in building high-performance teams. Many proven resources are available to help us learn about ourselves and how we can meld with others. Ironically, most models are based upon 4 key dimensions. Coincidence? I think not.

DiSC, Myers-Briggs, and StrengthFinders 2.0 are tried-and-true examples. Other popular personality type assessment tools include the Enneagram model, Hartman's color code, and the DeBruce Foundation's Agile Work Profiler. Regardless of which assessment tool you prefer, the important thing is to fully understand yourself and others so you can work more effectively and productively together as a diverse, yet cohesive team.

In addition to the various tools and resources for learning about ourselves within the context of our work/team environment, we must also understand the importance of our background and emotions in helping people understand who we *actually* are. You see, your backstory influences your behavior in more ways than you probably ever realize. Every single experience—good or bad—helps shape who you *actually* are.

The *I Am...* poem and the related *Life Journey Timeline* are two profound exercises I have participated in. In both cases, we were given a time limit to think introspectively and highlight key aspects of who we were and where we came from, and to chart both the highs and lows we've experienced. Once our time was up, we had an opportunity to present our "life stories" to the group. As each person stood up to speak, the energy and emotion in the room was palpable. In fact, some of us were moved to tears while teammates shared various events they had witnessed or experienced.

What an incredibly powerful way to get to really know someone's heart—someone who will work with you, sharing the same business values and objectives even though you may have subtle or even significant personality differences. In my view, we must endeavor to see each other as humans as opposed to merely a collection of experiences and skills—or as simply labels on a personality test. I believe this is even more important as we navigate through this new era of "The Great Repurposing."

Knowing someone's heart builds *trust* by giving us a more human understanding of *who* they *actually* are based on where they come from and what they've experienced. And we *all* come from somewhere and are imbued with a wide variety of experiences. This level of empathy provides an opportunity to give and receive grace when a comment or action appears out of character. And, according to Patrick Lencioni in *The 5 Dysfunctions of a Team*, trust serves as the foundation for the other essential team-strengthening elements.

Simply put, if you cannot trust your team—especially the leader—you don't really have a team. You merely have a dysfunctional group of individuals who happen to have the same logo on their business cards, Polo shirts, or uniforms.

Finally, from a strengths-based perspective, we can work to adapt our own behavior and work styles to get the very best out of each other as a fully functional, high-performance team, one that truly uses the power of its diversity to achieve shared goals. Every piece of a puzzle is a different size, shape, and image. Only when we fit them together do they reveal a clear picture.

Bottom Line: We are *all* different...and different is *good!*

> *"Your dignity can be mocked, abused, compromised, toyed with, lowered, and even badmouthed, but it can never be taken from you. You have the power today to reset your boundaries, restore your image, start fresh with renewed values, and rebuild what has happened to you in the past."*
>
> — Shannon L. Alde

DIMENSION 3: WHO OTHERS SEE YOU BEING

I believe a few sayings are important in helping us unpack the power of perception—how others view you. Essentially, how do your teammates say you typically "show up" based on your interpersonal behaviors?

The first saying comes from the great eighteenth century Scottish poet Robert Burns, who wrote, "O, wad some Power the giftie gie us/To see oursels as others see us!"

Yes, we humans crave feedback. I'm sure you've heard the phrase, "Feedback is a gift." Oh, it's a gift all right—that is, until it is given to you!

We *do* want feedback because we understand it is important to self-awareness and ensuring we show up in a positive, productive way more consistently when interacting with teammates. We just don't want it to hurt too much. Well, there's yet another popular saying, "The truth hurts." But it doesn't have to since "The truth can set you free!"

One of the most trusted and reliable techniques for providing feedback is the "360-Degree Survey" which invites feedback from those who work for you, peers who work alongside you, and the people you work for. It can even include external suppliers or agency partners with whom you interact.

To protect relationships, the survey results are anonymous—you know which segment the feedback is coming from, but not the specific individuals. The process is designed to encourage respondents to provide an honest and forthright perspective without fear of retaliation.

When it is done right, with a spirit of honesty, integrity, and candor, this technique can be incredibly valuable in helping us understand exactly how we tend to show up to each stakeholder level within the broader team. Wow, what a gift indeed!

Too often, we let avoiding conflict get in the way of our goal of developing truly authentic relationships with our teammates. In Kansas, we call it "Midwestern nice." We often let our feelings build up over time without addressing them in a healthy, productive manner. I can tell you from experience that sweeping things under a rug doesn't work. Issues merely fester and grow until they eventually surface. And when they surface, it likely won't be pretty.

In addition to conducting a 360-Degree Feedback survey, I have found another successful way to accomplish the same goal. It's not an anonymous survey. This process is 100 percent transparent and encourages more—and more frequent—face-to-face interaction. It is an integration of both the "Start, Stop, Continue" and "Do More Of, Do Less Of, Continue" feedback exercises.

In this case, we ask a team member to get feedback from others about *you*—including peers, subordinates, managers, and external partners—which can be summarized and aggregated into 4 categories related to the behaviors and related values one brings to the team:

1. **Do More Of**—The behaviors that add value to the team.
2. **Do Less Of**—The behaviors that dilute your value to the team.

3. **Continue Doing**—The behaviors that maintain your value to the team.
4. **Stop Doing**—The behaviors that erode your value to the team.

Opportunities for improvement must be couched in a positive, productive way within a safe and healthy environment. Everyone in the room should be treated equally lest anyone feel unfairly singled out. All must have an opportunity to request clarification (if necessary) while restating both the feedback they receive and the steps they plan to take in addressing their specific areas in need of improvement. This includes asking for support from the team, making it a two-way, interactive process.

"Your success is based upon how many uncomfortable conversations you are willing to have."

— Tim Ferris

Seeing one handle feedback in a positive, productive way gives those who provided it a sense of relief, making it easier for them to come to you directly with future feedback (and vice-versa). Like any relationship, when issues pile up without being addressed in a safe and respectful way, there is usually some event—maybe an unpleasant written or verbal exchange—that sets off the "pressure cooker," causing a much more damaging and potentially long-term situation that likely could have been avoided.

To ensure issues are recognized early, this exercise should not be a "one and done" activity; rather, receiving feedback should be integrated into your broader goal setting and performance management plan. This will provide an opportunity to get regular feedback as opposed to the most dreaded feedback process—the (gasp!) Annual Performance Appraisal. More on this later....

DIMENSION 4: WHO YOU DESIRE TO BECOME

We've saved the best for last. Obviously, you aspire to become a better version of *you*, or you wouldn't have picked up this book. But before we get started, I want to share these words of advice said by Steve Jobs just before he passed away:

> Your time is limited, so don't waste it living someone else's life. Don't be trapped by dogma—which is living with the results of other people's thinking. Don't let the noise of others' opinions drown out your own inner voice. And most important, have the courage to follow your heart and intuition. They somehow already know what you truly want to become. Everything else is secondary.

Who do you want to become? And how badly do you want to get there? If you were to fulfill your growth potential, what would that look like? Who would you be? What would you hope to accomplish? What *living* legacy would you like to build? How might that change your family, your friends, your coworkers, your community, and the world? What would it be worth to you? How would you measure its value? What currency is most motivating to *you*?

"What great thing would you attempt, if you knew you could not fail?"

— Anonymous

I have always loved the above quote because it provides a unique perspective and challenges us to think big. However, I feel replacing a few key words would make the quote even more powerful. Given the fact the writer is anonymous, I'm sure they won't mind.

"What great *purpose* would you *fulfill*, if you knew you could not fail?"

More than just "attempting a great thing," which comes across as a somewhat vague, one-off activity, *fulfilling our great purpose(s)* is a life-long quest. Are you clear on what you want? It might include:

- Financial security
- Personal freedom
- Purpose fulfillment
- Growth and development
- More time with my family and friends
- Leaving a "living" legacy
- Meeting others' needs
- Other?

Now, let me turn this around and ask you an equally (if not more so) important question.

What will your life be like if you don't find purpose in fulfilling your true growth potential?

- Financial insecurity
- Personal failure
- Squandering gifts/talents
- Surviving instead of thriving

- Letting family down
- Crippling regret
- Envying others
- Other?

> *"Someone once told me the definition of Hell; on your last day on earth, the person you could have been become will meet the person you became."*
>
> — Anonymous

Ouch! That would certainly be an extremely unsettling image.

I know which direction I would choose—*do you?*

I also know finding your purpose and fulfilling your growth potential takes intentional work. You must have clarity about *who* you serve, *why* you exist, *how* you invest yourself, and *what* you will do to get "there." My goal is to help you create a powerful and inspiring personal brand that will accentuate your unique assets and equities in highly attractive ways.

CHAPTER 9

WHO IS BRAND *YOU?*

"A brand is what other people say about you when you're not in the room."

— Jeff Bezos

Now that you have explored yourself across 4 dimensions to understand who *you* are, who *you* serve, and who *you* desire to become, it's time to pull together your Personal Brand.

The term "brand" or "branding" can have several different connotations from the direct, such as an intangible marketing or business concept that helps people identify a company, product, or individual, to a bit more esoteric, like creating an image of a product or service in your target audience's mind.

Based on my experience helping build great brands, I like to keep things simple. I believe brands are nothing more than a collection of promises. Great brands keep their promises. Those that *do* earn trust, and trust is the foundation of any lasting, loving relationship. What is *your* brand? What promises will you make to yourself and others so you stand out in a competitive, complex workplace while achieving the personal and professional growth you desire?

Whether you realize it or not, *you* are a brand. In fact, let's call you: Brand *You*. Throughout my career, I was blessed to work for some amazing brands and a host of extremely talented marketing leaders and agency partners. Like these great brands, there are several tried-and-true methods available to help you grow into your personal brand and fulfill your life's purpose.

Relax! You don't have to have a marketing background to follow this personal brand building process. It's simple and intuitive, and I will walk you through it step-by-step. The good news is that by going through this process, you will gain a deeper understanding of key marketing principles that can make you a better team member regardless of your area of expertise. Whether you are in human resources, sales, finance, accounting, operations, training, IT, legal, or customer service, like a corporate brand, *you* have a personal brand that must also be carefully cultivated to fulfill your growth potential.

Let's start by building a foundation for Brand *You* with, arguably, the most fundamental marketing model of all—The 4 Ps of Marketing (also referred to as the Marketing Mix), which provides a framework for making marketing decisions. It is defined as: "The set of marketing tools that a firm uses to pursue its marketing objectives in the target market."

Originated by E. Jerome McCarthy back in the 1960s and popularized by Philip Kotler (the "father of modern marketing") over the next several years, the original 4 Ps of Marketing stood for product, price, place, and promotion.

But because I like to shake things up a bit, I will change out product for problem, price for packaging, and place for performance—all revolving around purposeful growth. I believe these changes will make this exercise more relevant and useful in building your purposeful leadership brand...Brand *You*!

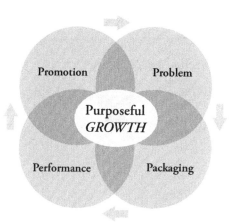

1. **Problem**—What problem does Brand *You* uniquely solve?

2. **Packaging**—How does Brand *You* look, write, and speak?

3. **Performance**—Does Brand *You* live up to your promises?

4. **Promotion**—How does Brand *You* stand out from others?

Let me explain how each of these 4 Ps can be translated from a commercial brand to a simple model that can help build your purposeful leadership brand—Brand *You*—starting with problem.

1. PROBLEM

What problem does Brand *You* uniquely solve?

> *"Marketing is best when it is need-oriented, when it is really solving a customer problem."*
>
> — Philip Kotler

According to a Show Me Scholars presentation developed by the Missouri Chamber of Commerce in 2018, we're only a few years away from a completely reshaped workforce. It is no coincidence the ability to solve problems is at the very top of the list of workplace attributes.

The top ten skills needed by 2025 are:

1. Problem Solving
2. Critical Thinking
3. Creativity
4. People Management
5. Coordinating with Others
6. Emotional Intelligence
7. Judgment and Decision Making
8. Service Orientation
9. Negotiation
10. Cognitive Flexibility

More than just skills, problem solving to drive growth must be woven into one's DNA. Regardless of the adoption of AI or VR, we're still people who must lead in empathetic, humanistic ways to work together to solve complex problems within a team structure.

By 2025, jobs will be based on three key human qualities:

1. Our ability to use our intellect for complex problem solving.
2. Our need for more immersive experiences and entertainment.
3. Our ability to empathize with others.

While the *external* customer is the end-user—the one whose ultimate problem you are solving—you are also serving several *internal* customers who create the product or service solution.

Of course, depending on your team or organization, many other important roles are involved in helping you fulfill your growth potential. And, as you will hear me say many times, it takes a well-coordinated *team* effort to solve a problem—any problem—whether it is related to the external customer's original problem or an internal customer's specific area of responsibility in solving that problem.

As consumers, we have things we want (e.g., flashy new car) and things we need (e.g., affordable, reliable transportation) along with a combination of both *rational* and *emotional* reasons for wanting/needing each. That said, we typically purchase a product or service because it solves a specific problem. Similarly, companies hire new employees (or promote existing ones) to help them solve specific business problems.

As a result, you must come up with a Unique Selling Proposition (USP) for Brand *You*. What makes you unique in helping solve the business challenges of your current (or desired) employer? What role can you uniquely play to support team efforts in achieving your shared goals?

- I'm a sales rainmaker—I love to grow sales opportunities.
- I'm a tech guru—I keep business systems up and running.
- I'm a finance whiz—I analyze numbers to achieve the best results.
- I'm a marketing maven—I build brand recognition that drives sales.

- I'm an operations person—I improve productivity at all levels.
- I'm a non-profit servant—I put the needs of others first.
- I'm a customer service rep—I resolve issues/rebuild trust.
- I'm an HR pro—I help attract, grow, and retain our people.
- I'm an accounts payable clerk—I make sure everyone gets paid on time.
- I'm a legal eagle—I ensure our "assets" are protected!

Aligning your purpose across all the dimensions of Brand *You* to solve problems is fundamentally important. How you communicate your product's USP to your target audience is where the magic lies. To start, let's look at packaging Brand *You*.

2. PACKAGING

Like a product on a retail shelf, Brand *You* has a "package" representing your personal brand. Now, don't get this twisted—I'm not referring only to one's surface level or outer appearance (although that is certainly part of it). I'm much more focused on how people come across to others on a broader, deeper, more holistic basis. In my experience, your packaging is defined by the way you *look*, *write*, and *speak*.

Let's start with your look—how you present yourself. To be perfectly clear, I don't care about age, gender, race, height, weight, sexual orientation/preference, tattoos, body piercings, multi-colored hair, or baldness. I care about whether you are appropriately dressed for your work environment and your personal grooming and hygiene are properly maintained. Duh.

Carrying yourself with confidence is important, as are interpersonal cues exhibiting an outwardly positive demeanor and a warm, cheerful, helpful aura. These traits make you more attractive to others. You want others to naturally gravitate to you and/or actively seek you out. And like a product on the shelf, your visual "merchandising" is what people see first—it's just a fact. And we all know how important first impressions can be. How Brand *You* "shows up" matters—a lot!

Once we pick a product off the shelf and understand its fundamental purpose, we can read more about how it may solve our problem from what's written on its packaging.

Let's address the importance of the written word. In our digital age, good business writing has gone from a critically important discipline to an almost antiquated art form because of our new communications culture that relies more on email, texts, instant messages, chats, posts, pins, videos, and tweets. Regardless of platform, we still need to write well to communicate our ideas clearly, concisely, and powerfully to get results.

I confess I struggle in this area. In fact, I may be one of the world's worst at self-editing. When I was a young executive at Pizza Hut, Claude Caylor, our sage (and sometimes rather blunt) media director took me aside after receiving a lengthy email from me and said, "Less is more, Mark.... Less is *more!*" But I'm an "explainer," so less is very difficult for me. I have to work hard to convey my thoughts in writing without being verbose.

Does that sound like you, too?

But truly good writing takes more time than volume. When Ben Franklin wrote to a member of the Royal Society in London to share the results of his experiments with electricity in 1750, the legend goes, he started the letter with, "I apologize in advance for the length of this letter. I would have made it shorter if I had more time."

It takes discipline and time to edit oneself to:

- Briefly summarize a given problem and/or opportunity.
- Hit the high points of the key issues—including the "size of the prize" for prioritization.
- Provide a short-list of potential solutions (pros and cons).
- Propose the best solution with supporting rationale.
- Ask for approval and/or support to move forward.

During my graduate work at Northwestern University, we used Harvard Business School case studies in many of my classes. (Hey, there's no shame in that. I understand Harvard is a pretty good school too.) We were given only one piece of paper (front and back) to dissect a forty- to fifty-page case following the steps above. As a result, I learned to write a well-thought-out, yet succinct summary of a business challenge and/or communicate a strategic growth proposal. I was amazed as my career progressed at how many executives—even the most senior—struggle mightily with this.

When I was in account management at Leo Burnett working on the McDonald's business, the memos we sent out to our clients were often scrutinized by three or four managers. We had a consistent format we were trained to use that started with the sentence, "The *purpose* of this memo is…." Using this technique helped us come across as professional and unified as a team on behalf of our clients.

Today, we use digital technology beyond email like project management or internal communication tools such as Trello, Slack, Asana, and SharePoint. Regardless of the platform, good, solid writing is fundamental to Brand *You*'s success. Learn and practice writing skills to communicate clearly, sound professional, and, most importantly, show you are a helpful, problem solver.

"Take advantage of every opportunity to practice your communication skills so that when important occasions arise, you will have the gift, the style, the sharpness, the clarity, and the emotions to affect other people."

— Jim Rohn

Here are 4 growth tips to help you write better:

✓ **Be Clear**

Ensure your message is *crystal clear*! Nobody has time to decipher vague or murky prose or fill in the gaps for you—so don't make them. Simply put—make your purpose clear and tell the reader what you want them to *do*.

✓ **Be Concise**

Assume everyone is at least as busy as you and be as *concise* as possible. Provide only essential information. Filler is unnecessary! I assure you, taking time up front to self-edit (or get someone to help edit) will pay off big on the back end.

✓ **Be Compelling**

State your case *compellingly* by using data (describe scope of the benefits) or desired outcomes for the reader (i.e., "What's in this for *me*?"). We're all being pulled in many directions, so no one is sitting around waiting to hear from you. If you're writing an email, start with an attention-grabbing subject line and follow through with text that compels the reader to take the desired action.

✓ **Be Contextual**
   While listed fourth, *context* is as important as clarity, conciseness, and compelling content. As such, sometimes a brief note is appropriate and other times a more in-depth explanation is warranted. The key is to know the difference and choose the appropriate length and style to accomplish your specific objective based on audience, platform, and desired outcome.

As the Canadian philosopher Marshall McCluhan said in the 1960s, "The medium is the message."

As you continue to build Brand *You*, let's turn our attention to how you *speak*.

Given the importance of speech in influencing people and outcomes, let's tackle one of most people's least favorite things…the oral presentation. (Gasp!) Just the thought of getting up in front of a group of people can make some people so nervous they hyperventilate and/or break out in a cold sweat, hives, or worse. I've been there.

Relax…you've got this. Here are 4 growth tips to help bring any presentation to life with 100 percent confidence:

✓ **Plan:** First, establish your topic, what you want to accomplish, and how you plan to communicate it. Are you planning to use PowerPoint or another type of presentation program?

Will you use charts and graphs that require explanation? Are you thinking of including graphics or possibly video clips to enhance your thesis, or some combination of the above?

Who on your internal or external team are you counting on to provide information or technical expertise? Be sure to give them enough time to properly prepare.

Finally, what is your timeline? How much time do you have to present and to pull the entire project together? Put together a *work-back plan* that starts with the presentation date and works backward to today highlighting key milestones along the way.

- ✓ **Prepare:** After you develop a high-level plan, Brand *You* can start preparing materials. If you are using slides, try to make them simple but engaging to ensure your key points come across clearly and powerfully. A summary headline with a key visual and a few brief bullet points to support your thesis in a logical, well-orchestrated manner will do the trick.

  Once you have your materials, I have found it incredibly helpful to practice the presentation alone in front of a mirror. This will enable you to see and hear what the audience will see and hear. Specific movements, hand gestures, and eye contact in concert with voice tonality, projection, and inflection are important elements that must be carefully rehearsed, in addition to identifying when to pause. I know it may feel kind of funny, but trust me, it works.

- ✓ **Perform:** Okay, enough planning, preparing, and practicing—Brand *You* has put in the work and is more than ready. The time has come to perform. Notice I didn't say, present? The truly memorable and most powerful presentations I have seen are, in fact, performances.

Like any good performance, it is important both to convey the necessary information *and* tell a powerful and emotionally evocative story. Do not use verbal crutches like "Umm…" and/or merely read your slides—the audience can read. These practices sound like nails on a chalkboard. Like the children's learning toy I had growing up (remember the See 'n Say?), please make your performance multi-dimensional; bring your content to life with interesting and compelling prose. You want the audience focused 100 percent on Brand *You*.

Likewise, always make eye contact with various people in the audience. Wait for each to nod at you (and they will) before moving on to someone else. This is your way of connecting on a human level. Ensure everyone "feels" you, so they understand your passion for the subject matter, retain your message along with a sense of trust and confidence in Brand *You*, and are motivated to move forward with your recommendations. (Think Jedi mind trick.)

Finally, be prepared to answer questions. By distributing your presentation far in advance of the big day, you should be able to anticipate most questions. Hint: The CFO will always want to understand the numbers involved in your recommendation.

- ✓ **Post-Analyze:** After your performance, take time to get feedback. What was the overall reaction? What did they feel you did well? What areas need work?

Do this as soon as possible while everything is still fresh in your and their minds. This discipline will build the necessary muscle memory for improving your performance next time and the time after that.

Remember, some people may make presenting in front of groups (large or small) look easy, but I assure you, it is not. Like mastering any skill, it takes patience and practice. Just ensure you are getting the *right* practice, or much like my golf swing, you'll do nothing more than cement bad habits, which is counterproductive.

Bonus Tip: The approach above works equally as well in job interviews as it does in making oral presentations.

3. PERFORMANCE

As stated earlier, a brand is nothing more than a promise. Beyond its packaging, which can stimulate an initial purchase, the most attractive thing about the brands we love is that they do a good job at consistently delivering on the promises they make to us through packaging, advertising, social media, buyer reviews, etc. Much like a personal relationship, we are let down when promises are not kept, which is upsetting. Building trust requires consistent performance.

According to the 2021 Edelman Trust Barometer, 88 percent of consumers surveyed value trust in a brand, which carries more weight in buying decisions than their love for the brand. In fact, a consumer is seven times more likely to buy from a highly trusted brand.

Simply put, people want to be associated with brands—and people—they can trust, which usually includes shared values and reliability. Edelman's research shows that younger consumers, Millennials and Gen Z in particular, buy based on trust, shared values, and consistency. The same can be said for Brand *You*. Are you committed to keeping your promises to both your organization and the members of your team? Does your performance demonstrate that commitment consistently?

> *"We are all doing the same exact thing: No matter what your business is, your product would not exist if it did not solve problems for people, if it did not make people's lives easier, more enriched, and better. And it's got to work. It's those two things: It has got to be necessary, and it has got to work."*
>
> — Danny Meyer, *Five Lessons from Customer-Obsessed CEOs*

In the military, soldiers are trained to have each other's backs in combat. In combat, soldiers are fighting for the person next to them. "No soldier left behind!" This mantra helps build trust, confidence, and camaraderie while allowing them to perform at the highest possible level under the most stressful situations. For them, commitment to one another could be the difference between life and death.

Regarding Brand *You*, would you say you consistently perform at a high level, living up to the organization's mission and your personal commitment to the team? Essentially, can you be trusted? Is your team confident you will do your job? As I said, first impressions are always important; however, in a work environment, you will have many interactions that will confirm or refute their perceptions of you. Indeed "perception is reality" as we learned earlier.

To ensure your interactions are favorable, you must work to build *Emotional Intelligence* (EQ). As stated previously, EQ focuses on one's ability to get along with others. Are you a collaborative, collegial team player? Or are you always the smartest guy/gal in the room? Are you someone who handles their emotions with class and dignity? Or do you pout, grumble, cross your arms, shake your head, or audibly sigh in meetings when you don't get your way?

At the same time, you must demonstrate *Results Intelligence* (RI) by living up to your commitments to the team or organization in achieving shared goals. Regardless of potential barriers you may encounter, can you be counted on to deliver on your assigned tasks by leveraging available resources in a high quality, accurate, and timely manner? Are you focused on results, or merely going through the motions, working hard, but not necessarily in a thoughtful, planful, and productive manner?

The bottom line is, as you advance in your career as a leader, you are living in a fishbowl with everyone judging both your words and actions, including the meaning behind them, real or perceived. The sum of your words and actions will add up to Brand *You*, and like it or not, a misperception of your personal brand can easily become your reality—one that can be very difficult to shake.

Popularized by GE several years ago and still relevant, the term "Net Promoter Score" (NPS) is the net difference between the positive and negative interactions one has with a given brand. This is essentially a feedback mechanism that allows the brand to determine how likely a customer is—based on direct experience—to recommend the brand to others, which is a key barometer of revenue growth.

Just think: How many of us would even consider buying anything of value without reading the product reviews first?

If you were able to use a similar NPS approach, how would you "net out" with respect to the packaging of Brand *You* based on your personal appearance, written and oral communications, and demonstrated behaviors that lead to your performance in solving a given problem? Can you be trusted to live up to your commitments? Would you have more promoters or detractors?

Bottom line: Would they recommend Brand *You* to others?

4. PROMOTION

Once a brand defines its problem-solving purpose, distinguishes itself through packaging, and keeps its promises through consistently high performance, it is time to focus on the *promotion* necessary to fulfill its growth potential.

With respect to Brand *You*, make no mistake there is most definitely a right and wrong way to promote yourself to achieve your career growth objectives.

Let's focus on promoting Brand *You* correctly. And like any great brand, it should not come across as "promotion" at all; rather, we want to internalize these traits so they become natural, recurring characteristics you can hone over time. Here's what I look for when considering someone for a promotion—I call these 4 growth tips my Killer Be's:

- ✓ **Be Industrious:** Work hard at whatever you are asked to do and maintain a positive, can-do attitude; always be willing to take on the toughest challenges; offer solutions instead of focusing on problems. (I'm already aware of what's wrong.)

- ✓ **Be Curious:** Ask good questions and listen well; search for best practices; avidly seek and share new lessons; challenge the *status quo*; always ask: *Why?* or *What if…?*

- ✓ **Be We Instead of Me:** Do not self-promote; "if you mess up, fess up," as humility goes a long way; serve others; be a helpful team player; earn the respect of the team by living up to your commitments and go the extra mile.

- ✓ **Be Results-Driven:** Establish clear metrics; be fact and data based; communicate outcomes with transparency; learn from mistakes; celebrate team successes.

If you are diligent in pursuing these 4 "character"-istics within the shared values of the team or organization, you will stand out and put yourself in a solid position for promotion. And everyone will cheer your success because it will be obvious to both your team and the organization that you earned it.

I reject the myth "It's not what you know, it's who you know." I believe *who you are* matters most.

No hiring manager or supervisor worth their salt would bet their career on someone based on a personal relationship. That relationship may help you get a foot in the door, but in a performance-driven world, one must get through the door on merit because everyone involved in the hiring process will be held accountable if it doesn't work out. And the risks involved in making a bad hire or promoting someone before they are ready can be extremely high financially and waste company time and hiring opportunities.

Now, don't get this twisted. Obviously, it is vitally important to work hard at building authentic relationships above, below, beside, and outside of Brand *You* to achieve your professional growth objectives. I put heavy emphasis on the word "authentic." I am a huge advocate for networking within industry associations, peer groups, business development events, and, of course, LinkedIn when done properly. However, in my experience, building inauthentic, politically motivated relationships tends to end badly. No one likes or respects a brown-noser.

How do we capture the essence of the 4 Ps of Brand *You* by integrating them into what is called a Brand Positioning?

From the halcyon days of advertising on Madison Avenue back in the '60s—glorified in TV shows from the comedy *Bewitched* to the more recent dramatic portrayal in *Mad Men*—we've seen ad campaigns pitched around the power of a slogan.

This isn't that.

Brand Positioning is very much aligned with your higher purpose. It must be unique, discernable, authentic, and memorable. It's also known as a Value Proposition because any business relationship is essentially a value exchange: What do I get in exchange for what I pay?

Start by defining your target audience (e.g., current employer, team leader/members, clients, prospective new employer, etc.) and identify their specific problem. Then list the benefits of working with Brand *You* to solve them. Performing with credibility and reliability will make Brand *You* more valuable. It is just as important that they will likely tell others about their positive experience with Brand *You*, thus influencing others on your behalf.

That's it.

Based on your brand architecture, you can begin to properly promote Brand *You*—helping you find, focus on, and communicate the power of your unique purpose to fulfill your true growth potential. As you formulate your communications plan, you must focus your message on *who* you are trying to appeal to and the specific objectives you want to achieve.

I subscribed to the Think-Feel-*Do* guest behavior model we used when I served on the agency side of the marketing business years ago, which featured three inputs and the related outcomes. Given the importance of positive word-of-mouth, prevalence of customer review sites, and the goal to create relationships over time, I have since added a fourth objective that I feel is equally important… *Relate*.

Again, this is not a linear or sequential step-by-step process. Rather it is integrated across each of the 4 communication objectives—all revolving around purposeful *GROWTH*.

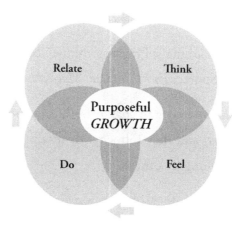

Think: What *do* you want people to *think* about Brand *You*?

- Create awareness among your target audience of what problem you solve better than others. (Head = Rational)

Feel: How *do* you want people to *feel* about Brand *You*?

- Engage your target audience in an emotionally evocative way to make them "feel" you. (Heart = Emotional)

Do: What *do* you want people to *do* because of Brand *You*?

- Encourage your target audience to take desired actions. (Hands = Behavioral)

Relate: What *do* you want people to *say* about Brand *You*?

- Encourage your target audience to serve as advocates to influence others on your behalf. (Mouth = Relational)

Rolf Jensen, the director of the Copenhagen Institute for Future Studies and author of *The Dream Society*, said, "The ability to create and relate stories" is now at the top of the list.

> "Brands are built around stories. And stories of identity—who we are, where we've come from—are the most effective stories of all. This [storytelling] is a powerful way to bring [brands] to life."
>
> — Bill Dauphinais, PricewaterhouseCoopers LLP
> Source: *Fast Company Magazine*

Good stories compel people to change both thoughts (rational) and feelings (emotional) and they influence or modify behaviors. Great stories get passed along by others.

When you are looking for a promotion or a new job, you must weave a narrative that connects Brand *You* highlights with your audience's needs. Like all great stories, you must appeal to people on both a rational and emotional level.

- **Rational:** Connect your competencies, experience, and results to the specific points outlined within the job description. Demonstrating your ability to fulfill the job requirements is merely an important first step. Those who do will likely move on in the search process, whereas those who do not will get quickly passed over.

- **Emotional:** Communicate your passion for the industry and the specific company you are speaking with both in writing and in person/online during interviews. Taking time out to highlight key nuggets of information about the industry and your experiences therein will demonstrate you are emotionally engaged and worthy of further consideration.

"These days, the camera is the new printing press: a full 80 percent of all internet traffic is video consumption," according to Andy Fuller with *Higher Ed LIVE*. Leveraging the benefits of what I refer to as "site, sound, and e-motion," you must look for ways to bring the Brand *You* story to life digitally and on social media. In addition to your resume, LinkedIn profile, and social media presence, some people have created their own website, blog, vlog, or podcast to provide greater depth and credibility. Regardless of platform, you want to ensure Brand *You* is seen as integrated, consistent, and compelling. Savvy employers will want a deeper understanding of who you are, what you're passionate about, how you think, and how you communicate. Remember to always use your authentic voice. Do not be afraid to let your personality show—that's why it's called a "personal brand."

In a recent CareerBuilder survey, 54 percent of employers reported online content led to hiring when the:

- Candidate's background info supported their professional qualifications for the job (37 percent).
- Content demonstrated the candidate's creativity (34 percent).
- Candidate's professional image was available online (33 percent).
- Content showed the candidate as well-rounded, with a range of interests, and suggested a good fit with the company culture (31 percent).
- Content demonstrated the candidate had strong communications skills (28 percent).

One important word of caution—be very careful what you post on social media. Your employer (or prospective employer) will check to see if your social media threads align with your personal brand story. Right or wrong, I have seen candidates get passed over because of posts indicating the candidate didn't reflect the organization's values.

As you continue to learn about yourself and reflect on your own growth experiences in various seasons, your Brand *You* distinctions and related story will no doubt change.

What's your Brand *You* story?

"You get whatever accomplishment you are willing to declare."

— Georgia O'Keefe

CHAPTER 10

GET THE FUDD OUT!

"So much of what we suffer from, that I suffer from, my mind creates. And if we can actually clear our minds of that old stuff, we can be in the present and we don't have to create Hell in our lives."

— Dr. Gabor Maté

Carly Fiorina, the former CEO of Hewlett Packard, said in a speech to our executive board during my tenure as chairman of the Promotion Marketing Association, "It seems that everyone wants to go to Heaven, but nobody wants to die."

So true.

How many people really want to take the steps to bring their vision to life? Why so few? I believe it's because, at our core, we're all creatures of habit—we simply don't like too much change. Changing our habits is disconcerting at best and sometimes even painful. That kind of thinking is not how we start a revolution on any level.

If we truly want to bring about purposeful change, I believe we must overcome some deeply rooted psychological issues. I have found fear, uncertainty, and doubt (often shortened to FUD) are primarily responsible for delaying our progress in fulling our unique purpose.

In the world, FUD is sometimes used as a disinformation strategy in sales, marketing, public relations, talk radio, politics, religion, and government to further an agenda that benefits those using the strategy.

Many people tell lies to get what they want. It is and always has been a problem within the human condition.

FUD is generally the use of negative, dubious, and/or false information to appeal to fear. We are also prone to creating this type of campaign in our own mind, limiting our ability to manage change personally and professionally—representing the lies we tell ourselves. Often the result of FUD is another word I'll add as a *fourth* letter to the acronym: D for delay.

I will unpack FUDD (sorry, no connection to our ol' cartoon pal, Elmer) in a way I think we can all relate to when examining our own lives. Again, I will employ the powerful "from X to Y" repurposing technique to guide the process.

The good news is we have an antidote for FUDD to help us grow into our unique purpose from the seeds we have sewn into our hearts.

FEAR

—What will happen if I fail, and if so, then what?

Many of us have heard the acronym FEAR (False Evidence Appearing Real). That is certainly accurate, but fear is a response, both rational and emotional, to unknown or difficult circumstances. Some claim to be driven to attain success by their fear of failure, whereas others become paralyzed by it. Others may be afraid of success.

Of course, it is only natural to be afraid of the unknown; however, the Bible tells us that faith can overcome fear. Depending on which version you read, in the Bible God tells us approximately 365 times not to fear. Why? God does not want us to live in fear.

Be. Not. Afraid.

> *"Don't let what you are afraid of keep you from what you were made for."*
>
> — Bob Goff

Most have heard Franklin Delano Roosevelt's famous line from his first inaugural speech, given at the height of the Great Depression: "So, first of all, let me assert my firm belief that the only thing we have to fear is fear itself—." However, I wager most don't know the rest of the sentence: "—nameless, unreasoning, unjustified terror which paralyzes needed efforts to convert retreat into advance." While the first part is no doubt true on many levels and makes for a great sound bite, I believe the second part is even more important. It is a call to move forward in fulfilling our purpose.

To help us overcome our fears and live a life of purpose and fulfillment, we must first grow from *fear* to *purposeful faith*. Or said another way, we must have the faith to be courageous and act boldly by standing up to the fear of the unknown and attacking it head-on. Think David and Goliath. It was David's faith in God and God's purpose for him that gave him the courage to take on Goliath when no one else dared to. FDR's faith led him to take action by creating the New Deal, which created jobs, financial reforms, and infrastructure projects as catalysts for a new era of growth and prosperity.

From Fear to Purposeful Faith

My fears are only lies in my head. I choose not to give them power. Instead, I will choose to have faith that I may overcome my fears by becoming bold and courageous as I seek to grow into my purpose. I *can* do this!

> "What a liberation to realize that the 'voice in my head' is not who I am."
>
> — Eckhart Tolle

And when you are laser-focused on *who* you serve, you begin to see they have faith in *you* and indeed are counting on you not only to grow but thrive.

What are *you* afraid of?

UNCERTAINTY

—Dare I risk what I have for what I desire?

Fear of failure almost always leads to *uncertainty* as we weigh the risk-reward benefits of any decision. When our fear of failure outweighs our vision of success, we tend to avoid taking the necessary risks to change the *status quo*. Many people who claim to be dissatisfied with their lives remain stuck because they don't want to risk what they do have. On the other side of the coin, I marvel at entrepreneurs who believe so strongly in their ideas that they are willing to risk everything. Some get rich and thrive that way; others remain poor and merely survive.

> *"And the day came when the risk to remain tight in a bud was more painful than the risk it took to blossom."*
>
> — Anais Nin

The next step in the process of managing self-change is choosing to grow from *uncertainty* to *purposeful hope*. If we are truly living our God-given purpose and have a keen understanding of exactly *who* we serve, then we must see the risks involved are well worth the rewards we are meant to achieve. Again, this turns the hope we have in our heart into the positive, purposeful actions needed to bring our vision to life.

For those who smugly profess the time-worn adage, "Hope is not a strategy," I respectfully disagree. Remember, hope can and should be an active—not passive—strategy that, when combined with tactical execution, *will* lead to success. And the opposite of hope is "hopeless" which is, well…er, "less" than a winning strategy. And "hopelessness" suggests a deep, dark state. But for hope to work for us, we cannot be timid and merely dip our toes into hopeful waters; we must be open and willing to take the leap, diving deep!

From Uncertainty to Purposeful Hope

I will choose to take on the risk of uncertainty because of the hope I have in the greater benefits of growing into my purpose. My plan *will* work!

"Death is not the biggest fear we have; our biggest fear is taking the risk to be alive—the risk to be alive and express what we really are...."

— Don Miguel Ruiz

Are *you* open to taking a risk?

DOUBT

—I'm not worthy. Isn't success for "other" people?

If *fear* leads to *uncertainty*, then most assuredly this combination leads to *doubt*. Negative thoughts can easily creep into our heads and cause us to doubt ourselves. I've heard these called "background voices." I'm sure you can relate to them. Am I an imposter? Am I as good as them? Am I ready for this? Am I even worthy of success?

"Our doubts are traitors, and make us lose the good we oft might win, by fearing to attempt."

— William Shakespeare, *Measure for Measure*

Somehow, we think everyone else has their stuff together and we don't. And the truth is, they probably feel the same way. It's just that some are better at hiding it than others. Either way, self-doubt can quickly lead to self-sabotage, and often we don't even realize we're doing it. Our doubt becomes a self-fulfilling prophecy that reinforces the initial doubt—and the cycle continues in a downward spiral.

If we are bold and courageous in facing our fears through faith, we must be prepared to take the next step to grow from *doubt* to *purposeful belief*. Faith founded not only on being created in God's image and infused with a purpose in our hearts, but the belief that we are indeed worthy of an abundant life filled with love, joy, peace, and fulfillment.

From Doubt to Purposeful Belief

I've done this (many times) before; I believe I can do it again. This time, even better and more successfully than ever as I choose to focus on growing into my purpose. Why *not* me?

> *"Your belief determines your action, and your action determines your results, but you first have to believe."*
>
> — Mark Victor Hansen

What do *you* believe?

DELAY

—Can I survive the painful regret of missed opportunity?
Now, if *fear* leads to *uncertainty* and uncertainty leads to *doubt*, it stands to reason that all this negative energy would stop us dead in our tracks—resulting in the paralyzing inertia of *delay*. This is quite possibly the most damaging of them all as a delay in taking action may not only cause us to miss out on a life-changing opportunity, but it may also result in a deeper, more serious source of regret. *What did I do with my life?*

> *"Procrastination is opportunity's natural assassin."*
>
> — Victor Kiam

We can be brave in overcoming fears, turn uncertainty into calculated risk leading to the hope of greater rewards, and instill self-belief that erodes doubts through faith. All that is fantastic; however, we must grow from *delay* to *purposeful action* and do something about it. Otherwise, we will continue to remain stuck in second gear and may never fulfill our life's purpose. What a shame that would be, right?

But like taking our medicine, we know that embracing change is absolutely a necessity for proper growth and development within every single facet of life. But it is never easy or particularly fun.

From Delay to Purposeful Action

I will choose to move forward exercising my freedom to take actions that will help me learn, grow, and develop along every step of my journey until I reach my destination—celebrating my wins along the way. I freakin' *did* that!

> *"Between stimulus and response is a space. In that space is our power to choose our response. And, in our response lies our growth and our freedom."*
>
> — Dr. Viktor Frankl, *Man's Search for Meaning*

What choices will *you* make to just *do* it?

I assure you these 4 obstacles to growth are relevant to my life. I can't even begin to tell you what moving beyond my FUDD to take this book from epiphany to completion was like. But the *purposeful faith* I gained to overcome my fear with boldness and courage, the *purposeful hope* I held helped me take a calculated risk in overcoming my uncertainty, and the deep sense of *purposeful belief* that helped me overcome my doubt all led me to take positive, *purposeful action* and finally overcome my delay.

As I think back on my career, I recall saying yes to opportunities that often tested my FUDD factor. What if I had said no to them? I would have missed out on meeting great people and having experiences that changed the trajectory of my career and my life's purpose—and possibly even yours.

The term "analysis paralysis" is pretty common, and it is very real. In business, we know while waiting for all the information to arrive and align, we sometimes allow the competition to speed past us. My solution is what I call the "80 Percent Right Rule." We should be able to make the right decision with 80 percent of the information instead of waiting for 100 percent, which likely won't come anyway. In sales, we also know that "Time kills all deals."

To take full advantage of the growth opportunities that present themselves, we must overcome FUDD—Fear, Uncertainty, Doubt, and Delay—with Faith, Hope, Belief, and, most importantly, Action—all focused on *who* we serve and revolving around our unique Purpose.

Just *do* it!

> "Change can be scary. But you know what's scarier? Allowing fear to stop you from growing, evolving, and progressing."
>
> — Mandy Hale

CHAPTER 11

ARE YOU READY TO TURN OVER A NEW LEAF?

"To everything there is a season, and a time to every purpose under the heaven: A time to be born, and a time to die; a time to plant, and a time to pluck up that which is planted...."

— Ecclesiastes 3:1-2 (KJV)

The hit song, "Turn! Turn! Turn!" was written by folk singer Pete Seeger in the late 1950s (well, he added the title and six words to the King James version of Ecclesiastes 3:1-8) and was later made popular by the folk rock band The Byrds in 1965.

TURN! is an acronym for Teachable, Uncomfortable, Responsible, and No Return!

Think of TURN! as a guide to overcome FUDD—the fear, uncertainty, doubt, and delay that often holds us back from finding our purpose and fulfilling our true growth potential.

As I studied the word *turn* a bit closer, I saw a deeper meaning I believe you will find instructive in moving through the changing seasons of your life in a healthy, positive, and purposeful way. If we want to make significant change truly stick, we must employ this important process. I first heard a similar model from a pastor talking about our failure to keep most of our New Year's resolutions. My TURN! model is a blend of ideas with my own thoughts and personal examples thrown in to bring the concept to life.

Let's unpack each of these TURN! tenets in order.

TEACHABLE

To fulfill our true growth potential, we must come to grips with the cold, hard truth that we don't know it all—in fact, we often don't even know what we don't know. To overcome this natural state, we must be *teachable*: Open to advice, counsel, and instruction from those who have "been there, done that" and desire to convey their knowledge and experience to help us grow.

When we allow ourselves to be taught, we demonstrate humility and a willingness to challenge our thinking, which promotes personal and professional growth. When we avoid being dogmatic or clinging too tightly to our current understanding, we appear open to learning vitally important lessons that can help us grow into our purpose and fulfill our true growth potential. Being open and teachable may also lead to meeting and building relationships with some awesome people we might never have crossed paths with otherwise. Amazing!

Also realize we can learn from both our successes and when we come up a little short. In fact, I believe we learn much more from our challenges than we do our successes. Notice I didn't use the word failure. It sounds so final. Failure is never final if we learn from it because it can help us grow even stronger. Yes, I prefer to think learning from our mistakes is just part of purposeful growth.

Even though we may possess a wealth of experience and expertise on a given subject, we can't know everything. The most learned and experienced professionals continue to learn and grow every year to keep up with the latest developments in their respective fields. Doctors are always searching for innovation breakthroughs to ensure they can provide the best care for their patients. Even the most seasoned pilots must train to reinforce important flight safety procedures or learn new equipment details.

"When you stop learning, you start dying."

— Albert Einstein

Many of us go through seasons that are both exciting and scary. Given the diversity of my career choices, it has been very important for me to remain teachable so I can navigate the major changes, which provide significant growth opportunities.

Early in my career, when I worked at Pizza Hut, our senior vice president of marketing was David Novak. Research told us pizza was kids' favorite food. (We are so happy!) However, the incredible appeal of "Happy Meals" suggested McDonald's was kids' favorite place to eat. (We're not so happy.) After Pizza Hut's success from a holiday movie tie-in with Steven Spielberg's animated hit, *The Land Before Time*, David felt the time was right to go all-in to close the kid gap with McDonald's.

As a result, David promoted me to director and moved me into a new area of marketing called National Event Marketing. This included high-end premium promotions, sports tie-ins, and entertainment licensing opportunities with the goal of developing a kids' meal program of our own. I didn't know much about this kind of marketing, but I was determined to learn all I could as I grew into my new role. This move changed my career path and helped me become a well-rounded marketing professional with far more tools and skills.

After Pizza Hut, I went on to lead two promotional marketing firms working with global companies like PepsiCo, Frito-Lay, KFC, Taco Bell, Subway, Hershey, and M&M Mars. Later, I become director of sales planning and promotion at JCPenney and then senior vice president of sales and marketing at Universal Studios Hollywood. Each position helped establish a solid foundation I would build upon in my broader role as a C-level leader.

Outside of work responsibilities, I served as a long-time board member and, ultimately, chair of the Promotion Marketing Association in addition to roles on the California Travel and Tourism Council, Licensing Industry Merchandising Association, and No Kid Hungry advisory boards. None of those invaluable experiences would have been possible without David's faith and trust in me along with my willingness to be teachable and to grow outside of my comfort zone.

The cycle of learning by remaining teachable continues within every growth season.

Are *you* willing to be *teachable* as you grow into your *purpose*?

UNCOMFORTABLE

Most don't like being uncomfortable, but if we are to progress from one season to the next, transformation is required. Sometimes the transformation is physical; other times it is mental or emotional, and still other times, it is spiritual—or some combination of the above. To allow ourselves to be *teachable*, we must be open to becoming *uncomfortable*—at least for a season.

> *"We don't grow when things are easy.*
> *We grow when we face challenges."*
>
> — Anonymous

Being uncomfortable is all part of the growth process, so you've simply got to work through it. Notice I said, *work* through it. You shouldn't merely hope to endure or outlast; you've got to work through being uncomfortable without any shortcuts. That way, you will feel a greater sense of satisfaction and confidence as you move on to the next season of your growth cycle.

For example, you may have been the best player on your high school team, but then you graduated and are now a newbie on a much more competitive college team. Starting at the bottom again and having to work your way back up to the top might be uncomfortable, but you will learn many new things.

Or you may have worked hard to get promoted. You knew you'd have to learn the associated tasks, but you were working on that in advance so you are prepared. Then it happens—downsizing forces you to fill two roles that are now one job and you are unprepared for the new tasks.

Congratulations!

In most cases, a promotion means taking on new authority and responsibility. It probably means you will have to learn new skills, and you will be reviewed by your superiors based on a list of deliverables commensurate with your authority, responsibilities, and compensation. Not comfy! Be careful what you wish for.

After the euphoria of the promotion—and subsequent hangover from your well-deserved celebration—wears off, you will find yourself in the uncomfortable position of having to work your way back up to the same level of mastery that got you promoted. (Think Sisyphus rolling the rock up the hill.)

Pain is part of growth (growing pains) making it necessary for each of us to overcome physical, mental, relational, and yes, even spiritual barriers to grow into our purpose and fulfill our goals.

"If there is no struggle, there is no progress."

— Frederick Douglass

After graduate school at Northwestern, I moved to Dallas to begin my career. As a lifelong athlete, I still had the itch to compete and looked for an outlet to relieve stress, stay in shape, and meet other people. I joined a masters swim team, bought a fancy Trek carbon-fiber racing bike, some uber-cool Nike running shoes, and began to train for triathlons (swimming, biking, running), which are held from late spring through early fall.

As you may know, Texas gets miserably hot in the summer. In addition to the stress and strain of training for three different sports, I had to do so in uncomfortable weather, so I learned to play mind games to trick myself into thinking I was more comfortable than I really was.

These techniques included smiling (believe it or not, it works), prayer or meditation, "listening" to an inspirational song in my head, or repeating a positive, uplifting, and empowering phrase that matched the cadence of my breathing and related body movements:

"I...will...not...quit!"

"I...will...finish...strong!"

When the time came to compete, I found I could endure the pain throughout the race because I had trained myself to become "comfortable being uncomfortable."

Then one unfortunate training incident really challenged my will. One afternoon in late March, I was on a long ride to train for the upcoming season. Just before the halfway point, a pickup truck came up behind me over a hill. When we swerved away from each other, I hit the curb, which sent me flying over the handlebars. I landed hard on my left shoulder and broke my collarbone. I had crashed a few times before and walked away with nothing more than scrapes and bruises, but this was much different.

One night while trying to sleep, I decided to turn the situation into a personal challenge. I vowed to enter a triathlon by the end of the summer. While triathlons combine three physical sports, there is an equally important (if not more so) fourth element to train: The Mind.

Getting back on my bike was difficult mentally. As the summer progressed, though, I gained more and more confidence in my stamina and ability to test myself in a race. I pushed myself to my physical and mental limits (beyond maybe) in the Texas heat as I relearned how to be comfortable being uncomfortable.

That September, I entered a popular race in the Dallas-Fort Worth area. I am very happy to report I completed the race. I am even happier to report I actually *won* my age group!

I…will…not…quit!

I…will…finish…strong!

But it's not just about sports. Finding a way to get comfortable being uncomfortable is a major part of your growth journey in all areas. Understand it, embrace it, and then work to move past it. When you do (and you will), it will add a level of satisfaction while building layers of grit and resilience that will give you confidence when you face your next challenge (and your next one after that).

Are *you* willing to be *uncomfortable* as you grow into your purpose?

"A comfort zone is a beautiful place, but nothing ever grows there."

— Gina Milicia

RESPONSIBLE

As you build on being both *teachable* and *uncomfortable*, you must be *responsible* for your own growth journey. While you will most certainly require help along the way, you must take full responsibility for everything that happens to you. The words *you* choose to say, the actions *you* choose to take, and the decisions *you* choose to make are totally up to *you*, and *you* alone must take full responsibility for them. I cannot count the number of times *I chose* to say or write something stupid, hurtful, or insensitive, and later had to humble myself and apologize for my offensive actions.

> *"You and I are essentially infinite choice-makers. In every moment of our existence, we are in that field of all possibilities where we have access to an infinity of choices."*
>
> — Deepak Chopra

In fact, the legendary Michael Jordan—arguably the best to ever play the game—said, "You miss 100 percent of the shots you don't take."

You will make some shots and no doubt miss some, but both are part of your record. The important thing is to take responsibility for your misses, learn from them so you can improve, and get right back in the game. To illustrate this point, Jordan also said, "I've missed more than 9,000 shots in my career. I've lost almost 300 games. Twenty-six times, I've been trusted to take the game winning shot and missed. I've failed over and over and over again in my life. And that is why I succeed."

I know people who claim to be stuck in a rut at work and others who remain entangled in unhealthy or nonproductive relationships. Others face some form of compulsive behavior or substance abuse. We must resist the temptation to blame others or play the sympathy card. Yes, addiction and mental health issues are serious illnesses, and all people are worthy of our support, but each of us has to choose to get the help we need to control our afflictions. We must take responsibility for our choices, and more importantly, how *we* wish to move forward. Only those who take action—and *responsibility for* their actions—will ultimately overcome their barriers and fulfill their true growth potential.

> *"Self-leadership begins with this discouraging revelation: you have participated in every bad decision you have ever made."*
>
> — Andy Stanley

To that point, I am reminded of one of my favorite biblical stories, Matthew 25:14-30 (ESV), where Jesus uses The Parable of the Talents (the word "talent" referred to a form of currency or treasure) to convey his message that it is our responsibility to fully maximize whatever gifts we are given.

This parable was a favorite of my daughters—one I used to tell them at bedtime when they were little. While twins, they are very much fraternal, exhibiting totally different interests and aptitudes along with unique personalities and talents. The parable led to a discussion I have reinforced with them every season of their lives based on a simple, yet powerful request:

"JUST BE THE BEST MCKENNA, AND BRIANNA YOU CAN BE!"

In the parable, a man was planning to go on a long journey and decided to entrust his servants with his property while he was away. To one he gave five talents, to another two, and another one. The one given five talents doubled the amount as did the one who was given three talents. However, the one given one talent merely buried it in the ground.

When the master returned, he called his servants together to settle his accounts with them. When both the servants who had multiplied the talents proudly stated this fact, the master replied to each of them, "Well done, good and faithful servant. You have been faithful over a little; I will set you over much."

When the master learned the servant who was given one talent merely buried it and gave it back when the master returned, the master fumed, "You wicked and slothful servant!" He then took the talent and gave it to the servant with ten, saying, "For to everyone who has will more be given, and he will have an abundance. But from the one who has not, even what he has will be taken away." And he cast the worthless servant into the outer darkness. In that place there will be weeping and gnashing of teeth.

Yikes! Now that certainly paints a very visceral picture of the importance of maximizing our gifts, but also how taking responsibility for our actions (or inaction) can have very real, long-term consequences. Of course, I left that last part out of the story for my daughters' sake, or they never would have gone to sleep. But for mature adults we must understand and accept responsibility for whatever we *do* or do not *do*.

Are *you* willing to be *responsible* as you grow into your purpose?

NO RETURN

Here is the final test—once you have learned to become *teachable*, have come to terms with the being *uncomfortable*, and understand the importance of taking complete *responsibility* for your thoughts, feelings, words, and actions—you must build upon this foundation with a mentality of *no return*. Real growth is not possible if we give in to the temptation of going backward.

> *"Growth is seen as an endless series of daily choices and decisions in each of which one can choose to go back toward safety or forward toward growth. Growth must be chosen again and again; fear must be overcome again and again."*
>
> — Abraham Maslow, *Psychology of Science*

The oft-proclaimed idea of two steps forward, one step back is not the way to achieve *revolutionary* growth. To truly make significant progress along our growth journey, we must have the courage to take the same desperate attitude as the Spanish conquistador Hernán Cortés and "burn the boats."

According to legend, in 1519, Hernán Cortés, with some 600 Spaniards, sixteen or so horses, and eleven ships landed on a vast inland plateau, today's Mexico.

The conquistador and his men were about to embark on a conquest to subjugate and loot an empire that held some of the world's greatest treasures. A masterful communicator, Cortés filled his men's heads with grand visions of what this wealth could do for them.

Unfortunately, they would soon find themselves out-numbered, out-armed, and out-provisioned in taking on a well-entrenched, highly trained, and formidable fighting force. Visions of riches would simply not be enough to accomplish their bold objective.

But Cortés had a plan to summon every ounce of skill, courage, and bravery his men had—a strategy based on three profoundly simple, yet powerful words: "Burn the boats!"

This left Cortés and his men with only two choices—victory or death. There was no exit plan. We know today how Cortés' decision to burn the boats panned out—through boldness and a great stroke of luck, he conquered the Aztec empire. (Montezuma II, the Aztec emperor, had seen the Aztec downfall and his vision became a self-fulfilling prophecy.)

Whatever one thinks of the conquest of Mexico, Cortés was both bold and committed. Are you ready to "burn the boats" to find and fulfill your unique purpose, or will you settle for some sort of safe and comfortable Plan B or Plan C?

More directly, can you live with the pain of regret if you don't try to persevere and succeed in the attempt?

For perspective, here is a list of some of the world's most successful authors who were rejected over and over by publishers. Imagine if they had not persevered.

- **Agatha Christie:** Five years of continual rejection. Her book sales now exceed 2 billion copies.

- **J. K. Rowling:** Twelve rejections until the eight-year-old daughter of a Bloomsbury editor demanded to read the book. The rest is history.

- **Jack Canfield:** Rejected by 144 different publishers. *Chicken Soup for the Soul* has sold more than 125 million copies.

- **Margaret Mitchell:** Thirty-eight rejections. *Gone with the Wind* sold 30 million copies.

- **Stephen King:** *Carrie* was King's fourth novel, but the first published. It was originally a short story he threw in the garbage, but his wife rescued it and encouraged him to turn it into a novel. Good thing since King has now sold more than 350 million books and is the undisputed king of the horror genre.

I understand the publishing business is difficult to break into, but geez. Just imagine if these now-famous authors gave up on their dreams after so many rejections. Of course, many similar stories can be found in sports and the performing arts where supremely talented individuals worked hard at their craft while waiting to be discovered and given an opportunity to reveal their greatness. We all love a great rags-to-riches or underdog story with a happy ending.

> *"Our greatest weakness lies in giving up. The most certain way to succeed is always to try just one more time."*
>
> — Thomas Edison

In real life, millions of people give up on their dreams after experiencing rejection, or worse, from fear of rejection.

Are *you* willing to "burn the boats" as you grow into your purpose?

> *"Your playing small does not serve the world. There is nothing enlightened about shrinking so that other people will not feel insecure around you. We are all meant to shine, as children do. It is not just in some of us; it is in everyone, and as we let our light shine,*

we unconsciously give others permission to do the same. As we are liberated from our fear, our presence automatically liberates others."

— Marianne Williamson

!

But wait, there's one last device in the TURN! model we cannot forget. It is vitally important in creating change. The *exclamation point* is a symbol representing both heightened emphasis and a sense of urgency. Let me show you what I mean by harking back to the Parable of the Talents we discussed earlier.

My guess is that within this parable, each of the three servants had decisions to make that incorporated some or all of the TURN! tenets. Will I be *teachable* to learn new ways to grow what I've been given? Am I willing to be *uncomfortable* as I take a risk with something that was given to me in hopes of multiplying it instead of losing it? Will I agree to be *responsible* for the results of my decisions—no matter how they turn out? If so, will I commit to take the action necessary to accomplish my goals with a *no return* mentality? And finally, knowing the master *would* be coming back, but not necessarily *when*, did I place a major emphasis on the master's request while exhibiting a sense of urgency to serve in ways that would lead to maximum growth in my attempt to multiply the talents I was given?

Clearly, two of the three servants answered these questions well. The third servant got caught up in the barriers of fear, uncertainty, doubt, and delay that led to inaction, self-preservation, and justification—even going so far as blaming his master for his own inaction. Remember how these three servants were received by their master when he returned and asked for an accounting: "What did you *do* with the talents I gave you?"

If asked, what will your answer be?

Now that you understand these tenets for "getting the FUDD out" and achieving purposeful growth, let me ask again: Are you ready to TURN! over a new LEAF?

To illustrate my point, I am reminded of an ancient Chinese proverb which poses a riddle: "What are the two best times to plant a tree?" I know you're thinking this one's easy…spring and fall, right? Not so fast.

The first best time to plant a tree would have been twenty years ago. By now, the tree would be well-established and we could benefit from its beauty, shade, and fruit. Of course, the second best time to plant a tree is today, before yet another day passes. Because when you are trying to grow something unique and special, every day counts.

> *"Twenty years from now you will be more disappointed by the things that you didn't do than by the ones you did."*
>
> — Mark Twain

I often say, "There are things I think, things I know, and things I think I know." One thing I do know for sure is our time on earth is relatively short, and tomorrow is not promised to any of us.

When we look at our tombstone, we will see the date we were born and the day we died. A dash is between those two dates. Within that dash is the essence of our life on earth—a series of choices we *do* get to make—and live with for better or worse.

This is not meant to be morbid, or bring you down; to the contrary, it is designed to wake you up and inspire you to take purposeful action that can significantly enhance your life and the lives of others now.

> *"The most important time in your life is now. The most important person in your life is the one you're looking at right now. The most important thing you could be doing in your life is what you're doing right now. The best way to prepare for the fire is to be totally present in what you're doing right now. Remember, now is the moment that never ends."*
>
> — Deepak Chopra

Are you actively living your best life? Or are you just kind of treading water in survival mode—putting off pursuing your dreams until "someday"? Well, what if someday never comes? Sadly, there are countless stories of people whose lives were tragically taken by a sudden health issue, an overdose, an accident, or a freak natural event like a fire, tornado, earthquake, or mudslide. One day they were with us, and the next day, they were gone....

We can also look at the word, "dash" in terms of one of its other meanings, a foot race, emphasizing speed and productivity from the gun. For a constant reminder of the importance of maximizing every single day, I always put a dash in front of my name.

— Mark

I feel a sense of urgency because I know every passing day *leaves* me less and less time to grow into my unique purpose. At this point, I have made the choice to be more intentional about living up to my personal brand purpose statement—I truly want to make a difference in the lives of people by helping them find their purpose and fulfill their true growth potential while inspiring them to do likewise to help others along life's journey. *Pay it backward.*

That means *you*.

Every experience and every person with whom I have had the good fortune to interact along my growth journey has helped shape and mold me into the person I am today. And I believe I have helped to positively impact countless people at each stop as well. Of course, I am painfully aware that I have also made several mistakes along the way that served to humble and teach me, but never break me. Even with all my experience and lessons learned, I am still a work in progress with significant growth potential. We all are.

None of us can take back our past or change the choices we made, no matter how much we wish we could. Trust me, I've made some real doozies. But we *do* have a choice in how we "*Grow* 4-ward." No matter what season we are in, now is the time to join me on a revolutionary growth journey to discover our unique, God-given purpose and fulfill our true growth potential.

> *"You can't go back and change the beginning, but you can start where you are and change the ending."*
>
> — C. S. Lewis

Now that we have cultivated the field for Purposeful Growth and sown the seeds of our Purposeful Self, let's begin our Purposeful Work growth journey by unpacking the 4 revolutionary and purposeful processes that make up the 4 LEAF *GROWTH* model. I'll show you how to integrate specific actions into your routine to help you grow individually, as a team member, and as part of an organization while making the world around you better for all the lives you touch directly or indirectly.

Come along now—it's *GROW* time!

PART III

GROWING YOU 4-WARD FOR PURPOSEFUL WORK

"I asked the leaf whether it was frightened because it was autumn, and the other leaves were falling. The leaf told me, 'No. During the whole spring and summer, I was completely alive. I worked hard to help nourish the tree, and now much of me is in the tree. I am not limited by this form. I am also the whole tree, and when I go back to the soil, I will continue to nourish the tree. So, I don't worry at all. As I leave this branch and float to the ground, I will wave to the tree and tell her, "I will see you again very soon."' That day there was a wind blowing and, after a while, I saw the leaf leave the branch and float down to the soil, dancing joyfully, because as it floated it saw itself already there in the tree. It was so happy. I bowed my head, knowing that I have a lot to learn from the leaf."

— Thich Nhat Hanh

THE PURPOSEFUL LEADERSHIP REVOLUTION

A SEASON FOR PLANTING GROWTH

Planting:
To place a seed, bulb, or plant into the ground so it can grow.

CHAPTER 12

LEADERSHIP REVOLVES AROUND *GROWTH* 'C'EEDS

"For a seed to achieve its greatest expression, it must come completely undone. The shell cracks, its insides come out, and everything changes. To someone who doesn't understand growth, it would look like complete destruction."

— Cynthia Occelli

Within the 4 LEAF *GROWTH* model is a direct link to the primary elements of plants where each represents a revolutionary process for attaining growth in neither isolated or linear ways, but indeed interrelated and holistic. This harmonious balance simply must take place for a given plant to fulfill its growth potential. It also suggests a specific season represented by each of the 4 organic growth processes.

As with the structure and stability any plant needs, we must, of course, start with a seed, which will begin establishing a root system.

In nature, seeds are scattered from a healthy, fruit-bearing plant to produce new plants nearby or wherever the wind may blow them. Given its warmer weather and ample rain, spring is the perfect time for seeds to germinate in the soil and establish their roots.

In many trees like the mighty oak, the root system serves as a strong foundation. In fact, the root system of a mature oak tree splays out underground as roughly a mirror image of its scenic canopy high above. To support the growth of this magnificent tree, the root system must be long, strong, and highly productive in delivering enough water and nutrients from the soil to nourish the leaves and fruit.

Likewise, the undeniable foundations for the growth of any individual, team, or organization are the purposeful "seeds" and strong "roots" of leadership.

We all admire and value great leaders, don't we? Many people are fascinated by what makes great leaders effective and they become inspired by the results those leaders achieve. In fact, every movement that has revolutionized the world was led by someone in some way, shape, or form.

How do I know so many people want to learn about the leaders they admire? Well, for starters, if you search the words "leader" and "leadership" online, you will find a combined 1.7 billion hits. According to Amazon and Barnes & Noble, books on leaders and leadership are among the best-selling of any genre. And there are untold numbers of teachers, coaches, consultants, podcasters, and bloggers who actively engage in scholarly research and/or routinely opine on this topic from their own experience. Finally, we know people spend millions of dollars a year attending conferences, seminars, webinars, and workshops with the hope of learning how they can become better, more effective, and inspirational leaders.

And we know that leaders come in all shapes, sizes, colors, genders, religions, and ages, representing all walks of life.

> *"If your actions inspire others to dream more, learn more, do more, and become more, you are a leader."*
>
> — John Quincy Adams

While leadership is dynamic and multi-faceted, and every leader exhibits a different style relevant to their unique circumstances, it all comes down to this simple, undeniable fact: You cannot be a leader unless you have followers.

Scholars have studied leaders who changed the course of history somehow for millennia. And countless books, movies, TV shows, and documentaries have attempted to get inside the heads of these extraordinary people.

What makes them different from the rest of us?

Are leaders born or made—or possibly both?

We also look at the many styles of leadership in the context of macro- and/or micro-circumstances. Situational leadership means a different leadership style exists in response to a situation's specific circumstances. No one-size-fits-all category exists when evaluating the styles of leadership used by some of the most influential people in world history or business.

However, experts say we have six general styles of leadership:

1. **Visionary:** Articulating a shared mission and giving long-term direction

2. **Participative:** Building consensus to generate new ideas and build commitment

3. **Coaching:** Fostering personal and career development

4. **Affiliative:** Creating trust and harmony

5. **Pacesetting:** Accomplishing tasks by setting high standards

6. **Directive:** Pushing results with exact commands and clear consequences

Even within the same industry where two legendary leaders pursue the same goal, different styles can be equally effective.

For example, in the NFL, Vince Lombardi was the inspirational, tough-minded, and in-your-face coach who won Super Bowls with the Green Bay Packers. In contrast, Tom Landry possessed a much more stoic, cerebral, and caring persona, which served him well in winning Super Bowls with the Dallas Cowboys. In fact, instead of using film to point out all the mistakes players made in a game, he prepared video of each player's *best* plays to reinforce positive behaviors.

To that point, I look at the word, "supervisor" a bit differently than most. If split into two words, we get "super" and "visor." I believe everyone has a *superpower*—a special gift that makes them unique and valuable to the team. A leader's job is like a visor, eliminating glare or debris so they can focus on gifts and advise each player on how to get the most out of their superpower. This will enhance the individual's growth while helping the team achieve its goals.

"Quite simply, our success is measured in what others achieve."

— Gary Burnison, CEO, Korn Ferry

Regardless of their preferred styles, I believe great leaders share many characteristics. Their greatness was founded on following revolutionary leadership principles or more aptly, what I have named the Purposeful Leadership Revolution.

My definition of a leader is anyone who directly or indirectly influences the thoughts, words, and/or deeds of another in achieving a shared goal.

Congratulations! By that definition, you are more than likely a leader!

Based on my experience, observations, and lessons from subject matter experts, I have found there are 4 revolutionary LEAF *GROWTH* processes that can be linked to great leaders. I refer to them as *GROWTH* Ceeds.

In many sports, a letter C for captain is sewn on the captain's jersey. This C sets the player apart as undisputed leader of the team and as someone players and coaches can count on to represent them on the field. And almost always, the captain is elected by the team, ensuring a sense of ownership and accountability.

But here's some hockey trivia—the great Boston Bruins player Bobby Orr did not wear a C on his sweater. Having tremendous speed, fluid skating agility, bulldog tenacity, and an unquenchable will to win, Bobby Orr revolutionized the position of defenseman, a position that was not traditionally counted on to score goals, by scoring regularly and even winning the scoring title in 1969-70. Not only was he an extraordinary player who gave his all every single game, but he set a positive example that inspired his teammates to perform better. Of course, Orr did wear the number 4.

The true essence of leadership is earned every single day and seen in a variety of ways that serve to positively influence the thoughts, feelings, and deeds of others and lead to attaining the shared goals or objectives of the team or organization.

The captain of any team, whether in sports, business, or any organization, must be the undisputed leader. In fact, they must set a good example of what is expected by the rest of the team, so together they can accomplish the goals they set for themselves. The captain must also lift the team up and help make them better—more productive and effective in the pursuit of greatness—as individuals and as a collective. Finally, the captain must lead with consistency to retain their C.

Remember, if you directly or indirectly influence the thoughts, plans, or actions of another in achieving a shared goal, congratulations, you are a leader, the captain of your team.

There are many other C words I could have used to highlight the traits of a great leader, such as competence, courage, character, creativity, confidence, challenging, and charisma. Instead, I've chosen the 4 most powerful and integrated C words—*Clarity, Connection, Communication* and *Commitment*—all revolving around purposeful growth, to define what I call the Purposeful Leadership Revolution.

THE PURPOSEFUL LEADERSHIP REVOLUTION

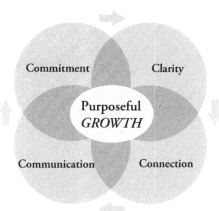

My sincere hope is you will find the revolutionary 4 LEAF *GROWTH* process helpful as you progress along your growth journey as an *individual, team member,* or part of an *organization* in ways that may benefit the *world* in each season.

CHAPTER 13

LEADING WITH CLARITY FROM PURPOSE TO PRIORITIES

*"True clarity and purpose emerge when
we see ourselves as we truly are."*

— Eleesha

Let's dive in to learn how important clarity is in helping us fully integrate our unique *purpose* into our stated business *priorities*.

No doubt the essence of true leadership lies in one's ability to identify and articulate the person, team, or organization's true purpose with razor-sharp clarity. Why do we exist? The French call this concept *raison d'etre*, which translates to the most important reason or purpose for someone or something's existence.

Wow, powerful stuff indeed.

- **CLARITY OF PURPOSE**

—**Why *do* we exist?**
As I said, it is 100 percent necessary to nail this down before anything else. While the word purpose is technically a noun and a verb, as I mentioned previously, the magic lies in using purpose as an action that inspires people to think, feel, and, most importantly, *do*

something of intrinsic value that makes a significant and lasting difference in the world. In fact, what good is having a purpose without acting in ways that help bring it to life and, ultimately, fulfill it?

> *"If we want to know what a business is, we have to start with its purpose. And the purpose must lie outside the business itself. In fact, it must lie in society, since a business enterprise is an organ of society. There is only one valid definition of business purpose: to create a customer."*
>
> — Peter Drucker, *The Practice of Management*

I believe the concept of purpose goes even deeper because it begs the question, what or who is a customer? Think of your team or organization's purpose as a compass with 4 different directions. Staying true to your purpose is like picking a direction and following it. Once we get off course, we must continually recalibrate until we find the path that will lead us to our destination.

To that point, we must not only be clear about our shared purpose, but we must connect it to our key priorities as a team and/or organization to fulfill our growth potential. If the two elements are incongruent, then we have not accomplished anything. In fact, we may have unwittingly created a bigger problem since few things are worse than an organization that touts an inspiring purpose but does not weave it into its business priorities. This is called, "Purpose Washing," and it is visibly inauthentic at best and causes brand-erosion. The concept of brand purpose requires us to be authentic—to do what we say we will do and be transparent as we do so, thus showing how and why our brand is relevant and trustworthy.

Be careful when you put your brand in others' hands, and ensure you have selected the right and best partner(s). Remember, in the end, it is your reputation. Once trust is broken, it is extremely difficult to get back.

Many organizations do live their purpose in every way—even when it may be much more profitable (at least in the short-term) to stray from time to time. The following are just a few examples.

Target has been living out its purpose for several years. Are you aware that Target donates 5 percent of its income to its local communities? For perspective, that's more than $4 million per week. It also provides human capital in the form of volunteerism among its store-level team members and makes significant donations of food. And it has been doing this consistently every year in every store since 1946!

Another great example of a company that lives out its purpose is Canva, a firm based in Sydney, Australia, that developed a globally accessible graphic design platform used to create social media graphics, presentations, posters, documents, and other visual content.

Canva has developed a very simple, yet extremely powerful and purposeful "Two-Step Plan."

Step 1. Build one of the world's most valuable companies.

Step 2. Do the most good we can do.

But instead of setting out to accomplish those goals in that order, Canva has committed to doing both since its inception in 2013.

As a user of Canva designs, I received an email recently thanking *me* for partnering with the company since 2017, along with the following updates on "our" progress together:

> We're excited to say that we now have 65 million people from 190 countries designing in Canva each month, who have created more than 7 billion designs. Our rapid growth wouldn't have been possible without your support.
>
> We now have more than 130,000 nonprofits on our nonprofit program (where we give away Canva Pro for free).
>
> Through our One Print, One Tree initiative where we plant a tree for every print order, so far, we've committed to planting more than 2 million trees.
>
> We're part of the 1 percent pledge where we have committed 1 percent of our profits, 1 percent of our product, 1 percent of our team's time, and 1 percent of our equity to be a force for good in the world, through the company values that our team tries to live every day, "be a force for good," "be a good human," and "empower others."
>
> We're excited to announce that we've made some great progress on both Step 1 and Step 2 in the past few weeks:
>
> - Canva is now valued at $40 billion (USD) thanks to some world-leading investors who want to support us on our mission to empower the world to design.
>
> - We have committed 30 percent of Canva's value to be used as a force for good to contribute to the world.

Our first project is with GiveDirectly, where $10 million will be given directly to the world's poorest people in Southern Africa.

So that's it. Just wanted to say a massive thank you for your contribution to Canva over the years; it's greatly appreciated. We hope you feel proud of your contribution to both Step 1 and Step 2. We truly couldn't do it without you.

We'll try to live up to the mammoth responsibility over the years to come.

The Canva Team

Wow, talk about a brand that lives its purpose, right? And they reached out to thank *me* for being a partner in their success?

Finally, I read a *Harvard Business Review* article highlighting an approach that big 4 accounting firm KPMG used to define its purpose. Instead of devising it within the C-Suite and merely trickling it down to its associates from on high, KPMG took a different tack. Through its Higher Purpose Initiative, KPMG reached out to its associates to help the firm define its purpose through telling stories of how their work helped make a positive difference in the world. Then, the company shared those stories throughout the organization to place the proper emphasis behind its unique purpose.

By employing a "bubble-up" approach that involved its associates in the process, KMPG created a much deeper emotional engagement than they would have built via a more traditional "top down" approach. This helped inspire KPMG's associates to pay more attention to the value they must continue to bring to their clients every day.

You see, purpose must be truly authentic, 100 percent believable, extremely relevant, and consistently applied throughout the organization. Like a magnet, if those elements are firmly in place, the business results will certainly follow.

A team or organization's purpose has 4 key components:

1. **Aspirational:** Aligned with long-term vision

2. **Inspirational**: Aligned with the daily mission

3. **Operational**: Aligned with strategic/tactical plans

4. **Institutional**: Aligned with shared values

As you can see, the common word across these components is "aligned." When gaps between an organization's purpose and its priorities exist, it causes a breach of trust across all stakeholders, internal and external. The erosion of trust is a killer, striking at the health and vitality of any relationship.

Once we've defined our individual purpose, we must ensure it is aligned with the purpose of our team and organization. Then, together we can craft a vision for where we'd like to grow by some point in the future.

• CLARITY OF VISION

—Where *do* we want to grow?

> *"Vision is a picture of the future that produces passion."*
>
> — Bill Hybels

In establishing a vision, I prefer to use ten years as a time horizon for a few reasons.

First, I think most people can conceptualize this span of time—any less and it may feel too soon or unrealistic; any longer and it may feel too distant or unattainable.

Second, one of the greatest and most widely recognized examples of the power of vision in setting the tone for an organization was John F. Kennedy's Rice University speech in 1960. President Kennedy painted a vivid picture of *why* it was important for the United States to take the lead in space exploration—landing on the moon and returning safely to earth *within the decade*.

I am well-aware this particular example has been used many times, and I'm sure many other good examples supporting ten years as a good time horizon for a vision statement exist; however, given the tremendous power of this particular example, I'm inclined to stick with it as one of the best examples that an inspired and aligned vision can be fulfilled. In his speech, Kennedy stated:

> We choose to go to the moon! We choose to go to the moon in this decade and do the other things, not because they are easy, but because they are hard; because that goal will serve to organize and measure the best of our energies and skills, because that challenge is one that we are willing to accept, one we are unwilling to postpone, and one we intend to win.

Kennedy's speech featured 4 integrated strategies for creating a compelling vision for your team or organization—all revolving around purpose:

1. **Inspiring:** It is emotionally evocative, uplifting, and highly motivating to all stakeholders.

2. **Challenging:** It appeals to our sense of awe, wonder, and natural curiosity while stoking our competitive fires.

3. **Empowering:** It creates a sense of personal investment and pride in the work and ownership in the outcome.

4. **Fulfilling:** It provides the higher order benefit of fulfilling our unique purpose as a species.

"That's one small step for man; one giant leap for mankind."

— Neil Armstrong

Wow, talk about a vision. How inspiring that speech must have been for those in the audience that day? It is incredible for me to imagine how, as the result of a faithful commitment and daily dedication to a shared vision, the team of NASA engineers and astronauts could be challenged, and indeed, empowered to achieve something so unique, so spectacular, and so fulfilling it would establish a benchmark of innovation excellence for many generations to follow.

Now, *that* is how creating a powerful and purposeful shared vision and working together as a fully aligned team can establish a legacy of greatness!

What is *your* vision for yourself, your team, and your organization over the next ten years?

- **CLARITY OF MISSION**

—How *do* we plan to get there?

Once we establish our overarching shared purpose and craft an inspiring vision of where we want to grow together, we need to develop our mission statement. This is essentially a statement that should answer the question: What must I (individually) and we (collectively) do every single day to achieve the inspirational and aspirational vision we are aligned and committed to accomplishing together?

I am not a fan of starting a mission statement with the word "To." I prefer starting with "I" for a personal brand mission statement to denote a personal commitment to taking action, and "We" for an organizational mission statement to put the emphasis on a spirit of unity and teamwork within the context of achieving a shared goal.

Just as important, if not more so, is following I or we with "believe," so the combination, "I/We believe" makes the statement personally relevant, emotionally evocative, and powerfully engaging to all.

Let's first take a look at the power of the word "believe" starting with its definition:

1. An acceptance that *a statement is true* or that something exists.

2. *Trust, faith, or confidence* in someone or something.

Now, let's review mission statements from some of the world's most successful organizations to see what they might look like with the modifications I propose:

- **Google:** *We believe* in organizing the world's information to make it universally accessible and useful.

- **Starbucks:** *We believe* in inspiring and nurturing the human spirit—one person, one cup and one neighborhood at a time.

- **Nike:** *We believe* in bringing inspiration and innovation to every athlete in the world. (If you have a body, you are an athlete.)
- **Lexus:** *We believe* in treating each customer as we would a guest in our home.
- **Southwest:** *We believe* in delivering customer service with a sense of warmth, friendliness, individual pride, and company spirit.

Here's one I found when I was ordering my "uze" at POUR, one of my favorite local coffeehouses. (Ahem…when I'm not at Starbucks.) It was written boldly on the side of a carton of Silk almond milk sitting on the counter:

- *We believe…* in making delicious, plant-based food that does right by you and fuels our passion for the planet to make *your* journey smooth.

In a similar vein, while I was serving as chief marketing officer (CMO) for **WOW**orks, a portfolio of fast-casual restaurants including Saladworks, Garbanzo Mediterranean Fresh, Frutta Bowls, and The Simple Greek, our collective mission was very powerful and purposeful:

- *We believe…* in fueling the passions of our team members, guests, business partners, and communities—giving everyone the opportunity to live their best life.

Do you see how changing "To…" (sounds a bit clinical, methodical, and somewhat distant) to "*We believe…*" makes each mission statement deeply personal, passionate, inspiring, and action-oriented?

This will instill a deeper sense of pride and personal commitment that will breed faith, trust, and confidence across all stakeholders.

Hey, it seems to be working pretty well for Ted Lasso, right?

The power of "believe" actually goes both ways, as studies show leaders who demonstrate strong belief in their team generate both better performance and loyalty.

> *"Outstanding leaders go out of their way to boost the self-esteem of their people. If people believe in themselves, it's amazing what they can accomplish."*
>
> — Sam Walton

Now, let's repurpose this technique and apply it to Brand *You* starting with "I believe…."

What does Brand *You* believe?

> *"I believe that we will win! I believe that we will win! I believe that we will win!"*

It gets me fired up every time I hear it. I really love this now-famous US soccer team cheer on many levels. From its first word, "I" yelled by the leader and then echoed in unison by the crowd to suggest solidarity as individuals coming together as one. Next comes the important coupling of words, "I believe…" which forms a deep emotional bond among the revelers. What follows is, "I believe that…" which serves as a bridge to clarify their belief; then comes the addition of "I believe that we…" which signifies who is involved (both the team and their loyal fans). And finally, the reveal of their shared goal, "I believe that we will win!"

Although winning the game is the obvious objective, the word, "will" is very important because it has a couple of different, but related meanings: 1) a demonstration of faith that a shared goal *will* be accomplished, and 2) through the collective *will* of an aligned team and its passionate legion of fans. We're in this together.

This cheer is an excellent example of harnessing the passion, belief, and power of a shared vision and mission in support of a sports team.

Now, let's look at how individuals tap into their respective beliefs to fulfill their purpose and related growth potential.

In my research on the power of belief, I came across a program called *This I Believe*. Originally conceived as a five-minute segment created and hosted by legendary journalist Edward R. Murrow, *This I Believe* aired on CBS Radio from 1951 to 1955. The show encouraged both celebrities and everyday people to write brief essays about their personal motivations to be read over the air.

The show was later picked up by NPR and became a phenomenal success from 2005 to 2009. According to its website (thisibelieve.org), *This I Believe* lives on as an international organization engaging people in writing and sharing essays describing the core values that guide their daily lives. Over 125,000 of these essays, written by people from all walks of life, have been archived, heard on Public Radio, chronicled through books, and featured in weekly podcasts.

We have all developed beliefs that serve as our guideposts in navigating our life journeys and as motivation for growing into our unique purpose. The most important part of developing beliefs is taking the time to think introspectively so you can develop your own belief, ideas truly authentic to you. Essentially, this is what makes you *you*.

> "*What you believe, you receive.*"
>
> — Gabrielle Bernstein

Your "I believe…" statement will serve as your personal guide and filter, sifting out what you, your team, and/or organization stand for, especially when times get tough, and what you won't stand for, which is equally important.

What do you believe is your purposeful mission?

- **CLARITY OF SHARED VALUES**

—What *do* we stand for?

The essence of any great organization lies in its ability to develop a culture whose shared values align with its purpose, vision, and mission. No easy task, it should not be crafted behind closed doors and later shoved in a drawer.

And, to place the proper emphasis on the word "shared," ensure your shared values are upheld by everyone in the organization lest they get dismissed as merely a list of eloquent, though ultimately meaningless platitudes.

As leaders we must understand we are always under a microscope—everyone is watching everything we say and do. Thus, we must truly embody the organization's shared values, serving as a role model for others to follow every single day in every circumstance.

As with one's personal values, the shared values of any team or organization must serve as a compass to help guide everyone's actions consistent with its shared purpose, long-term vision, and daily mission. We must ask and answer the question: "What *do* we stand for?"

- We stand for the Pledge of Allegiance.
- We stand for the singing of our National Anthem.
- We stand for the presentation of colors by our military.
- We stand for the sacred union of marriage.
- We stand for the funeral procession as it passes by.

All of these and many more are very powerful, emotional, and recognizable examples of shared values that unite us as Americans, family, friends, and loved ones, regardless of our many differences. And each of these examples is unified by 4 interwoven concepts: unity, action, respect, and trust.

Similar to the concept of starting with what we believe…in relation to a purposeful mission statement, it is vitally important to understand the importance of using "We Behaviors" (We-haviors, if you will) in relation to our shared values. Again, the use of "we" ensures a tighter sense of alignment and commitment among individuals and teams in support of shared values embodied by the organization.

At Saladworks, Jean Boland serves as chief people and culture officer. She and I led the entire organization, executive team included, in a multi-phased exercise to identify our shared values. We wanted the entire organization to participate in the development of shared values.

Given that I define shared values as the ways we must work together to achieve our daily mission and, ultimately, our purposeful vision over time, it makes perfect sense to involve everyone in the process.

This creates a deeper level of ownership and accountability when we are given a voice to share our thoughts and insights to help improve our workplace relationships and culture.

Saladworks' brand positioning is "Be Original," which relates to the common thread woven throughout its target guest persona, menu variety/flexibility, and organizational culture. As a result, each of its shared values starts with the word "be" to indicate a personal commitment in living them out. (Think Be-haviors.)

First, we used Survey Monkey to send out a broad list of proposed shared values and got team input on how to cull it down. We looked at what was left in our discussion of shared values. Then we ran a straw poll before scheduling a Zoom meeting with breakout rooms for seven to eight members representing several different parts of the company. We asked each group to come up with the most powerfully motivating word or words on the list. Once each team felt comfortable with their top five "Be" words, we brought everyone back together and asked one leader from each team to give us their chosen word/words and why they chose it/them.

Listening to excited chatter from each team and seeing nods of approval from the broader organization was awesome—even on Zoom. However, what made the session even more powerful was hearing specific names brought up as examples of those who live out each shared value. You see, more than just words, these shared values represented not only the way we would work together to achieve our mission, but the very essence of who we wanted to *be* every day.

Rather than stop at our five most culturally relevant shared values, our "Be-haviors," we decided it was important to dig much deeper to clearly define specific "We-haviors" representing each shared value. This is how we changed our mindset from the individual (be) to the team (we) to create a sense of clarity, accountability, and collective ownership in bringing our shared values to life every day.

BE PASSIONATE

- ✓ We are purposeful.
- ✓ We are energetic.
- ✓ We are engaged.
- ✓ We are fun!

BE INVENTIVE

- ✓ We are curious.
- ✓ We are solutions-focused.
- ✓ We are growth-minded.
- ✓ We are courageous.

BE ACCOUNTABLE

- ✓ We are trustworthy.
- ✓ We live up to commitments.
- ✓ We own our mistakes.
- ✓ We are a team together and apart.

BE FULFILLED

- ✓ We are all important.
- ✓ We are generous.
- ✓ We celebrate success.
- ✓ We take good care of ourselves and others.

BE REAL

- ✓ We are genuine.
- ✓ We are loving.
- ✓ We are hospitable.
- ✓ We are graceful.

Our Shared Purpose: **Be "WOW!"**

Do you see how inserting specific We-haviors under each shared value, the individual Be-haviors, helps unite the team by supporting each member in fulfilling the team's shared purpose?

In addition to serving as shared values, these Be-haviors and the related We-haviors also served to describe the essence of the company (the Brand Filter), which was summed up as Be "WOW!", which helped guide priorities and decision-making. If we couldn't make something truly a "WOW!", then we had no time for it. We even created a hand sign (Think two peace signs overlapped to form a "W") to symbolize our shared values—punctuating the end of each Zoom call with a hearty "BE WOW!" ending. Photographs of team members making this "W" symbol in our restaurants or even while on vacation were shared throughout the organization to help celebrate and reinforce our shared purpose.

This technique can work for any team or organization regardless of industry or category.

Remember, shared values must be practiced every day. Keep them in the forefront of all you do. Keep them dusted and well oiled, if somewhat worn through constant use. Ensure they are well-known, and more importantly, actively and evenly applied across the organization.

One excellent example I came across recently was from Arby's. After decades of starts, stops, and rebranding campaigns, Arby's looked at itself, evaluated its unique and relevant assets against its young male target audience, and came up with: Arby's… We have the meats.

Not only did Arby's come out with new menu items and clever ads, videos, and integrated marketing materials to reach its external stakeholders (guests, communities, suppliers), it also instilled this idea in its internal stakeholders (corporate support center, franchisees, team members, and investors).

Arby's highlighted the word "we" in both its outward brand positioning and inward shared values. According to Arby's CEO Paul Brown, "We work hard, we play fair, we get it done, we make a difference, we have fun, and, most importantly, we help our employees dream big."

I don't believe this was a coincidence.

But wait, there's more.

To ensure these shared values are not only understood and agreed to, but lived every day, nearly all 80,000 team members participate in an event called Arby's Brand Champ. Arby's Brand Champ is a half-day, off-site learning experience established to help team members deliver on Arby's purpose to set actionable goals and explore how they can make a difference in the lives of others.

The program has been a vital element in reinvigorating Arby's, and as of this writing, more than 170,000 participants have experienced Brand Champ. Brown claims that Brand Champ has not only improved guest satisfaction scores, but it has become a way for Arby's team members to bring these shared values into their personal lives.

Wow, walking-the-talk and very inspiring on so many levels.

Remember, your shared values should serve as a guidepost for your team or organization. To ensure they do not become merely a series of lofty phrases or empty platitudes, it is vital to connect them to your purposeful mission and vision. You want to make them stick in practical and relevant ways to help achieve business priorities while enriching your team and the guests and communities they serve.

How do your personal values fit with your team or organization's shared values?

Your organization's foundation, represented by aligning its purposeful vision, mission, and shared values with your own, will guide you in establishing personal and professional growth priorities with razor-sharp clarity.

CHAPTER 14

LEADING WITH CONNECTION FROM PRIORITIES TO PLANS

"Life is really simple, but we insist on making it complicated."

— Confucius

While clarity's importance cannot be overstated in developing a brand's foundation, whether it be personal, team, or organizational, it is merely the first of the 4 revolutionary leadership growth processes. The next step is connection, the ability of a leader to connect the key *priorities* founded on the purposeful vision, mission, and shared values of an organization in tangible ways that support its growth *plans*.

Many types of planning models are out there, from ten-year vision plans to three- to five-year strategic plans to one-year annual operating plans. While I'm not going to go into the nitty gritty of how to build out each of these types (you're welcome), I do want to highlight a few of them to demonstrate the importance of connecting your purpose to your plans.

Let's start with the ten-year vision plan. As discussed earlier, I believe in establishing a ten-year timeframe for achieving the organization's stated vision. Thus, it would seem to make sense to ensure we develop a plan to help get us there.

Within the restaurant industry, 4 key pillars lead to growth. I call these the "Big 4:"

1. **People:** Great people attract and take care of our guests.

2. **Guests:** Satisfied guests build sustained sales.

3. **Sales:** Sales delivers higher bottom-line profits.

4. **Profit:** Higher profits lead to enterprise growth.

Don't get this twisted. Building a successful restaurant brand is certainly not easy, but it's also not that complicated.

As a result, we must ensure our ten-year vision plan incorporates what we plan to accomplish across each of these 4 integrated growth pillars. But before we go any farther, I want to introduce you to a fun, interactive approach I used with my executive team when I served as president of Mimi's Cafe. It helped frame our ten-year vision plan in a personal and inspiring way.

For some background, *Nation's Restaurant News* is one of the leading trade magazines covering the restaurant industry. Almost everyone in the industry reads it cover-to-cover for the latest food and beverage trends, tips, and resources and the most up-to-date coverage on who is doing what to build their respective restaurant brands. Getting featured on the front cover is a high honor.

In one of our strategic planning meetings, I held up a copy of *Nation's Restaurant News* and then asked each member of the executive team to close their eyes for a few minutes and just dream a bit. Then I asked them to open their eyes and write down what the headline for Mimi's would be if we were featured on the cover ten years from then.

Admittedly, some anxious moments followed as the team looked at each other with question marks hanging over their heads. But soon, their eyes lit up and the ink started flowing.

Once they had completed their respective headlines, I had them each recite theirs in front of the rest of the team and provide the rationale behind it. After each headline, the team clapped enthusiastically for their peers as the excitement and energy in the room continued to build.

I went last because it was important for me as their leader to listen to them first before I jumped in with my headline. The good news was, despite some awkward syntax and differences in word selection, we had achieved two important goals: alignment and ownership.

If I had just started with my personal vision, we might have gained some alignment among the team, but we wouldn't have developed a true sense of personal or team ownership that would have been sustainable over time. Both are vital for any plan's success, and this exercise certainly made our time together much more productive in that meeting and all subsequent meetings as our plan began to take shape.

Let's go back to our Big 4 Growth Pillars—People, Guests, Sales, and Profit. My question to the team was simple: "What 4 big things do we want to achieve within each of these 4 Growth pillars to help us attain our vision?"

1. **People:** How can we leverage the value of our human capital?

2. **Guests:** How can we optimize our total guest experience?

3. **Sales:** How can we drive incremental sales opportunities?

4. **Profit:** How can we maximize our bottom-line profits?

That doesn't sound so daunting, does it? Regardless of your specific industry, I wager there are likely 4 growth pillars also driving your business. If so, just think if you could achieve 4 "big things" within each of those 4 key growth areas that would change the game for your team or organization. Wow, how powerful would that be?

Finally, at Mimi's Cafe we integrated our shared values within the context of our team recognition and rewards program. Every month, we held a company-wide meeting in the support center to gather all team members in one place. The purpose was to share not only what had transpired the previous month and celebrate our successes, but to communicate company updates, special events, and new initiatives for the following month.

Pretty standard stuff, right? But what made these meetings special (in addition to enjoying our legendary Mimi's Muffins) was the opportunity for individuals to recognize another for living out our shared values in a meaningful way that supported our purposeful mission. The recipient was called out of the audience to come up front and receive their award directly from the team member who recognized them.

The speeches outlined why the team member was worthy of the award and focused on each of our shared values while connecting them to our mission in a practical way. This created a very warm, human exchange that enhanced the relationship between the two individuals and brought together the entire organization. A photo taken at the end of the award speech helped capture this special moment for posterity.

We also held an end-of-year celebration where awards were presented to individuals who best represented our shared values in our daily mission. I then had the honor of giving out the president's award to one individual who lived out *all* our shared values throughout the year.

This individual recognition went a long way toward keeping the organization's shared values alive and focused on its related vision and mission. Using your shared values to recognize and reward individuals or teams is obviously a great way to show those values in a positive way.

At The Cheesecake Factory, we connected our purposeful vision, mission, and shared values to our business priorities on a much deeper, more personal level by establishing "19 Daily Commitments." Each daily commitment represented the granular aspects of the brand's mission statement: "To create an environment where absolute guest satisfaction is our highest priority."

Again, I feel this mission statement would have been even stronger if we used "We believe in creating…" instead of "To…." but I digress.

During the pre-shift meeting before the restaurant opens to serve guests each day, a different person is selected to recite their assigned daily commitment, emphasizing what that commitment means to them personally and how they can apply it in their specific job to help achieve the daily mission and key business priorities.

The Cheesecake Factory has a tremendous commitment to ongoing training across all levels of the organization. This allows it to manage its huge, 300-plus menu items—most of which are prepared fresh from scratch every day—along with hospitality that simply cannot be matched. In fact, the discipline of faithfully living up to its mission by emphasizing a specific daily commitment is what makes The Cheesecake Factory arguably the most distinctive and successful restaurant concept in the world.

Once you have established the foundation of your ten-year vision plan, it is much easier to translate it into a more specific three- to five-year strategic plan and likewise an even more detailed one-year operating plan. Regardless of your time frame, you need a strong connection between your purpose, priorities, and, of course, plans.

If the closest distance between two points is a straight line, think of a ten-year plan and imagine what would happen if your internal and/or external stakeholders were not aligned with that vision. While your basic direction must remain to reach your destination, the specific route you take often needs to be adjusted to ensure you stay on course. Otherwise, it is easy to find yourself stuck in a ditch somewhere out in the middle of nowhere. This can even happen with an annual operating plan as we'll discuss later.

In each of our plans, we must establish a strong connection to the "needs" of today while sewing "seeds" of innovation and growth for tomorrow. And, of course, we need to clear out any "weeds" that get in the way of achieving our shared goals. And leaders need to be able to communicate their vision from the board room to the break room, ensuring everyone responsible for bringing the plans to life is fully aligned and has a shared sense of commitment and ownership.

CHAPTER 15

LEADING THROUGH COMMUNICATION FROM PLANS TO PEOPLE

"Communication is power. Those who have mastered its effective use can change their own experience of the world, and the world's experience of them. All behaviors and feelings find their original roots in some form of communication."

— Tony Robbins

Traditionally, the work we have talked about up to this point is led by the CEO (and/or a skilled, experienced consultant) and built out by the executive team and key leaders within an organization. That is why they get paid the big bucks. Their years of experience and expertise mesh to chart the organization's course. It's like generals planning military campaigns for their troops to carry out. Now we must use effective communication techniques to move from *plans* to *people*.

Today, woke leaders are reaching out to team members throughout the organization for input on these important growth pillars. This listening demonstrates much deeper empathy and trust, providing a greater degree of ownership and loyalty. Like the earlier Saladworks example, I personally prefer this approach. With today's Millennial and Gen Z workforce, I think it is even more powerful to involve them in the strategic growth planning process. And the collective wisdom of an organization through crowdsourcing provides deeper input and feedback, boosting everyone's performance. Deep listening is at the root of great communication.

Regardless of the strategic planning approach, it is time for transparent communication. Simply put, a leader must clearly explain and disseminate the organization's purposeful growth plans to its people—the ones whose job it is to carry out the tasks necessary to achieve the desired results.

A leader must influence *all* stakeholders effectively—up and down the ladder, sideways, inside, and outside the organization—via the power of skillful communication. Again, this includes both internal and external stakeholders. Unfortunately, not everyone on the team may be fully on board with the direction, so careful attention must be paid to reach out to those team members and bring them into the fold. A good leader must be able to read the reactions to their message and course correct as necessary. What might be inspiring to some people may come across differently to others.

In fact, I believe internal and external communication is so important in establishing a growth platform that we should consider changing the meaning of CEO to Communication Executive Officer.

As we discussed briefly, for truly great communication, we need a balance between content (what is being said) and delivery (how it is expressed). Even the most compelling content poorly expressed can fall flat. Likewise, the most emotionally evocative expression of empty content is an equally wasted opportunity. This goes for every possible communication platform.

CHAPTER 15

LEADING THROUGH COMMUNICATION FROM PLANS TO PEOPLE

"Communication is power. Those who have mastered its effective use can change their own experience of the world, and the world's experience of them. All behaviors and feelings find their original roots in some form of communication."

— Tony Robbins

Traditionally, the work we have talked about up to this point is led by the CEO (and/or a skilled, experienced consultant) and built out by the executive team and key leaders within an organization. That is why they get paid the big bucks. Their years of experience and expertise mesh to chart the organization's course. It's like generals planning military campaigns for their troops to carry out. Now we must use effective communication techniques to move from *plans* to *people*.

Today, woke leaders are reaching out to team members throughout the organization for input on these important growth pillars. This listening demonstrates much deeper empathy and trust, providing a greater degree of ownership and loyalty. Like the earlier Saladworks example, I personally prefer this approach. With today's Millennial and Gen Z workforce, I think it is even more powerful to involve them in the strategic growth planning process. And the collective wisdom of an organization through crowdsourcing provides deeper input and feedback, boosting everyone's performance. Deep listening is at the root of great communication.

Regardless of the strategic planning approach, it is time for transparent communication. Simply put, a leader must clearly explain and disseminate the organization's purposeful growth plans to its people—the ones whose job it is to carry out the tasks necessary to achieve the desired results.

A leader must influence *all* stakeholders effectively—up and down the ladder, sideways, inside, and outside the organization—via the power of skillful communication. Again, this includes both internal and external stakeholders. Unfortunately, not everyone on the team may be fully on board with the direction, so careful attention must be paid to reach out to those team members and bring them into the fold. A good leader must be able to read the reactions to their message and course correct as necessary. What might be inspiring to some people may come across differently to others.

In fact, I believe internal and external communication is so important in establishing a growth platform that we should consider changing the meaning of CEO to Communication Executive Officer.

As we discussed briefly, for truly great communication, we need a balance between content (what is being said) and delivery (how it is expressed). Even the most compelling content poorly expressed can fall flat. Likewise, the most emotionally evocative expression of empty content is an equally wasted opportunity. This goes for every possible communication platform.

I have found 4 different, but very interrelated goals for communicating purposeful growth:

1. **Aspirational:** Make it Visual.
   Use storytelling techniques; I call this dream-casting.

2. **Inspirational:** Make it Meaningful.
   Invite them to become part of something bigger.

3. **Rational:** Make it Personal.
   Connect with people on a human level, supplying the WIIFM (What's in it for me?).

4. **Attainable:** Make it Real.
   Instill trust and confidence that the plan will indeed work.

I'm sure you can think of a leader who inspired you personally through their communications.

As you can imagine, each specific leadership style will naturally have an approach to communication that fits it best. Some areas will overlap between the styles, depending on the *content* being communicated, the *delivery*, and the situational *context*. Sometimes a leader must establish an aspirational vision; sometimes they need to inspire the team to perform at a higher level; sometimes they need to exude a calm, quiet confidence under pressure; and sometimes they need to exhibit a two-way, interactive, engaging style to elicit input/feedback from the team.

The point is to develop a primary communication style that fits you. Do not try to copy someone else's style; that will come across as inauthentic, unnatural, and ineffective. Your secondary and/or tertiary communication styles will develop over time as you gain more experience managing your message in different situations.

Bottom line: Regardless of your individual communication style, your *content* within its proper *context* must result in establishing a deep sense of confidence and trust in all stakeholders.

> *"Trust is the glue of life.*
> *It's the most essential ingredient in effective communication.*
> *It's the foundational principle that holds all relationships."*
>
> — Stephen Covey

To ensure your message is fully understood, easily repeatable, and spurs appropriate actions that will take root within the organization, you must repeat it several times. Stay on message! Look for opportunities to reinforce your key points across all levels of the organization and relevant stakeholders.

Think of a dandelion as it goes to seed. When you blow on it, its seeds scatter in multiple directions. The same is true with communication. If you do not have a strong, consistent message, you won't know what your team/organization might hear. Miscommunication is fertile ground for misalignment, and we've already proven the importance of alignment—which is the desired outcome of the Purposeful Leadership Revolution.

I've come into organizations and heard people say, "So, this is what we're doing now?" Others will say, "Don't worry. This is just another 'flavor of the month' program that will change again soon. I'll just wait it out."

Hearing both remarks, I think to myself, *Yikes! With this kind of strategic yo-yo communication going on, how am I going to get the team aligned behind the plan we all (or so I thought) agreed to go into battle with?* A leader must use appropriate communication techniques to ensure everyone on the team understands and is 100 percent aligned with the who, why, how, and what of our plans.

Check in with your team from time to time to ensure there is no confusion. Every member of any executive team should be able to recite the organization's purposeful vision, mission, and shared values and the key tenets of the strategic growth plans. In fact, have leaders support and reinforce your message across their spheres of influence. Better yet, have members of their departmental teams present their respective plans within the overarching growth plan. In addition to expanding the spotlight to as many members of the organization as possible, this creates a deep sense of alignment and personal commitment for achieving growth plans.

> "Ultimately, leadership is about inspiring others to believe. Our aspiration should truly be the inspiration of others."
>
> — Gary Burnison, CEO, Korn Ferry

By using appropriate communication techniques, you can stir the hearts of the people who must then perform specific roles to execute our growth plans. Once you have the team's hearts, their minds and bodies will naturally follow.

CHAPTER 16

LEADING WITH COMMITMENT FROM PEOPLE TO PERFORMANCE

"If you are a leader, the true measure of your success is not getting people to work. It's not getting people to work hard. It is getting people to work hard together. That takes commitment."

— John C. Maxwell

Once a leader communicates the growth plan to the team to ensure alignment at a conceptual level, the real work begins in outlining specific commitments necessary for *people* to achieve the desired *performance* goals.

Of course, establishing an inspiring vision is vitally important, but if we cannot lead the team to execute it, we end up with one of my all-time favorite quotes from Thomas Edison: "Vision without execution is nothing more than hallucination."

I love that quote because not only is it true, but it provides a very graphic reminder that we must integrate *both* components, vision *and* execution, to achieve our growth goals. Within the essence of leadership, there must be a commitment among the team members tasked with executing the plan.

Again, you can't be a leader without followers, right? And nobody achieves anything of significance all by themselves.

The term for this concept is "followership," which means a reciprocal commitment between leader and follower to work together to achieve a shared goal or outcome. Anyone drawing a paycheck will perform the duties they are asked to do to fulfill their job description at minimum or to avoid getting fired at worst. However, the true essence of "followership" is for the leader to inspire and motivate their team to perform up to their full potential, challenging them to reach higher than they previously thought possible.

That is why the 4 Ceeds of purposeful leadership start by clearly establishing the foundational principles up front, followed by ensuring a strong connection to key business priorities, and next communicating the plans to all stakeholders. If a leader brings the team along on the journey, a natural progression will follow, earning the leader trust and commitment from stakeholders.

Which is really only just the beginning. Wait…. What?

"Do your job."

— Bill Belichick, Head Coach of the New England Patriots

One reason the New England Patriots have been so successful over the last several years is they have developed a unique culture defined by excellence in execution. Head coach Bill Belichick is a mastermind in creating schemes to help put his players in the best position to be successful. Often, he picks apart his opponent's weaknesses by accentuating his team's strengths while attempting to take away what the other team does best. Check and mate! Once the game plan is in place, his mantra is simple, yet powerful: "Do your job." This mantra is well-known and, indeed, embraced by every single team member simply as part of their culture.

A great coach like Bill Belichick and his staff can draw up a fantastic game plan, but if the players do not do their given jobs, both individually and collectively as a team throughout the week and in the game, the plan won't work. "Do your job," is more than a catchy slogan or mantra; it is essential to the success of the individual players, the collective team, and the broader organization in achieving their shared objectives.

Nobody wants to let their teammates, coaching staff, organization, or fans down. They work extremely hard to live up to their commitments to each other so they can perform at the highest level on game day. String enough successful results together and you have, arguably, one of the greatest dynasties in professional sports. Six Super Bowl victories between 2001 and 2018 is nothing short of amazing. And yes, that Tom Brady fellow was pretty good too.

As my friend and former colleague Brian Ferris likes to say, "In making breakfast, the chicken is merely involved in the process, whereas the pig is totally committed to its success."

Very true, Brian.

To get every player on the same page and 100 percent committed to playing their individual role to the very best of their ability, we must be smart about it—figuratively and literally. You may have heard about using SMART goals in developing personal growth and development plans as part of an annual planning process. Why? Because they work.

> *"Connect the dots between individual roles and the goals of the organization. When people see that connection, they get a lot of energy out of work. They feel the importance, dignity, and meaning in their job."*
>
> — Ken Blanchard

SMART (specific, measurable, achievable, relevant, time-bound) goals represent a personal commitment to helping the team or organization execute its shared vision and achieve its business goals. Let's examine why SMART goals are important by outlining their ability to be the connective tissue that aligns the success of individuals, teams, and organizations.

SPECIFIC

What *specific* commitments are you making individually to help your team and/or organization accomplish its stated growth goals? This is no time to be vague or wishy-washy; a well-crafted SMART goal should be very specific.

Example: Develop, test, and implement a new menu entrée designed to increase traffic and profitable sales at lunch.

MEASURABLE

For anything to be considered a SMART goal, it must be *measurable*. Again, this isn't the time to be subjective, so be clear about how success will be measured in an objective, fact-based manner.

Example: Grow net sales revenue by 3 percent during lunch segment.

ACHIEVABLE

Some say the A should stand for "attainable," yet I believe "achievable" is more appropriate because it's a more positive, inspirational, and action-oriented word. We *can* do this!

Example: Increase guest counts by 2 percent with an increase in guest check totals by 1 percent.

RELEVANT

While this should go without saying, it must be emphasized—everything you do should be *relevant* to helping the team or broader organization achieve its strategic goals. If not, don't *do* it.

Example: Increase overall guest satisfaction score at lunch by 3 percent.

TIME-BOUND

Where is the finish line? All SMART goals must be *time-bound*, with key milestones along the way, to ensure each goal is achieved by a clear and acceptable date.

Example: Test market new lunch menu entree by April 1.

SMART goals provide a clear direction individual team members must commit to in pursuit of broader team and/or organizational goals. And, as we'll discuss later, they provide the foundation for developing an interactive performance management plan. But instead of a broad array of disparate individual SMART goals, management must synchronize the growth priorities, including objectives, strategies, and tactics, of the team or organization with the available resources.

One way to do this is to integrate individual SMART goals into a "4 x 4 x 4 Growth Plan/Structure" (4 objectives, 4 strategies per objective, 4 tactics per strategy). This can work equally well within a 3 x 3 x 3 structure depending on the number of growth priorities you and your team are willing to commit to.

> *"Leadership is lifting a person's vision to high sights, the raising of a person's performance to a higher standard, the building of a personality beyond its normal limitations."*
>
> — Peter Drucker

That's right, Pete—Purposeful Leadership revolves around *GROWTH* Ceeds!

THE PURPOSEFUL LEADERSHIP REVOLUTION

Clarity

Connection

Communication

Commitment

=

ALIGNMENT

Alignment behind these 4 revolutionary *GROWTH* Ceeds will provide a strong, healthy root system, creating a solid foundation of trust for the Purposeful Leadership Revolution.

Are you, your team, and your organization *aligned* for the Ceeds of revolutionary growth to take root?

THE PURPOSEFUL ENGAGEMENT REVOLUTION

A SEASON FOR TRANSFORMING GROWTH

Transforming:
To make a thorough or dramatic change in the form, appearance, or character of; become transformed.

CHAPTER 17

ENGAGEMENT REVOLVES AROUND *GROWTH* SAVIA

"Engaged employees are in the game for the sake of the game; they believe in the cause of the organization."

— Paul Marciano, PhD

I grew up in Kansas. We're probably best known for wheat, but we also grow lots of corn and feed crops to support the state's massive livestock business. While our family lived in Wichita, my great-grandmother Ella Owens owned a farm south of there in a tiny town called Oxford. We used to drive down on Sundays after church to visit her. Born in 1875, Ella was a remarkable woman who lived to be ninety-nine years old—just a few months shy of one hundred!

As a young boy, I loved roaming Ella's property and listening to her tell stories about what it was like growing up in rural Kansas and traveling with her family by wagon train as a young girl when they moved to California to grow oranges. She had a huge wrap-around porch, and it was fun to sit out there with her as we talked and watched the beauty of nature all around us. Ella loved to grow all kinds of plants and flowers; she especially loved to raise irises and would walk me around the garden to inspect their growth and beauty from one visit to the next. In fact, I can still remember the sweet smell of those flowers mixed with rain from a summer thunderstorm building up on the horizon.

On one of those visits, I first heard the phrase, "knee-high by the Fourth of July," referring to how tall the corn should be by that milestone. Just months before, seeds were sown and roots were formed to support plants transforming into maturing corn stalks right before our eyes.

Several years later, the concept of transformation took on a new meaning when Allan Huston was named the new president of Pizza Hut. As we gathered around him in the spacious, open-air atrium of the corporate office to hear his speech, a buzz was in the air. Allan pledged to embark upon a new era of growth that would seek the contributions of every one of us in the room and throughout the far-flung reaches of a restaurant system featuring more than 7,500 locations in the US and several countries around the world.

During his speech, Allan implored each of us to join him in committing ourselves fully with our head, heart, and hands to achieve our daily mission, so we could eventually attain the broader vision for the Pizza Hut brand. Allan talked about the importance of transformational growth—how appropriate.

I felt inspired, with a deep sense of personal engagement I'm not sure I had ever felt before. I was invited to become a "part of the plan," which was very exciting. The image of Allan and his definition of personal engagement that day made a deep impression on me, which persists more than thirty years later.

That said, I think Allen's head, heart, and hands model lacked one important component if we want to truly engage people on a deeper, more emotional level.

I believe we must first get team members (the who) to engage their heart (the why), their head (the how), their hands (the what), and their habits (the when). This is a vitally important addition to the definition of engagement that leads to *empowerment*, which is truly the result of a fully engaged individual, team, and organization.

In fact, the profound effect of engagement and its importance in complementing the revolutionary processes in fulfilling the leadership principles outlined in the previous section are why I believe it deserves its own section within the 4 LEAF *GROWTH* model.

You see, I believe that aligned leadership provides the foundation or root system essential in supporting growth; however, the trunk, branches, and nourishment system must be built upon that foundation to ensure it thrives in any environment to create transformational growth. In Spanish, this nourishment is called *savia*. Translated into English, it literally means "life blood."

Through the miracle of photosynthesis, which include trapping carbon monoxide within a plant and releasing oxygen, a pumping system is instigated by the leaf. This process is called xylem, and it stimulates the *savia* (water, minerals, and nutrients) to move from the soil through the roots to each area of the plant. The fact that this process is self-sustaining, allowing molecules to move up through the plant in a net-neutral manner without investing a single molecule of energy is absolutely mind-blowing.

But that's not the end of the process. When photosynthesis occurs in the leaf, it creates phloem, a process that sends nourishment back down through the plant to create two-way, interactive engagement that enriches the plant for growth.

In my mind's eye, this is exactly how I envision the Purposeful Engagement Revolution.

As we will learn in the next section, the life blood of any team, organization, or community is its people. And highly engaged people—revolving around their powerful and inspirational purpose, aligned and enmeshed with the organization's purpose—is the best way I have found to create transformational growth.

> *"Quite simply, our success is measured in what others achieve. One thing I've learned in my 15 years of being a CEO is that strategy is 90 percent execution—and 90 percent of execution is people."*
>
> — Gary Burnison, CEO, Korn Ferry

Strategic plans devised in a boardroom are great, but the people serving on the front lines who transform aligned strategic plans into aligned tactical actions are the true drivers. With a feeling of trust and empowerment, those actions lead to achieving desired results—or purposeful accountability—and a deep sense of personal satisfaction, which can result in purposeful fulfillment (which we'll discuss in more detail later).

WASH. RINSE. REPEAT.

Engagement represents the bridge between plans and results. It is more than a buzzword. It is how people become motivated to live out their purposeful vision, mission, and shared values to accomplish their given tasks every single day in helping to fulfill their team or organization's growth goals.

According to Pricewaterhousecoopers (PWC), 73 percent of employees who say they work for a purpose-driven company are engaged. By comparison, only 23 percent of those who do not work for a purpose-driven company report being engaged. Wow, that's a significant difference.

When you think of it in a personal context, engagement is a very powerful word. If you are married, I'm sure you remember what it was like to get engaged. Engagement represents the beginning of a process where two people come together as one. In a similar way, we can apply the word engagement to participating on a team or working within an organization.

- **We wear a ring** = Promise and Commitment
- **We tell everyone we know** = Excitement and Celebration
- **We make plans together** = Growth and Development
- **We keep our commitments to each other** = Love and Loyalty

According to Gallup:

> An engaged employee is involved in and enthusiastic about his or her work. Engaged employees are 100 percent psychologically committed to their roles. They thrill at the challenge of their work every day. They are in roles that use their talents, they know the scope of their jobs, and they are always looking for new ways of achieving the outcomes of their roles.

Based on more than 35 million employee surveys conducted over thirty years, Gallup suggests there are three types of employees:

1. **Engaged:** Employees work with passion and feel a profound connection to their company. They drive innovation and move the organization forward.

2. **Not-Engaged:** Employees are essentially "checked-out." They're sleepwalking through their workday, putting time but not energy or passion into their work.

3. **Actively Disengaged:** Employees aren't just unhappy at work; they're acting out their unhappiness. Every day, these workers undermine what their engaged coworkers accomplish.

Why is engagement so important? According to *State of the Global Workplace*, the most engaged teams in Gallup's database when compared to the least engaged teams experience an average of:

- 41 percent% Lower Absenteeism
- 24% Lower Turnover (in high turnover organizations)
- 10% Higher Customer Metrics
- 17% Higher Productivity
- 20% Higher Sales
- 21% Higher Profitability

Wow, all good stuff.

How is Gallup's approach set up to reliably and consistently determine these predictive outcomes? Based upon their vast experience, Gallup concluded there are twelve questions that link powerfully to achieving key business outcomes based on the importance of moving beyond mere job satisfaction to establishing deeper, more emotional team member engagement.

These are referred to as their Q12. Based on my experience administering and taking the Gallup employee satisfaction survey in different companies, the same key areas seem to rise to the top *every single time*.

> "Research indicates that workers have three prime needs:
> Interesting work, recognition for doing a good job,
> and being let in on things that are going on in the company."
>
> — Zig Ziglar

News flash! According to Gallup, more than 51 percent of employees are actively looking for a new job. Yikes. And as a result of the impacts of COVID-19 in the workforce, government labor reports and related research studies suggest that number will continue to rise. Unless there is a (much) higher emphasis placed on the people in an organization.

But there is hope. I believe if leaders within the organization practice the tenets outlined within the Purposeful Leadership Revolution section we just covered, many (if not all) of these key areas could be flipped around. In fact, they would get a considerably positive gain in perpetuating highly engaged team members, eliciting the desired response, "I love my job, my teammates, my company, and the customers we serve!"

Again, engagement is not merely a buzzword. Like the *savia* of a tree, it is the transformational life blood of any individual, team, or organization that desires to fulfill its purpose and achieve its full growth potential. Our work should not be considered merely a means to an end; rather it should play an integral role in fulfilling our purposeful growth plan.

Let's walk through the 4 growth processes within the Purposeful Engagement Revolution—engaging the *Heart, Head, Hands,* and *Habits*—that center around the *who* which, in this case, happens to be you or members of the team and/or organization you lead.

THE PURPOSEFUL ENGAGEMENT REVOLUTION

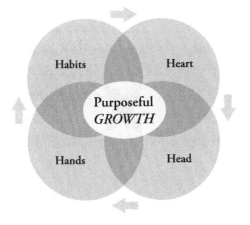

CHAPTER 18

ENGAGING YOUR HEART FROM PURPOSE TO MOTIVATION

> *"Leaders engage their teams by giving them a sense of purpose, providing them opportunities to develop and advance, and putting them into positions where they can be successful."*
>
> — Gordon Tredgold

Once we have established *who* we serve, let's cover the importance of engaging your heart—transforming from *purpose* to *motivation*—so you know *why* you do what you do.

Many research studies have been conducted to better understand the mindset of Millennials (and Gen Z right behind them as well as "Zillennials," an overlap of the two). The perception of Millennials being lazy, entitled, fickle, and unmotivated is just plain wrong. Growing up in the digital age, their world is obviously much different than that of Baby Boomers or Gen Xers. It's not wrong; it's just different—and as I've said many times—*different is good!*

Given all the books, seminars, webinars, and research I have personally seen—coupled with a good portion of my work experience (not to mention my having twenty-four-year-old daughters)—it is my thesis that the Millennial Mindset can best be summarized as the "4 Me" generation.

No, this is not to be confused with the "Me" generation of the 1980s, which was characterized by money, greed, power, and narcissism. (Think Gordon Gecko, the slimy, villainous corporate raider played by Michael Douglas in the movie *Wall Street*.)

In fact, the truth is just the opposite. As the name implies, there are 4 key tenets that summarize the 4 Me mentality we find in today's Millennial-focused world. These 4 key tenets—Personalization, Customization, Self-Expression, and Connection—are based on the appropriate balance of Hi-Tech (digitization) and Hi-Touch (humanization) interactions:

1. PERSONALIZATION

—Get to Know Me

- I'm a living, breathing, feeling human, not merely a collection of "1s and 0s."

"Words have meaning, and names have power."

— Author Unknown

In the Bible, God changed the names of certain people called to carry out God's plan—a transformational, repurposing process to help them grow *from* who they were *to* who they were meant to be. God changed Abram's name to Abraham, Simon's name to Peter, and Saul's name to Paul. The names and labels you bestow upon yourself and the names and labels other people give you have power.

When I dine in a restaurant or walk into any retail establishment, I make a special point to learn and use people's names. Name badges make it easy, yet people often seem startled when I call them by name. For those not wearing a name badge, I simply ask. In both instances, I see their eyes light up and a smile crease their face. They are no longer a server or cashier; they are a living, breathing, and feeling human—just like me!

> *"A person's name is the greatest connection to their own identity and individuality. Some might say it is the most important word in the world to that person. It is the one way we can easily get someone's attention. When someone remembers our name after meeting us, we feel respected and more important."*
>
> — Joyce E. A. Russell, *The Washington Post*

Even in the digital age with rapid improvements in artificial intelligence and machine learning, the last I checked, we are still human. Not only do we have a brain, but the ability to sense and feel. Until robots (or zombies?) come to take us away, I believe the notion of personalization will only grow stronger—not weaker—as we continue to adapt to technological advancements over time that can learn our unique preferences.

2. CUSTOMIZATION

—Make it for me

- I have specific color, style, function, budget, and timing requirements; I want it "my way."

In addition to obvious examples of customizing a meal in a restaurant, we customize a wide variety of products and services.

- ✓ Cars
- ✓ Athletic Shoes
- ✓ Furniture
- ✓ Entertainment
- ✓ And More

Building on the concept of personalization, we see a growing trend toward *mass customization*. Remember the quote from Henry Ford, "You can have any color of Model T you want as long as it's black." Well, today you can go online to customize almost any vehicle to create the perfect combination of exterior paint, interior, wheels, and a variety of related accessories. All custom-designed to fit your specific desires, personality, and budget. This is also where the concept of freedom and flexibility come in since team members today are looking to flip the emphasis to "Life/Work Balance"—work opportunities they can customize to fit their life stage and lifestyle. Even if it means accepting less in compensation.

3. SELF-EXPRESSION

—Let me be me

- I'm very social and I "like" to "share" my life experiences with those I "love."

As humans, we have always had a need for self-expression. This goes back to cave drawings or just good ol' fashioned sharing stories around a fire. For those of us old enough to remember the '60s and '70s, we can recall it coming in the form of long hair, bell-bottom jeans, protests, and music (among, ahem, other things).

Today, social media gives us a platform to express ourselves by posting a cute baby photo, a special occasion, or possibly a funny cat video with merely a few clicks. We use social media to share life's special moments and our opinions on what matters to us—from social to political to religious opinions and everything in between. Freedom of self-expression has become a form of art with some people spending a lot of time ensuring they post or tweet exactly the right words, photos, memes, videos, etc. within the context of their personal brand.

4. CONNECTION

—Connect with me

- I want relevant content in context with my specific life stage/lifestyle, and I want to connect with a higher purpose, something bigger than myself.

Yes, we've all heard the phrase "something bigger than yourself" or some such. There's even a TV commercial for Volkswagen that righteously jumps on the bandwagon by saying, "Drive something bigger than yourself." Huh? Last I checked, *all* cars are bigger than me.

Even though I feel the above example is a bit misguided and a cheap way to glom onto a societal trend, that an advertising message was built around this concept merely supports my point. Millennials are motivated by taking action that leads to improving their world and leaving a positive, living legacy for those who follow.

For Millennials—and Gen Z right behind them—connecting their unique purpose to their world in meaningful and relevant ways creates an emotionally evocative bonding opportunity that can build a lasting and loving relationship over time. This is especially important given that many things are somewhat "disposable" to them. Hey, if this isn't working for me, then I will simply move on. "Time to bounce." Not a great time to be a brand or organization if you do not perform up to (or exceed) their expectations. They'll drop you like a bad habit. That's why I prefer the term engagement (two-way/interactive/relational) over loyalty (one-way/singular/transactional).

To that point, according to a McKinsey research study conducted in August 2020 among over 1,000 US-based employees, nearly two-thirds surveyed said that COVID-19 has caused them to reflect on their purpose in life. And nearly half said that they are reconsidering the kind of work they do because of the pandemic. Millennials were three times more likely than others to say that they were reevaluating work.

A summary of the research findings published in an article written on April 5, 2021 by Naina Dhingra, Andrew Samo, Bill Schaninger, and Matt Schrimper stated, "For starters, we know that employees at all levels of the organization say they want purpose in their lives. Eighty-nine percent of our survey respondents agreed, a proportion that tracks closely with academic research."

"Seventy percent of employees we surveyed said that their sense of purpose is largely defined by work. Senior executives in our sample nudged that average upward, but even so, two-thirds on nonexecutive employees said that work defines their purpose. This signals the clear opportunity for employers and leaders—an open door to encourage your employees at all levels to develop and live their purpose at work."

"Such findings have implications for your company's talent-management strategy and its bottom line. People who live their purpose at work are more productive than people who don't. They are also healthier, more resilient, and more likely to stay at the company. Moreover, when employees feel that their purpose is aligned with the *organization's* purpose, the benefits expand to include stronger employee engagement, heightened loyalty, and a greater willingness to recommend their company to others."

From a career-building perspective, younger Millennials and their Gen Z counterparts are less interested in financial compensation than flexibility and a sense of autonomy and freedom. Simply put, they want to be part of a "movement." They want to be part of something bigger than themselves.

There, I said it. But this isn't something entirely new, nor is it motivating only to Millennials and Gen Z. I believe the power of purpose holds a special place in the hearts of us all and has since time began. Given the effects of COVID-19, this desire for flexibility and the pursuit of greater life/work balance has been both highlighted and amplified.

> *"Be not simply good; be good for something."*
>
> — Henry David Thoreau, *Familiar Letters*

Today, we are just more in tune with our thoughts and feelings and have various outlets to express them—both socially and professionally. Indeed, the convergence of our social, family, work, and spiritual lives is at the very heart of engagement. Beyond working as a nine-to-fiver or pulling a shift and getting paid every other week, we all want *more* out of our jobs.

Many cause-related marketing campaigns have gone well beyond fundraising efforts. They have mobilized people to establish a movement. Think back to the humble beginnings of some now well-established charities:

- ALS (Lou Gehrig's Disease) "Ice Bucket Challenge"
- American Heart Association "Go Red For Women"
- Alex's Lemonade Stand Foundation for Childhood Cancer
- Susan G. Komen "For the Cure" (Breast Cancer)

In addition to these great charitable organizations, there are a host of examples within corporate America where brands are tapping into this powerful, purpose-based "movement mindset," or what I call, "The Great Repurposing."

- **#MeToo:** Sexism and Gender Equality
- **Black Lives Matter:** Civil Rights and Racial Equality
- **Environmental:** Climate Change and Sustainability
- **Conscious Capitalism:** Business and Ethics

While each of these 4 Me tenets has its merits, the fourth—connection—is most relevant to the concept of purposeful engagement among Millennials and Gen Z from an employment perspective.

Let me give you a few real-world examples I had the distinct honor to take part in. They will help bring this concept to life for you.

- The Cheesecake Factory's "Drive Out Hunger" tour partnership with Feeding America.
- Noodles & Company's partnership with Share Our Strength's No Kid Hungry campaign.
- "Mimi's for Miracles" partnership with Children's Miracle Network, tie-ins with the American Heart Association's "Go Red for Women" and the National Breast Cancer Foundation.
- Saladworks' "Fives for Lives" fundraising/food donation program to support local healthcare heroes during the height of COVID-19 and "Million Meals Challenge" in partnership with No Kid Hungry.

By leveraging our assets and equities—including mobilizing our thousands of passionate, highly engaged, and motivated restaurant-level team members—we were able to accomplish 4 key purposeful growth objectives:

1. **Awareness:** Placed a spotlight on important causes that help people in need in our local communities, across the country, and in some cases, the world.

2. **Engagement:** Created emotionally evocative, interactive approaches to fully engage our team members, guests, and communities.

3. **Actions:** Enlisted our guests, team members, and business partners to participate through product donations or financial contributions.

4. **Relationship:** Encouraged our guests and team members to exponentially expand our reach by becoming brand ambassadors—tapping into their social communities.

Working in a restaurant in any capacity from serving guests to preparing the food is highly stressful and exhausting. I've always said if you want to be successful working in the restaurant business, you must share a deep love for both people and food—in that order. I have found the people part is actually the most attractive. That is where bonding takes place and a sense of family is established. Simply put, we are in the *people* business. We just happen to sell food.

In his book *Drive: The Surprising Truth About What Motivates Us*, Daniel Pink suggests there are three ways to genuinely motivate people: autonomy, mastery, and purpose. I agree with Pink on this list, and we will be discussing each one within this section on the Purposeful Engagement Revolution. However, I believe these areas of motivation are listed backward—to me, purpose should always come first, and mastery should come before autonomy. To me, there is a fourth area missing—a deeply emotional sense of duty.

Whether you were in Cub Scouts or Girl Scouts, the military, or competed in team sports, you likely learned early on about the importance of duty as a key motivator for improving performance. Among other things, duty includes honor, courage, perseverance, and trustworthiness.

Now, let's bring this concept even closer to home. For those of us with families, the deep sense of duty to provide for them might actually be the strongest motivation. In fact, I believe the external motivation around one's duty to others supersedes the other areas of internal motivation. This is a very human instinct that has existed for centuries.

When I think back over the course of my thirty-five-year career to all the early mornings, late nights, weekends, long commutes, flights, rental cars, and hotel stays in every kind of weather imaginable, I distinctly remember *who I served*. And when times were tough and stress was elevated, I relied on a mental image of those within my spiritual, relational, professional, and personal realms. They are the ones who truly motivated me to stay fully engaged, true to my purpose, to strive for mastery, and to seek autonomy based upon the awesome power of duty all based upon a foundation of unconditional love.

Again, whether it's a spiritual deity, a spouse/partner, your family, a teammate, guest/customer, yourself, or the soldier fighting next to you, duty may provide the greatest motivation to engage (or remain engaged) at the highest level. And when every member of a team is fully engaged, it builds a deep sense of confidence that both our individual and collective team or organizational purpose can be fulfilled.

We all have a deep yearning to feel connected with others; however, the need to feel needed by others may be more powerful. Again, when we capture the heart, the rest of the mind and body will follow.

"Every human being who works has to know what they do matters to another human being."

— Patrick Lencioni

CHAPTER 19

ENGAGING YOUR HEAD FROM MOTIVATION TO MINDSET

"Now the peculiar excellence of man is his power of thought; it is by this that he surpasses and rules all other forms of life; and as the growth of this faculty has given him his supremacy, so, we may presume, its development will give him fulfillment and happiness."

— Will Durant, *The Story of Philosophy*

We covered the importance of *who* we serve and *why* we do what we do. Now let's take this concept a bit deeper as we learn how to transform the vision of your heartfelt purpose by engaging your head—from *motivation* to *mindset*—so that you know *what* to *do*.

On one of my many travels, I had some time to kill in the airport before my flight was ready to board. Given my love for books and learning in general, I strolled over to a bookstore to browse a bit. There in the window was a book that immediately caught my attention.

It was called, *Mindset: The New Psychology of Success—How We Can Learn to Fulfill Our Potential* by Dr. Carol Dweck. After many years of studying achievement and success, Dr. Dweck, a world-renowned

Stanford University psychologist, proposed that one's mindset is a much bigger determiner of success than talent or ability. Specifically, Dr. Dweck cites the dichotomy between those who harbor a "fixed mindset" and those who exhibit a "growth mindset" and how that difference influences their success in parenting, business, school, and relationships.

At a high-level, a person with a fixed mindset believes they possess specific and self-limited knowledge, talents, and abilities that cannot be changed. These people tend to peak early and fail to live up to their full potential. On the other hand, people who exhibit a growth mindset believe they have the ability to actually increase talent, ability, and even intelligence via a combination of curiosity, learning, and discipline. This results in a self-belief that their potential is unlimited.

> *"The world as we have created it is a product of our thinking. It cannot be changed without changing our thinking."*
>
> — Henry Ford

To put the concept of mindset in perspective, let me give you an example. I serve on the Board of Directors for the New Frontier Educational Foundation in support of the Frontier Charter Schools in Kansas City. Early in my time on the board, I was invited to take a tour of one of the Frontier Charter Schools with Greg Rieke, who co-founded Frontier as a STEM-based educational model years ago with a bold vision to help educate the most underserved communities in the city and provide a bridge to a brighter future.

On the tour, I came across a handmade poster on the wall in the main hallway. On each side of a drawing of the human brain was a column featuring different ways of thinking about the same situation.

One statement came from a fixed mindset and the corresponding statement came from a growth mindset—sound familiar?

Fixed Mindset	Growth Mindset
"I give up."	"This may take some time and effort."
"This is too hard."	"I'll use some of the strategies I've learned."
"I can't do Math/Science/Social Studies/Read."	"I'm going to train my brain in: Math/Science/Social Studies/Reading."
"I can't make this any better."	"I can always improve; I'll keep trying."
"I'm not good at this."	"What am I missing?"
"I'll never be as smart as them."	"I'm going to figure out what they do and try it."
"I made a mistake."	"Mistakes help me improve."
"It's good enough."	"Is this really my best work?"
"I'm asesome at this!"	"I'm on the right track."

Do you see the difference in mindset represented in each of these parallel statements? The mind is an incredibly powerful tool. If used correctly in a growth-centric way, it can be trained to overcome barriers and accomplish important tasks. Conversely, if left to its own devices, it can lead to a fixed perspective that can be self-limiting and grow increasingly challenging to overcome.

"The happiness of your life depends upon the quality of your thoughts."

— Marcus Aurelius

But as much as I agree with this bifurcated fixed versus growth mindset model, I believe two more important distinctions lurk within the voices we often hear in our heads representing both our foreground and background messages.

Like the angel on one shoulder, our foreground voices are often the self-talk we listen to when we're totally honest with ourselves, truly authentic, and growing into our purpose. I like to think of these voices as adding positive energy or possibly the harmony to a favorite song.

Unfortunately, like the devil on our other shoulder, we also hear background voices projecting an unconscious stream of negative messages. This often happens when we are gripped with fear, uncertainty, doubt, and delay (FUDD) and feeling stuck in the muck and mire of inertia.

On one end of the axis, we have foreground voices that contribute to a "victor mindset." On the other end of this axis are the background voices contributing to a "victim mindset."

You recognize those voices as:

- ✓ **Victor Mindset:** Speak it into the universe. I'm just going to will it to happen. If it is to be, it's up to me. Failure is not an option. No retreat, no surrender.

- ✓ **Victim Mindset:** It's not my fault. I never seem to catch a break. Some people have all the luck. Why (not) me? Seriously? Again? This always happens to me. If only…. Would'a, could'a, should'a.

I envision our minds like a beautiful garden, one that needs to be cultivated and nourished for each individual plant to grow in beauty by fulfilling its purpose. Unfortunately, weeds can set in and quickly grow up around the plants. If left unattended, it is easy for the weeds to choke out the beautiful plants. If each plant symbolized a thought, imagine how many positive thoughts it would take to overcome our negative thoughts? We simply must eliminate the weeds in our head to develop a positive, healthy outlook that leads to becoming victors.

"Progress is impossible without change, and those who cannot change their minds cannot change anything."

— George Bernard Shaw

A growing segment within the life coaching industry is centered on how we can harness the awesome power of our minds. In fact, the ability to control one's mind is at the heart of Napoleon Hill's landmark tome *Think and Grow Rich*, in which he studied success patterns among the most respected and successful leaders of his time.

While I am no psychologist, I have found through personal experience and many others' observations throughout my career that our minds can work both for and against us. This is often the most important distinction between those who fulfill their wildest dreams and those who fall short.

I have identified 4 key mindset themes (two victim-related and two victor-related) that I believe we must honestly assess if we are to authentically grow into our purpose to fulfill our true growth potential.

1. Self-Limiting Beliefs

2. Imposter Syndrome

3. Mind Mapping

4. Mindfulness

1. Self-Limiting Beliefs—As I stated in describing the victim mindset, many of us hear background voices that often limit our growth opportunities. These negative voices center on FUDD—the confluence of fear, uncertainty, and doubt that leads to delay.

Of course, these background voices are not true unless we give them power. When we do, it is like wet cement beginning to harden. The voices become louder and more persistent until they turn into rock-solid, self-limiting beliefs.

The power of belief can be an incredibly positive force for personal and professional growth, or it can be a devastatingly negative force that can limit your true potential. You get to choose. Here is where positive self-talk comes in because you must drown out the negative voices with ones of assurance, confidence, and "relentless optimism"—a term I used among our executive team at Mimi's Cafe as a foundation for turning our business around.

"Hey, we're down double-digits in sales with a brand that has lost its way and is dragging down the stock of its parent company. That's the bad news. The good news is that today (and every day) is a new day, and we must remain relentlessly optimistic if we are to weather the storm and achieve our ambitious growth goals. Challenges will no doubt crop up unexpectedly and we will suffer through some bad days; however, if we string enough good days together, we will build confidence among the team that, over time, we can do this!"

Yes, we *can* do this, but only if we leverage the techniques we learned earlier in the book to help us retrain our brain and turn the negative background voices of FUDD into positive, uplifting, and hopeful foreground voices that speak our truth through repurposing the negatives into positives. Remember, purposeful faith is greater than unfounded fear; purposeful hope is greater than risk uncertainty; purposeful belief is greater than self-doubt; purposeful action is greater than the paralysis of delay.

We can break this down into 4 questions I have heard from several mindset coaches:

- Why do I believe this thought is true?
- Do I believe this is really *my* truth?
- What do I believe is actually true?
- What action do I need to take to move forward?

These daily affirmations over time and with consistency will serve as an antidote for each negative FUDD background voice, helping to repurpose your mindset from victim to victor.

Essentially, you are who you think you are.

> *"Every time you are tempted to react in the same old way, ask if you want to be a prisoner of the past or a pioneer of the future."*
>
> — Deepak Chopra

2. Imposter Syndrome—Everyone else is fully adept in their roles with far superior knowledge, expertise, and experience to offer the world than you are, right? Wrong! We are all works in progress and, at any given season, we are merely at different stages of our respective growth journeys.

I'm sure we've all heard the phrase, "Fake it 'til you make it." Nobody has it all figured out; however, some people are better at projecting confidence than others. And that's not such a bad thing.

As I'm sure you've picked up on throughout this book, I am a huge believer in the importance of confidence. It's a very attractive force that builds camaraderie and trust among leaders and their teams. But if you don't have confidence in yourself, how do you expect to earn the confidence of others?

We already have too much pressure and stress caused by forces we have no control over, so why would we want to add pressure and stress through an internal force we *do* control?

Give yourself a break and allow yourself some grace—the opportunity to learn and grow by running your own race at your own pace.

"Come home to yourself. Stop running. Stop hiding. You are worthy, enough, magical, capable, and so much more. Come home to yourself. You are allowed to rest here."

— MB

By asking questions, demonstrating humility, being diligent in knowledge and skill-building and learning from your mistakes, you will naturally build confidence. Over time, your growing sense of confidence will lead to mastery, and, of course, to new growth opportunities where the cycle continues.

3. Mind Mapping—Like a computer, our mind represents an intricate map of plans, commands, actions, and learning opportunities. We consult a map when we need directions. But as the saying goes, "If you don't know where you're going, any road will take you there." Where are you going?

This is why it is so important to obtain clarity of your purpose. Like a map, you must write down where you want to go so you can map out a plan to help get you there. Otherwise, you may find yourself like the Griswold family in the movie *European Vacation* where they drive continuously in circles around a roundabout in London. And like any journey, you must map out key milestones along the way. As Stephen Covey says in his landmark book *The 7 Habits of Highly Successful People*, "Start with the end in mind." If you found and fulfilled your unique purpose, what would it look like? Where would you be? Now, map out the right/best route to get there.

> *"You have power over your mind—not outside events. Realize this, and you will find strength."*
>
> — Marcus Aurelius

After living in the Los Angeles area for eight years, I can attest that it has earned its reputation for presenting drivers with systemic traffic challenges. However, with the benefit of GPS mapping, I realized I could reach my destination via another route if the route I had originally chosen was backed up. The point is maps can help us reach our destination *and* provide opportunities to reroute if/when necessary.

Likewise, we must remain true to the power of our purpose (our destination) yet stay flexible in how (and when) we arrive. Enjoying every step of the journey can be difficult for many who are considered Type A personalities—impatient and goal-oriented. At the risk of sounding corny, we must stop and smell the roses along the way, understanding that we are all on different growth journeys with different timelines.

Remember, we need to mind map our journey with tremendous clarity, focusing on specifically where we want to go, so we can reach our destination one mile at a time, while looking out the window to enjoy the scenery along the journey.

4. Mindfulness—A lot has been said and written over the last few years about the importance of mindfulness in achieving personal and professional growth. To me, mindfulness has many aspects, from prayer or meditation to deep-breathing exercises, inner/outer-directedness, yoga, or guided imagery. Some of us prefer to listen to music, go on a nature walk, or elicit positive affirmation through self-talk.

Any (or possibly all) of these elements of mindfulness can provide positive benefits to help center your mind and emotions. However, when I think back to my competitive sports days, one technique seemed to work best—visualizing the race from start to finish, culminating with a sense of how I would feel afterwards.

I don't view these techniques as simply mind games; rather they are a way to imprint on our brain the specific thought patterns needed for successful outcomes. I'm sure you've heard interviews of great athletes who suggest they could "see" their victory before they even started the race.

I first heard the term "guided imagery" from a psychology teacher in high school who took our class on a mental journey. As we closed our eyes, she spoke to us in a calm, soothing tone, telling us when and how to breathe, and helping us fill our heads with vivid images of where we were and what we were doing, seeing, smelling, tasting, etc. To this day, I incorporate similar techniques, but with an important twist: I envision exactly how I want to feel in each scenario. I have found that additional sense makes all the difference.

When I think of mindfulness in relation to job performance, I think of a phrase we used when I led Mimi's Cafe: "Be here now!" This meant to be both physically and mentally present, living in the moment with no distractions. Focusing on the specific issue at hand, but more importantly, on its positive outcome.

We often get caught up in the swirl of the day-to-day, and it becomes easy to feel overwhelmed. We multitask to try to get everything accomplished, but in doing so, we don't necessarily do our best work. However, when we are totally present and focused on solving the most urgent issue of the day, we can feel good about the accomplishment. Then we can tackle the lesser issues with no stress. If we press forward by accomplishing the small stuff first, we may feel a sense of immediate gratification. But we will still have the most stressful project hanging over our head like some sort of "Sword of Damocles" to deal with later.

The good news is our minds can be (re)trained to align our heartfelt purpose with a brave and confident mindset—and it's never too late to start!

> *"Keep your thoughts positive because your thoughts become your words. Keep your words positive because your words become your behavior. Keep your behavior positive because your behavior becomes your habits. Keep your habits positive because your habits become your values. Keep your values positive because your values become your destiny."*
>
> — Mahatma Gandhi

CHAPTER 20

ENGAGING YOUR HANDS FROM MINDSET TO DEVELOPMENT

"The way of success is the way of continuous pursuit of knowledge."

— Napoleon Hill, *Think and Grow Rich*

We've covered the importance of engaging you heart and head, so let's now talk about engaging your hands—transforming from *mindset* to *development*—so you know *how* to do what you do.

A question often asked on employee satisfaction surveys or corporate culture questionnaires is: "Do I have the necessary training, tools, and resources to do my job to the best of my abilities?" While I believe any team or organization is responsible for providing appropriate training, basic tools, and resources, I feel it is incumbent on us to fill in the gaps on our own.

Long gone are the days when a company would pay for a three- to four-day conference held at some exotic resort. Even one-day seminars or workshops are being curtailed. While most of this change is due to COVID-19 or the tremendous cost of these external events, there is an even bigger reason.

We live in the Information Age!

Given the advent of search engines, which provide almost effortless access to relevant content from a wide variety of expert sources, we can enrich our knowledge and continue training in a highly targeted way. This is much more productive than sitting in a huge auditorium or hotel ballroom hoping to glean a few insights from the roster of speakers. Beside the high cost of traveling and attendance, we simply cannot "afford" to be out of the office so long. Work has a habit of piling up.

In this age of lean manufacturing and the need to use fewer resources and work smarter, we must adapt to a new way of learning. We have a plethora of digital platforms available: blogs, vlogs, podcasts, audiobooks, webinars, videos, tutorials, electronic newsletters, social media—all featuring thought leaders and subject matter experts in whatever area we are interested in.

I guess I am still a bit old school since in addition to still reading the newspaper every day, I am also a huge fan of reading books. I love books! My library (and basement) is filled with nonfiction books I have read and sometimes reread to help me learn and grow both personally and professionally.

New school, old school, or somewhere in between, there are simply no excuses for not taking growth opportunities into your own hands instead of counting solely on your employer to provide them. And I assure you, it is never too late to learn new ideas, techniques, or tools to enhance your job performance. With the increasingly rapid pace of change, this is not a nice-to-do—it is a must-do if you want to remain relevant and valuable to any employer.

According to the global executive recruiting firm Korn Ferry, based in part on their nearly 70 million assessments, "Learning agility is the number one predictor of success. It takes mental agility, people agility, change agility, and strategic agility—all of which is founded upon the broader concept of learning agility."

We've talked about the importance of establishing a growth mindset. The key to growth lies in our ability to stay curious and open to learning new ideas, concepts, and skills.

In addition, we have a powerful tool at our disposal for information gathering—our mouths. Huh? That's right—ask (more) questions. The people around us have subject matter expertise and would love to help us. You can learn new things in group or departmental meetings, or you can schedule time with your peers or leaders in other departments to learn how the puzzle pieces fit together. This also works when working remotely.

I'm reminded of the movie *Glengarry Glen Ross* starring Jack Lemon and Alec Baldwin. Baldwin's character is the boss of a real estate sales firm in New York. His "pep talk" to the team regarding improving sales performance is punctuated by what he calls, "The ABCs of sales," which stands for "Always be closing." I like to twist this phrase by replacing the last word with "curious" because I believe curiosity is relevant to our lifelong pursuit of knowledge and growth.

Always be curious by asking powerful questions. Then peel the skin off the onion by following up and asking more detailed questions. What's the question behind the question? Your intellectual curiosity will become a valuable tool in learning more, better, and faster, and it will send the powerful message that you are humble enough to learn from others' wisdom and experience. I have received this important feedback on more than a few occasions.

> *"Curiosity is an act of vulnerability and courage...
> we need to be brave enough to want to know more."*
>
> — Brené Brown, *Braving the Wilderness*

I am a big believer in the power of mentoring. From college and graduate school professors to business leaders, supervisors, and peers, I have been blessed with several inspiring mentors who helped me progress along my growth journey. And I have done my best to serve as a mentor to many others.

Accepting help from a mentor entails 4 very positive benefits:

- You'll see things from a totally different perspective.
- You'll get new ideas you may never have thought of otherwise.
- You'll receive wisdom from someone who's "been there."
- You'll be inclined to "pay it backward" and mentor others.

To keep things simple, I suggest finding two mentors, one to help navigate your growth journey who is proficient in the soft skills (EQ) required for building positive, productive relationships within your teams. Then, find another mentor who can help improve your hard skills (RI), the ones needed to perform your job. Like the yin-yang symbol, your skills will be in balance to provide fertile soil for personal and professional growth to transform you into a more well-rounded leader.

But in some industries, the hard skills require an extra level of attention. Given our rapidly changing world—with technological innovations like big data, digital and social media, AI/machine learning, robotics, 3-D printing, and virtual/augmented reality, etc.—we have a new wrinkle on this concept called "reverse mentoring."

Reverse mentoring is where younger people who grew up "digital natives" help mentor their leaders who did not. In many cases, middle- to upper-level managers and department heads have significant practical knowledge, business savvy, and real-world experience; they are just not (yet) as adept at applying technological solutions to business challenges. By working together to take advantage of their respective areas of expertise, experience, and wisdom, the work gets done more productively with a greater sense of mutual participation and ownership.

When he was eighty-seven, the year before his death, Michelangelo reportedly wrote *ancora imparo* on the edge of a drawing, which means "I am still learning."

Me too, Mikey. Me too.

Although the continuous learning process will no doubt help you master your current job, it can also help you land a promotion or attain a new position somewhere else. You see, the world keeps spinning on its axis and revolving around the sun whether or not you are ready. As a result of COVID-19, several industries are having a difficult time filling open positions. At the same time, competition for high-level positions will always be stiff, so you must get yourself ready if you want to continue growing a fulfilling career long into the future.

To help accomplish your goals, I suggest putting together a written career growth plan. Simply take out a piece of paper and divide it into two columns, one labeled Current Role and one Future Role. Then do the following for each column.

1. CURRENT ROLE

Ask yourself: What do I need to learn to be the very best in my current job?

You may think you are working hard and being proficient at what you do, but are you really doing your job to the best of your ability? Are you standing out as a team member with high potential? Unfortunately, employee satisfaction surveys suggest many supervisors are not providing enough feedback to keep you informed on how you are doing. (We will cover this in greater detail later.)

But don't let that stop you.

Take time to dig out your last few performance reviews and make a list of your strengths and areas of opportunity as outlined by your supervisor. This information traditionally lives in the personnel files within your HR department, so it represents your reality and a great starting place.

You should schedule time with your supervisor to supplement this information with real-time feedback. I assure you that when an individual demonstrates an authentic desire to learn how they can be a better, more productive, and effective team member, any supervisor worth their salt will want to help.

Finally, keep your eyes and ears open to gauge how you are performing relative to team members with similar responsibilities. This combination of inner and outer awareness will serve you well at each stage of your career journey.

2. FUTURE ROLE

Ask yourself: What do I need to learn to grow into a promotion or compete for an opportunity elsewhere?

Here is a brief list to get you thinking at a macro level. Of course, your particular industry and related responsibilities will dictate a much more specific list:

- ✓ Microsoft Office (Word, Excel, PowerPoint, Outlook)
- ✓ Finance and Accounting
- ✓ Business Plan Writing
- ✓ Strategic Planning
- ✓ Personal Branding
- ✓ Presentation Skills
- ✓ Writing Skills
- ✓ Digital Creative Skills (Photoshop, Illustrator)
- ✓ Emotional Intelligence
- ✓ Results Intelligence
- ✓ Business Intelligence (Data Analysis, Dashboards)
- ✓ Artificial Intelligence
- ✓ Leadership Development
- ✓ Organizational Behavior
- ✓ Managing Difficult Conversations
- ✓ Time Management
- ✓ People Management
- ✓ Project Management (Sharepoint, Slack, Trello, etc.)
- ✓ Program/Process Management (Lean Six Sigma, etc.)

Depending on your age and the school(s) you attended, you may have been exposed to the core concepts in many of these areas. However, the pace of change has become so rapid that you may need some "fertilizer" to help stimulate new concepts or methods to grow your performance to a new level.

Remember, exceptional doers get promoted and become managers. Most of what we learn helps us become better doers, not necessarily better at leading and managing others. It is vitally important to invest in learning management skills if you want to grow into/as a leader. This means you must balance the hard skills with the soft skills to earn the confidence and trust of those you lead and those who lead you.

Now, make a list of potential resources you can access to help you master each area on your personal growth plan. As I mentioned, there are a ton of free or almost free resources to help you along your growth journey. Simply connect the dots between your top career growth goals and the best resources for learning how to reach them. Just think—if you added one area each quarter, it would allow you to achieve 4 times the growth every single year.

In many communities and/or online, you can also earn certification in several of these areas that will look good on your resume. Employers love to see candidates who exhibit a growth mindset. It demonstrates you have an unquenchable thirst for knowledge and a desire to apply the right/best tools and resources to excel at your job. Who wouldn't want to hire or promote that?

With a growth mindset, you will learn to master your current role and set yourself up to compete for internal promotion or look attractive for an exciting new opportunity elsewhere.

> *"Whatever we plant in our subconscious mind and nourish with repetition and emotion will one day become a reality."*
>
> — Earl Nightingale

CHAPTER 21

ENGAGING YOUR HABITS FROM DEVELOPMENT TO MASTERY

"The successful person has the habit of doing the things failures don't like to do. They don't like doing them either necessarily. But their disliking is subordinated to the strength of their purpose."

— E. M. Gray

So far in this section, we've covered the importance of engaging your heart, head, and hands in helping you purposefully grow into your best you. Let's pull it all together by engaging your habits—transforming from *development* to *empowerment*—to help you know *when* to do what you do. All with a high level of discipline, consistency, and the pursuit of excellence.

Depending on who you listen to, it can take somewhere between twenty-one and sixty-six days to form a habit. Keep in mind, these could be habits with positive or negative consequences in finding your purpose and fulfilling your growth potential.

"We are what we routinely do. Excellence, then, is not an act, but a habit."

— Aristotle

In *Outliers: The Stories of Success*, Malcolm Gladwell claims it takes 10,000 hours to master a subject. While that may be true for some situations, I do not believe it is true for everyone in all situations. We've all heard the saying "practice makes perfect," right? While I believe we need practice to get better in any endeavor, it is not that simple. Another school of thought comes to us via legendary Green Bay Packers coach, Vince Lombardi who said, "Practice does not make perfect. Only perfect practice makes perfect."

If you've ever seen my golf swing, you know without instruction I could spend 10,000 hours on the range and not come away with a perfect swing. Oh, I'm sure I would probably hit several really sweet shots along the way; however, it would not likely result in a repeatable, sustainable swing. Instead, all I would end up with is blistered and bloodied hands and the same doggedly optimistic, though ultimately frustrating, swing I started with. Trust me, I would love to be wrong on this because I absolutely love golf, but I tend to play consistently inconsistent even on my best days.

Some of you may remember Olga Korbut from Russia or Mary Lou Retton of the United States—world-class Olympic champion gymnasts from the 1970s and '80s respectively. Both earned perfect tens, which is incredible. However, today we are watching the most amazing and truly transcendent gymnast in the world—Simone Biles—performing routines nobody can come close to matching. She, too, has earned perfect tens in various competitions. The point is, there is always room for improvement because perfection is merely relative and, by definition, unattainable.

Unfortunately, no one is perfect, so without a coach to help us make the proper adjustments—in our golf swing, in our life, in our career, or in our relationships—all we can realistically hope for is to make some small improvements. On our own, we may be mired in bad habits leading nowhere, leaving us stuck in the mud of inertia and/or indecision without taking action at all. *"FUDD!"*

While I've found several great books on the topic of habits written by subject matter experts such as James Clear, Charles Duhigg, and Brendon Burchard, here's what has worked for me and some other successful people I admire. Remember, we all have both good habits we want to build on and bad habits we'd like to eliminate.

> *"Excellence is not a gift, but a skill that takes practice. We do not act 'rightly' because we are 'excellent,' in fact, we achieve 'excellence' by acting 'rightly.'"*
>
> — Plato

We tend to do repeatedly what we feel rewarded for doing. The reward can be life-affirming and healthy, or more often, unhealthy, the kind we know we ought to change but have trouble with because changing it runs counter to our desires. That's why our annual New Year's Resolutions don't last, right?

We do what we do because we are all creatures of habit. And we tend to repeat behaviors that give us a sense of comfort. But, as I said, there is no growth when we are stuck in the quicksand of comfort.

I believe in accentuating the positive as opposed to focusing (too much) on the negative. So, let's focus on 4 habits we should all start doing to help us fulfill our true growth potential.

THE 4 HABITS WE SHOULD START DOING

1. SET BOLD GOALS AND BE INTENTIONAL

The first habit features the importance of two interrelated actions. Set bold goals for yourself that will stretch you past your "comfort zone." In Jim Collins' landmark book *Good to Great*, they're called BHAGs which stands for Big Hairy Audacious Goals. Whatever you want to call them, the first thing you must do is *have* some. Write them down and post them where you can see them every single day. Recite them silently or aloud to speak them into existence. Without a set of bold goals, you are just wandering aimlessly—possibly working hard yet getting nowhere.

The second part is even more important than the first. I believe in the power of being intentional with our thoughts, words, feelings, and actions to be more consistent in driving results. Maybe not from a linguistic perspective, but from a metaphorical one, the word "intentional" could have come from the root word "intense." I believe we must be *intense* about developing, nurturing, and growing habits that lead to positive behaviors and outcomes.

If we are to grow into our purpose, our habits must intentionally reflect that goal as opposed to random scatter-shooting. Becoming "intensely intentional" about what we choose to think, say, feel, and *do* will provide a foundation upon which all other habits can be built.

2. ADOPT AN ATTITUDE OF GRATITUDE

The legendary Zig Ziglar was fond of saying, "Your attitude is your altitude." While I love me some Zig Ziglar, and we all understand the power of a positive, can-do attitude, I feel this phrase would be more helpful by exchanging "attitude" with one important word—*gratitude*.

According to studies, many positive behaviors and related outcomes come from adopting an attitude of gratitude:

- ✓ Shields you from negativity
- ✓ Makes you happier
- ✓ Rewires your brain
- ✓ Eliminates stress
- ✓ Heals
- ✓ Improves sleep
- ✓ Boosts self-esteem and performance
- ✓ Enhances the Law of Attraction
- ✓ Improves relationships

Studies confirm we develop and grow faster, stronger, better—and with a much deeper sense of joy and fulfillment—when we are grateful for what and who we have in our lives.

In fact, most life coaches recommend developing a *gratitude journal* to take stock of the many positive things we have, which tends to make the negative things seem less important. I wholeheartedly agree with this practice, but I'm not as concerned about whether you write them down in a journal, pray them silently or aloud, or merely meditate on them in your own way. The important thing is to be intentional about being grateful every day. The power of gratitude is tremendously beneficial because it shapes your heart, head, hands, and habits. And what a great way to start each day as a brand-new gift to be grateful for.

In addition to what we have (things), it is equally, if not more important to take stock in and give thanks to who we have (people) in our lives. Here's an example of 4 in each category I came up with off the top of my head. I'm sure you can come up with many more specific and relevant to you.

What We Have...

- Health?
- Food?
- Shelter?
- Employment?
- Other?

Now, if you can say you have all 4 of these important basic needs fulfilled, congratulations! Unfortunately, according to Gallup's *Basic Needs Vulnerability Index*, in 2020, 750 million people could not make that claim. It puts things in perspective for us, doesn't it?

Who We Have...

- Spouse/Family/Significant Other?
- Friends?
- Teammates/Coworkers?
- Mentor/Coach?
- Other?

If you have at least 4 people who fulfill one of the above roles, you are also doing very well. The ability to cultivate close, trusting, loving relationships provides a community feel that makes our "things" (what we have) worthwhile.

> *"Gratitude is the golden frame through which we can see the meaning of life."*
>
> — Brendon Burchard

3. DISCIPLINE YOURSELF

We often think of the word "discipline" as something that happens to us when we make a poor choice and get in trouble. Been there. But there is an even more powerful definition when used in the context of making positive, productive, and proactive choices.

For an athlete, those choices may include eating right, staying hydrated, stretching well, and getting plenty of rest so they can maintain a specific training regimen. In business, the choices may include a variety of self-disciplinary techniques that prepare you to reach peak performance at work.

Following are 4 of the most important choices for improving self-discipline:

1. **Manage Your Time and Energy:** As the saying goes, "Time is money." More than that, time is a great equalizer since we may not all have the same resources, but we all have twenty-four hours in every day. We must use this time wisely, setting daily milestones that will help us achieve our ultimate goals. We often hear coaches say, "No wasted reps," or "No wasted days." They believe intense focus on the present will prepare their teams to reach their aspirations.

When confronted with a formidable challenge requiring a quick solution, a former ad agency supervisor of mine would say, "There are twenty-four hours in a day and we can get a lot done together in that time, so let's order some pizzas and get to work!" Sometimes this kind of commitment and intensity is called for. However, it cannot become the norm because it will soon burn out everyone.

We can find a ton of self-help tools and resources to maximize our time. However, I have found no silver bullet solution to time management. Rather, it is merely self-discipline and must be accomplished using whatever tools and resources work for you—digital or analog.

President Dwight D. Eisenhower developed a model for evaluating the best ways to maximize productivity within the massive responsibilities of the office. It was a simple 4-box matrix on which the X-axis used the terms Urgent and Not Urgent, and the Y-axis used Important and Not Important.

Within this framework, "The Eisenhower Principle," he separated his key priorities and related action items into 4 categories:

- Urgent/Important = Do
- Not Urgent/Important = Plan
- Urgent/Not Important = Delegate
- Not Urgent/Not Important = Eliminate

> *"I have two kinds of problems:
> the urgent and the important. The urgent are seldom important,
> and the important are seldom urgent."*
>
> — Dwight D. Eisenhower

Sounds simple, right? But how many of us get sucked into wasting time chasing after the not urgent and not important while avoiding letting go and delegating the urgent and not important. Remember, what we say no to is every bit as important (if not more so) than what we say yes to.

We must have a better way of ensuring we are using our limited time productively. Good news! We have one, and it's called a to-do list.

Some people prefer to get up early and make to-do lists for what they plan to accomplish that day. Other people, like me, prefer to make them the night before. Having it all on paper means I can rest easier knowing my next day's plan is already written. I actually use a hybrid approach where I will plan out my week on the weekend, usually Saturday morning, so I can enjoy the rest of the weekend without thinking (too much) about work. This also makes the dreaded "Sunday night effect" easier to manage. The key is to match your biggest, most thought-related tasks with the time of day when you traditionally have the most energy to fulfill them.

And yes, like Eisenhower, I believe in an established hierarchy of priorities for to-do list items. Whether listed as simply A, B, C, or D, or something more visceral like "Hair on Fire!" "Get 'er Done," "Smoldering Embers," or "Back Burner," whatever works best for you is fine as long as you do it in an intentional, disciplined, and consistent way. As I mentioned, my old boss at Pizza Hut told me, "Just get it from 'to-do' to 'to-done'!"

Just *do* it!

2. **Create Success Routines:** The YUM! Brands culture has a disciplined approach to improving operational excellence called Success Routines. In essence, it takes the daily personal to-do list concept and applies it on the team or organizational level. When everyone understands what excellence looks like, and they buy into the daily success routines required to achieve it, positive results naturally follow.

   Having written success routines included in quarterly business plans and approved by the leadership chain ensures everyone knows the specific goals that must be accomplished every day to meet team and/or organizational goals.

   Your personal success routine should incorporate ways to enrich your mind, body, spirit, and soul every day to ensure your health and wellbeing as a whole person. For example, if you don't incorporate some form of exercise along with healthy eating and sleeping routines, your body will not be nourished to fuel your growth goals. Some people like to start work early; others are night owls. Some people like to work out first thing and others prefer to do so later in the day or at night. Some people are vegan or vegetarian while others prefer meat.

Likewise, you need a positive, productive mental health and wellbeing routine to maintain the focus and cognitive skills necessary to achieve your growth goals. One example is "The Pomodoro Technique" whereby you select a task and work hard for twenty-five minutes, followed by a five-minute break. After 4 of these "sprints" (tech term), take a longer break. And make sure to give yourself some type of reward for every sprint completed. This will help you remain focused and mentally engaged and optimize your work performance and sense of accomplishment.

We're all wired differently. You will be more productive and successful when you establish a personalized *success routine* that works for you. Don't worry about what works for others.

3. **Be a Purposeful Learner:** I think every company probably considers itself a learning organization in some way, shape, or form. However, as the Purposeful Engagement Revolution teaches us, opportunities exist for individuals, teams, and organizations to employ learning techniques to engage their team members on a much deeper level.

   According to a recent survey conducted by LinkedIn of 2,000 of its members, "People who learn are 24 percent more likely to feel happy at work."

   We will talk about the importance of learning best practices in the next section. For me, what it really means to be a learning organization rests on the ability for management to be comfortable with the concept of temporary failure. To that point, I hate the word "failure" because I believe it connotes a sense of finality as opposed to a spirit of continuous improvement—or what I call "purposeful growth." In my view, failure is only final if you don't take away key lessons to help make future improvements.

You may have heard the phrase "Fail early. Fail small." I don't want us to fail at all. By practicing purposeful growth habits, we create a spirit of continuous improvement based on 4 revolutionary components:

- ✓ Plan
- ✓ Test
- ✓ Learn
- ✓ Optimize

WASH. RINSE. REPEAT.

You see, when a plan comes together and is executed well, yet does not achieve the desired results, mistakes made along the way can be corrected. In fact, I believe we grow more from our mistakes than our successes. When we're successful, we can become complacent. Whereas when we make mistakes, we feel a sense of urgency to learn from and correct them as soon as possible.

4. **Perform Post-Analysis**—Looking backward allows us to (try to) understand what we've done and how we might use those lessons to make improvements going forward. In the military,

they call these important activities After Action Reports, whereas sports teams call them Film Sessions.

Many large corporations employ a similar discipline with what is commonly referred to as a post-analysis. (I hate the term post-mortem because it sounds like someone died—I hope not!) This is when a project team comes back together after project launch to analyze the results—what went right, what went wrong, and any surprises they encountered. A disciplined post-analysis is designed to help the team learn from the past to plan and prepare for greater success going forward.

Be aware that the swirl of the day-to-day can easily get in the way of taking time to conduct a thorough and systematic post-analysis—if you let it. Regardless of the size of your team or organization, I have found the post-analysis process is one of the most important disciplines a team can undertake. In addition to the lessons the current project team can learn, it can also provide a road map to help get a new project team up to speed quickly.

4. SERVE OTHERS

As I mentioned, when you are growing into your purpose, you are likely serving others in some way. Again, I believe *who you serve* is even more important than *why* you do it. When you make things personal or give them a human face, you tend to get a deeper sense of daily emotional engagement.

Think back to when you learned to ride a bike. If you're like me, you started with training wheels. Then, when you developed a keener sense of balance, it was time to take the training wheels off. Taking the training wheels off doesn't mean your initial rides were completely successful—you probably fell down a few times. But when you did, instead of walking the bike back to the garage and quitting (even if it took some prodding from your parents), you dusted yourself off and got back on the bike. You kept trying until you felt more confident, absorbing the (painful) lessons of your prior attempts and making corrections until riding was second nature. What a sense of freedom and accomplishment. You may have even gone on to learn to "pop wheelies" and, like me, jump trash cans *à la* Evel Knievel—a hero from my misspent youth. Just remember, someone helped you along the way, and I believe we are all called to likewise serve others along their growth journey.

Within a team or organization, leaders must allow members to make mistakes *and* be there to pick them up, dust them off, and get them back on the bike. Imagine the confidence the team will gain knowing they can play with a free mind. It's like a quarterback who is allowed to play through mistakes without fear of getting benched after one turnover. This confidence breeds a deeper level of emotional engagement that, over time, leads to superior results.

Of course, I'm not talking about rewarding individuals or teams for poor planning, effort, or execution. I'm talking about encouraging folks to plan strategically, take reasonable risks, and execute to the best of their abilities. Otherwise, the organization may invest its limited time and resources for very little gain. That is not the way to achieve step function change growth. Mistakes are okay; however, we must learn from and correct them to move the team forward. That is why I prefer a purposeful learning approach to help move us toward our goals as opposed to seeking perfection, which as I previously mentioned is unattainable.

"Empowerment is all about letting go, so others can get going."

— Kenneth Blanchard

THE PURPOSEFUL ENGAGEMENT REVOLUTION

Heart

Head

Hands

Habits

=

EMPOWERMENT

If the Purposeful Leadership Revolution leads to *Alignment*, then the Purposeful Engagement Revolution leads to *Empowerment*.

And we know that aligned and empowered team members who feel emotionally and physically engaged—taking ownership of the outcome—are happier and more fulfilled. Empowerment will support business growth and result in higher retention rates. As I've seen on many occasions, experienced teams tend to be more profitable to the enterprise. And this is more important than ever because of "The Great Repurposing" era that was kicked into high gear by COVID-19.

To that end, let's move onward from The Purposeful Engagement Revolution (Transforming Growth) to The Purposeful Accountability Revolution (Harvesting Growth).

THE PURPOSEFUL ACCOUNTABILITY REVOLUTION

A SEASON FOR HARVESTING GROWTH

Harvesting:

To gather (a crop) as a harvest. A supply of anything gathered at maturity and stored: a harvest of wheat. The result or consequence of any act, process, or event.

CHAPTER 22

ACCOUNTABILITY REVOLVES AROUND *GROWTH* OFFSHOOTS

"The law of harvest is to reap more than you sow.
Sow an act and you reap a habit.
Sow a habit and you reap a character.
Sow a character and you reap a destiny."

— James Allen

Fall has always been my favorite time of year for its warm, sun-filled days that give way to cool, crisp evenings and the faint smell of logs burning on some distant fire. Football tailgate parties, hayrides, pumpkin patches, candy apples, Halloween trick-or-treaters, and steaming hot mugs of apple cider complete the vision of fall in my mind's eye.

Fall is when the full bounty of nature is revealed in beautiful, brightly colored leaves and fresh, juicy, well-ripened fruit and vegetable harvests. It's a time of celebration in agrarian communities, honoring the physical manifestation of the hard work of farming from spring through summer before achieving its unique purpose by harvesting in fall.

As I've said, leaves come in many different shapes, sizes, colors, and textures based on the equally unique purpose of a plant's genus. Leaves serve as the catalyst for growth through the magic of photosynthesis—generating a green pigment called chlorophyll that provides energy to the tree. What I find fascinating is the way nature uses the fall season to change the color of a leaf from green to a spectrum of vibrant yellows, golds, oranges, reds, and purples—colors that were already present in the leaves, but hidden by the more dominant green chlorophyll. As the nights get longer and the air temperature cools, the leaf no longer needs to produce chlorophyll for food as the tree prepares itself for its next season.

What "colors" might be present, yet hidden, within yourself, your team, and/or your organization to provide opportunities for both current and future growth?

In addition to serving as the growth engine for a given plant or tree, that's not all leaves do. Leaves help the plant bear nuts or fruit that provide nourishment for people and animals. They also contain seeds to be scattered to reproduce the plant leading to new growth opportunities. For an example, the fig tree in my backyard has an accountability to develop fig leaves and fruit as key measures of its success.

Within this book's organic 4 LEAF *GROWTH* metaphor, the concept of Purposeful Accountability "revolves around" these growth offshoots. As someone who has been blessed to serve in several different leadership positions, I believe that you simply must be as passionate about accountability as you are about leadership and engagement. In fact, given the strong headwinds we face in navigating an increasingly competitive, globally connected, technologically advanced, performance-driven business climate, we need to be exponentially more focused on accountability across all stakeholders. This means accountable to ourselves, the teams we play on, the organizations we're employed by and, of course, the *WHO* we serve.

Remember the concept of transformational "Step Function Change" growth I spoke about earlier? I will build on that foundation throughout this section as we learn how to master 4 key elements that comprise the Purposeful Accountability Revolution— *Outcomes, Obstacles, Outliers,* and *Obsolescence*—by measuring what matters most and remaining flexible and resilient while incorporating a best-practice mindset within a spirit of continuous improvement.

THE PURPOSEFUL ACCOUNTABILITY REVOLUTION

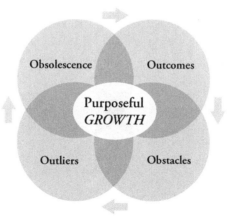

CHAPTER 23

ACCOUNTING FOR OUTCOMES FROM PURPOSE TO MEASUREMENT

"Measure what is measurable and make measurable what is not so."

— Galileo

Regardless of which business you are in, it is important to keep score—moving us from *purpose* to *measurement* to achieve our desired outcomes. If we are to be performance-driven individuals, teams, and/or organizations and achieve our goals, we must have a system for measuring results that emanates from our shared purpose and facilitates accountability. Like the instrument panel we depend on when driving, we call this accountability system a dashboard and it helps us display the measurements that matter most. This information helps us learn how to become brilliant at the basic drivers of our business.

One year, Ram Charan was the keynote speaker at the annual Restaurant Leadership Conference held in Scottsdale, Arizona. In his illustrious career, Charan has been a board member, highly acclaimed author, award-winning Harvard Business School and Northwestern University professor, and a sought-after executive consultant. Charan has a brilliant mind and a special gift for simplifying the execution of complex business processes to help maximize growth potential for individuals, teams, and organizations.

According to Jack Welch, former Chairman of GE, "He (Ram Charan) has the rare ability to distill meaningful from meaningless and transfer it to others in a quiet, effective way."

One key takeaway I internalized from Charan's presentation is relevant to this section. Charan said, "In any business, I have found that success comes down to two key variables: Velocity and Yield." In this model, velocity represents the speed and volume of "turn" for a given product or service, whereas yield represents the profit margin associated with each turn, as in one widget sold represents one turn.

WASH. RINSE. REPEAT.

Okay, great—let's all go to happy hour!

Here, I am using "turn" as we used it at Universal Studios Hollywood to refer to the number of guests we served. Guests entered the park through turnstiles, so each turn represented a customer, a sale, and revenue. In my role as senior vice president marketing and sales, this model was relevant for me and my teams. In addition to building the overall brand, our job was to: 1) drive incremental net sales (gross sales minus discounts, promotions, etc.) by maximizing attendance (turnstile "turns" representing velocity) while, 2) providing additional sources of revenue ("VIP Experience," VIP parking, "Front of the Line" pass, "Buy a Day, Get a Year!" annual pass promotions, merchandise, concessions, etc.) to maximize our yield, or profit per guest.

Think about NASCAR—standardized chassis and components, rules and regulations—all to ensure a level playing field. The crew chief, driver, mechanics, and pit crew need to work together to establish a plan to gain an edge when dealing with the same track and weather conditions. As you can imagine, state-of-the-art technology (hi-tech) must be balanced with the driver's feel of the car on a given surface (hi-touch) to give each team its best shot at winning.

Finding even a few tenths' improvement in speed can equal multiple-second advantages during a 400- or 500-mile race. Often, this tiny advantage can lead to taking the checkered flag, Victory Lane, and a champagne (or beer, soft drink, milk—depending on the sponsor) bath for one driver and team. For the rest of the pack, it's back to the garage to look for an edge to help them do better the following week.

As the "legendary race car driver," Ricky Bobby said in *Talladega Nights*, "If you ain't first, you're last." Ricky said lots of dumb things.

While I'm certainly no "gear head" who can tell you how to fine-tune a race car, I can teach you an approach I've used successfully in building brands. It came to me when Sean Covey gave a keynote address at our Focus Brands Global Franchise Conference a few years back. The talk was based on Covey, Chris McChesney, and Jim Huling's book *The 4 Disciplines of Execution*. Their thesis is simple, yet powerful, outlining 4 key disciplines to help drive what they call "4DX Growth":

> **Discipline 1**—Focusing on the Wildly Important
> **Discipline 2**—Acting on Lead Measures
> **Discipline 3**—Keeping a Compelling Scorecard
> **Discipline 4**—Creating a Cadence of Accountability

Based on my entertainment, retail, restaurant, and hospitality experience, including Universal Studios Hollywood, the two variables of *velocity* and *yield* are indeed foundational. However, they are simply not enough by themselves because they do not incorporate the equally important human factor that represents our team members and guests.

I believe, in virtually any business, success comes down to a combination of 4 interrelated and revolutionary growth metrics that are included in the concepts of *velocity* and *yield*. These are the critically important human factors that lead to success in meeting our goals:

- ✓ **People** (to serve Guests/Customers)
- ✓ **Guests/Customers** (to build Sales)
- ✓ **Sales** (to generate Profits)
- ✓ **Profits** (to drive Growth)

WASH. RINSE. REPEAT.

While this model may sound simplistic, I assure you it has several layers that need to be peeled back to identify what truly drives business success.

And given the nature of today's dynamic and highly competitive business environment, it is vitally important to find the right/best set of metrics to provide a competitive edge for our brand so we can maximize sales and market share as profitably (and reliably) as possible.

The concept of reporting and analyzing both *lead* and *lag* measures really resonates with me since any decent manager knows how to call balls and strikes—the lag measures. However, an excellent manager knows how to identify and impact the most salient lead measures in achieving lag desired measures. This is where the magic lies.

Within the digital media world, the concept of lead and lag measures is fairly straightforward given the breadth and depth of objective metrics one can track within a sales funnel that leads to a purchase (e.g., send rate, open rate, read rate, click-thru rate, time on page, conversion rate, shopping cart sales, abandon rate, etc.). Let's look at a real-world example in an operational situation we uncovered while I was at Mimi's Cafe that led to an important breakthrough on hourly labor productivity, a key measure of profitability.

First, a little background. In the restaurant industry, the combination of labor costs and cost of goods sold (COGS) is known as the "Big Two" because they represent the biggest line items on the profit and loss statement.

Given the rising costs of healthcare, minimum wage hikes, competition for staffing, and the growing number of dining options, all exacerbated by COVID-19, we find a scarcity of high-quality talent to fill open positions. Thus, digging into the dynamics of labor to find even small savings and/or increased productivity is vitally important.

Most restaurant and retail managers use some sort of labor-centric lag measurement; however, when you consider Mimi's offers table service for breakfast, brunch, lunch, and dinner, there is a very important human element involved. A server can literally make or break you. Given the tasks and turnover of each position within the restaurant, one can easily see a pattern emerge. To paraphrase the famous line in George Orwell's political satire *Animal Farm*: "All labor hours are created equal—some are more equal than others."

Given that we know when most guests prefer to dine with us, we must not only be fully staffed at the appropriate times—that's a given—but we must have the right/best team to ensure our labor hours are as productive as possible.

Here's what I mean. Breakfast is the busiest and most profitable time at Mimi's, so scheduling is vitally important in maximizing sales. Let's say we have a long-time, well-liked server (we'll call them Dakota) who, for whatever reason, is just not as productive as another server (we'll call them Denver). Denver is an authentically charming "go-getter" who has only been with us a short time. As a result, Dakota earns $15 an hour and Denver earns $12.

While Dakota is chatting up the guests, Denver is building a relationship with guests in a different way. You see, Dakota is engaging on a surface level, but it has nothing to do with the guests' expectations about their dining experience.

On the other hand, Denver is helping guests enjoy a great dining experience by recommending featured menu items (read profitable), prepared in a special way (cha-ching), with a round of our unique sparkling wine flights (cha-ching). Returning to the table at the end of the meal, Denver offers to box up some of our famous Mimi's Muffins for the guests to take with them (cha-ching!). Finally, Denver warmly thanks the guests for coming in and invites them to come back soon—and, "Ask for Denver."

Simply put, Denver is giving our guests more of what they love about Mimi's in a very real, authentic, and hospitable way. This equates to a higher guest check, and equally important, increases the likelihood the guests will come again and refer Mimi's to their friends, family, and coworkers. Or maybe Denver's guests will then think of Mimi's for a catering occasion, or ordering a family meal online.

By the way, a bigger guest check means a bigger tip for Denver. Just sayin'.

Based on the ability to obtain server-level detail from our point-of-sale system, we were able to rank each server during each shift every day. This allowed us to recognize and reward the most productive servers while giving them an opportunity to share best practices with the others and elevate the whole team's productivity.

But we all love Dakota, who is always so friendly and appears to be very busy; however, this is no way to run a business. Yes, we must remember our team members are humans whose livelihoods we either control or significantly contribute to. We have to care. And we have to find the balance between being compassionate and being competitive. If we go too far in either direction, we lose.

Whether in the context of a restaurant, a retail environment, or virtually any type of team or business organization, there are Dakotas and Denvers. The key point here is we must control what we *can* control. We cannot fixate on the number of guests on a given day—only what we *do* with them.

We must measure what matters *most*.

And we must be transparent about sharing our results with the team to foster a sense of trust that goes along with accountability. When I worked at Pizza Hut years ago, our president, Steve Reinemund, had a bell outside the door of his office he would ring when we beat our weekly sales goal. Today, there are no shortage of metrics we can use to gauge our performance. But it is vitally important that we, as leaders, share as much information as possible with our team. This will ensure they take personal accountability in doing what is necessary to achieve our shared goals.

Much like driving a car or flying an airplane, having a dashboard with "drill down" areas representing cost-benefit analysis related to our teams and locations can bring a sense of clarity and transparency. This makes management decisions so much easier and less subjective or emotional. Remember, most managers earn a performance bonus based on their ability to exceed stated key performance indicator (KPI) thresholds, so they have a personal incentive to use the appropriate data to help them achieve both the company's objectives and their own.

"Accountability is the glue that ties commitment to the result."

— Bob Proctor

Let's look at one more real-world example by examining the lead measures that comprise our lag measures—our sales plan. Within the restaurant industry, the following variables represent a dashboard for both short- and long-term success.

Guest Counts

- Lag Measure: Total Number of Guests
- Lead Measures: New Guests (Acquisition), Repeat Guests (Frequency/Loyalty/Engagement/Advocacy)

Guest Check

- Lag Measure: Guest Check Dollar Average
- Lead Measures: Pricing, Menu Mix, Add-Ons

Guest Experience

- Lag Measures: Overall Satisfaction, Intent to Return, Intent to Recommend

- Lead Measures: Friendliness, Cleanliness, Food Quality, Speed of Service, Order Accuracy

But wait…there's more. Within the guest experience section, it's great to have these lead measures, which will no doubt lead to their respective lag measures. We can also identify the importance of proper staffing, training, rewards, and recognition that enable the execution of any marketing or menu-related plan to attain the desired guest experience.

You can't drive (profitable) sales—either guest counts or guest checks—if the cashier, waitstaff, or kitchen crew aren't properly trained to execute a given menu/marketing program.

You can't have outstanding guest experience metrics if you don't have the appropriate staffing, training and feedback loop to live up to your brand promise.

And, of course, with every restaurant there could be other business channels that drive sales growth (e.g., online ordering, delivery, catering, ecommerce), which requires a consistent guest experience across digital platforms.

As I mentioned, growing sales is not easy, but it's not complicated either. In fact, I had a phrase I used with marketing teams that reflected my folksy Midwestern upbringing. Simply put, our job is to work together with our training/operations teams to build sales: "Invite 'em in! Serve 'em up! Bring 'em back!"

Remember, we are in the *people* business.

You see, if we only looked at the lag measures, we would merely be skimming the surface. Only by diving deeper into the lead measures can we create actionable programs (e.g., menu, marketing, media, merchandising, hiring, training, reward and recognition, etc.) to maximize our sales growth opportunities across all business channels. And this disciplined approach to measuring outcomes—and sharing results with the team—applies to any type of business.

Like the ultimate measure of any crop is its yield (what you can sell in the market), so too is the measure of our business activities (what you can take to the bank). Increasing velocity will obviously accelerate growth potential, but so will the vitally important human elements that revolve around your team or organizational purpose to help maximize yield.

CHAPTER 24

ACCOUNTING FOR OBSTACLES FROM MEASUREMENT TO ADAPTABILITY

"The best laid schemes o' mice an' men gang aft agley [often go awry]."

— Robert Burns

The progression from purpose to measurement in determining outcomes now takes us to the concept of how we can overcome obstacles by moving from *measurement* to *adaptability*.

By this point, your purposeful business plan is firmly in place and well-communicated across all stakeholders. Everyone is thoroughly engaged in helping to bring the plan to life. You also have appropriate performance metrics and related recognition and reward mechanisms firmly in place. An air of confidence permeates the enterprise as all signs indicate the successful execution of your ambitious growth plan.

It's time to "*GROW* up"!

Until some unforeseen obstacle(s) get in the way… Oops!

- Security breach
- Government regulation
- Competitive intrusion

- Health/Safety accident
- Product recall
- Legal actions
- Financial malfeasance investigation
- Activist investors
- Trademark/Intellectual capital infringement
- Supply chain distribution challenge
- Product procurement issue
- Commodity price surge
- Labor scarcity
- Marketing performance
- Weather trends

Or a global pandemic….

In my career, I have worked in organizations that have encountered nearly every one of these obstacles at one time or another. Not all at the same time, thank God. In each case, our plans had to change to accommodate the issue, some certainly much more so than others. And as the former great heavyweight boxer Mike Tyson said, "Everyone has a plan until they get punched in the mouth."

So true, Mike…so true.

Remember the character "Mayhem" in the All-State Insurance TV commercials? We refer to obstacles during our planning phase as mayhems to watch out for. What could possibly go wrong? Would we be prepared if something did go wrong?

Unfortunately, the majority of these obstacles are unavoidable and time-sensitive; they can arise without warning, and they require immediate resolution. Who could have foreseen the devastating effects of COVID-19 at the beginning of its surge in March of 2020? Remember how we all had to "pivot" (the official word of 2020) our business interactions. Instead of business as usual, we had to learn to communicate remotely. Zoom…Zoom. Phrases like, "You're on mute" (the official meme of 2020) and "Can I share my screen?" (the official question of 2020) were part of our new-normal. And we had to adopt new practices while we were forced to hole up at home trying to figure out how to keep our businesses operating.

"What stands in the way becomes the way."

— Marcus Aurelius

However, some of these obstacles can be planned for, at least to some degree.

For example, when I was at The Cheesecake Factory, a few early adopting states and/or municipalities required restaurants to put nutritional information on their menus. Given the abundant portions at The Cheesecake Factory—not to mention the…well…let's just say "flavor-enhancing elements" in the recipes of its uniquely craveable menu items—there was initial worry this government regulation could negatively affect sales. At the same time, the economy was entering into "The Great Recession" caused by the collapse of the real estate market.

As the great Winston Churchill said, "Never let a good crisis go to waste." We should all strive to turn negative situations into positive outcomes. While complying with this new menu nutritional labeling regulation, we stepped up our message of "sharing"—a key element of The Cheesecake Factory's appeal is not only that its portion sizes are big enough to share, but the celebratory dining experience makes it a popular destination for its guests to share life's special moments.

In fact, this led to a comprehensive marketing, menu, and partnership campaign featuring quarterly, themed "sharing" events. Each event was linked to the brand's key assets with both calendar-relevant and guest-centric initiatives while providing an opportunity to share with those in need within the communities we serve.

1ST QUARTER: *SHARE THE LOVE*

During the "season of love" anchored by Valentine's Day, our *What's Your Flavor?* Cheesecake recipe contest garnered more than 10,000 recipe submissions, culminated in five finalists of which "Stefanie's Ultimate Red Velvet Cake Cheesecake" was voted the winner by the public, and was rolled out on "National Cheesecake Day" as our featured cheesecake for the year. We contributed $.25 to *Feeding America* for every slice sold.

To generate personal engagement among our legions of fans, we also hosted a cheesecake personality quiz featuring a list of questions that would determine which of our thirty cheesecake varieties was a perfect love match for you. As you can imagine, we received a flood of likes on Facebook and lots of cheesecake personality quiz comments and shares.

To this day, the Ultimate Red Velvet Cake Cheesecake™ remains the number-one-selling cheesecake variety by a wide margin.

2ND QUARTER: *SHARE THE CELEBRATION*

The Cheesecake Factory is a perfect place to celebrate special occasions, so during this quarter, which includes Mother's Day, Father's Day, graduations, and weddings, we asked our guests to "share" those special memories with us.

In addition to providing each guest a complimentary slice of cheesecake for every $30 spent with us, we created a highly engaging promotion on Facebook where we asked them to share a particular reason they had for celebrating.

The very personal and emotionally evocative submissions we received were incredibly powerful (to say the least). That our guests were so comfortable sharing their personal lives with us demonstrated the trust we had established with them. This just doesn't happen for most brands.

Based on the thousands of submissions we received, we selected a winner and sent them on an all-expenses-paid trip to Celebration, Florida, which just happens to be near the Disney World Resort. I love it when a plan comes together.

3RD QUARTER: *SHARE THE SPIRIT*

During this time, we wanted to focus our efforts on a unique corporate social responsibility (CSR) campaign that demonstrated a spirit of giving back to our communities.

In partnership with Feeding America, the nation's largest network of food banks, we created the *Drive Out Hunger* Tour featuring a converted bread truck, a team of drivers, and an inspiring song ("New Day" by Universal Music Group recording artist Tamar Kaprelian) to serve as our anthem.

During the thirty days of September (aka Hunger Action Month), we started in Los Angeles and snaked our way across the country, visiting a different city every day until we reached Washington, DC.

At each stop, we collected cans of soup for Feeding America and gave out slices of our new Ultimate Red Velvet Cake Cheesecake™.

During our final stop at the Capital Area Food Bank, we revealed a "Can-struction" sculpture of our Ultimate Red Velvet Cake Cheesecake™ featuring 30,000 cans of soup as we announced the successful results of our *Drive Out Hunger* Tour.

4TH QUARTER: *SHARE THE JOY*

During this season, we honored the universal concept of joy by inviting our guests to share their joy with us, each other, and those they love.

To accomplish this, we gave out a *Slice of Joy* card good for a complimentary slice of cheesecake for every $25 gift card purchased—either in our restaurants or on our website.

The idea was for guests to *Share the Joy* of the season by celebrating with friends, family, and coworkers at The Cheesecake Factory. The $25 gift card earned them a slice of cheesecake worth $7.50 retail for themselves.

The "Share"-themed campaign helped The Cheesecake Factory overcome food labeling obstacles and a recession. And in doing so, we built up both our external brand (guests and communities) and our internal brand (team members and business partners). This was especially important during such an uncertain time.

Another example of turning obstacles into bridges happens when a team or organization doesn't meet revenue targets and uses that to motivate the organization. Whether part of a small to medium size privately held organization, or a large, publicly traded global enterprise, we *all* have to achieve specific performance milestones each day, week, period, quarter, and year.

Steve Davis, the former chairman and CEO of Bob Evans, Inc., which was the parent company of Mimi's Cafe when I served as president, said, "Mears, if you and your team miss this quarter, what are you going to do next quarter to make it up?"

Like having a second parachute, one should always build contingencies into any annual operating plan. However, pulling that chute may merely be a trade-off between current business needs and future growth opportunities. Sometimes you must throw the original plans out the window and develop new (and better) plans to get the business back on track. A sense of urgency among team members is important in this situation.

Mimi's Cafe was suffering double-digit sales declines when I started there. The executive team had to take immediate action to reverse this trend. After reviewing the data, industry trends, and our business model, we created a comprehensive and integrated sales-building plan.

As a memorable way of packaging this series of programs internally, we called it...

OPERATION: ROLLING THUNDER!

Our goal was to drive sales via compelling, relevant, and brand-centric programs throughout the day—giving our guests "more of what they love" about Mimi's:

Breakfast: "Muffins To Go" highlighted the opportunity for our guests to take a package of our legendary Mimi's Muffins home to their families or back to their offices to share with coworkers.

Brunch: "Wine Flights" featuring three white wines and three red wines along with our innovative "Sparkling Wine Flights" featuring a split of sparkling wine and three juice mixes.

Lunch: "Express Lunch" featuring a fifteen-minute guarantee and a "Soup to Go" program highlighting our delicious made-from-scratch soups in a quart-sized container for only $5.

Dinner: "Bistro Meals" featuring several three-item meal options for $10.99 and "Family Meals to Go" featuring an array of ten different meals starting at $25 that could feed a family of four to six.

Bar: "Happiest Hour" featuring glasses of wine, bottled beers, well drinks, and appetizers—all for $5 each.

Operation: Rolling Thunder! promotional activities were complemented by exciting and flavorful new menu items, new menus, and merchandising along with revised guest satisfaction training. This helped us overcome our sales obstacles and begin to turn the brand around.

Arguably the most impactful business obstacle in recent memory we can all relate to is linked to COVID-19. I have been heartened to hear countless examples of how great leaders used many of the same leadership techniques we're discussing here—designed to *grow* their businesses—have been repurposed to literally *save* their businesses and the livelihoods of their team members.

As I mentioned, I have been involved in organizations that have suffered through and ultimately overcome some serious obstacles that could have eroded public trust if not handled in an appropriate and timely manner.

While every obstacle is different with varying degrees of severity, there are some common elements to them all. Based on my C-Suite experience and serving as a company spokesperson for several brands, I want to share 4 key takeaways I feel are helpful in similar situations:

1. **Transparency:** Say what you know and when you found out about it. Taking too long to comment suggests you have something to hide and you hope the issue will go away on its own. It almost never does. If there is an ongoing investigation, stay out in front of the situation by scheduling press updates regularly. Again, state very clearly what you know and what you don't know to provide helpful, credible updates to all stakeholders.

2. **Responsibility:** "If you mess up, fess up!" Accepting full responsibility takes courage, especially when the stakes are high. However, taking responsibility turns the conversation away from unproductive finger-pointing and blaming to a more positive, productive, solutions-oriented perspective.

3. **Authenticity:** You can't fake contrition. We must understand brands (both our personal brand and corporate brand) represent more than merely a logo and catchy tagline; they are a manifestation of our human interactions with each of our stakeholders. If we, as leaders within an organization, do not authentically reflect our shared values, how can we expect our team members to do so?

4. **Trustworthiness:** As we know, actions speak louder than words. Provide frequent updates on the steps you have taken to repair the immediate damage and the future steps you will take to ensure the issue doesn't happen again. This is how you rebuild trust with your stakeholders—both internally and externally. Trust—like leadership—must be earned, not taken for granted.

When faced with obstacles, one must continuously take purposeful action—progressing from *measurement* to *adaptability*—to help the team or organization navigate the choppy waters in an authentic, transparent, and brand-appropriate way.

As my father has said since I was a child (based on a quote from the Greek philosopher Epictetus), "It's not what happens to you, but how you react to it that matters."

CHAPTER 25

ACCOUNTING FOR OUTLIERS FROM ADAPTABILITY TO EXCELLENCE

"The definition of insanity is doing the same thing over and over again, but expecting different results."

— Albert Einstein

The study of outliers—incorporating a best practice mindset to learn from others—leads us from *adaptability* to *excellence*.

To attain excellence in any endeavor, one must build on the fundamentals through repetition and consistency, which create muscle memory. Athletes know this as they incorporate routine exercises into their overall training regimen. But to make dramatic improvements in performance, they seek out new techniques to essentially shock their system. This creates a process of continuous improvement that builds on the foundation laid by their former routine.

In business, the process of continuous improvement is similar because we are all interested in performance growth. No one is celebrated when sales and/or profits are flat. Now, in the case of a dramatic economic downturn or other significant event, a short-term case can be made for "flat being the new up"—it's certainly better than being down. Having served in both publicly traded and privately held organizations, I can assure you that sentiment doesn't last long. More often, stakeholders ask, "What have you done for me lately?"

We live in a world where performance is often defined by comparable, time-based improvement. For example, sales and profit this period compared to last period and/or the same period last year, or quarter over comparable quarter and year over comparable year.

Like athletes, we cannot merely do the same things over and over and expect a different result. You don't have to be an Einstein to figure that out, right? We must seek continuous improvement through a variety of sources to *attain*, and more importantly *sustain*, excellence over many seasons of growth. This positive momentum attracts additional investment that can be applied to the care and feeding of new and/or improved growth initiatives.

We all agree we need to move beyond the status quo in pursuit of continuous improvement that leads to future growth and sustained excellence. Well, how do we get there?

To begin with, every person on our team and/or in our organization must adopt a "Best Practice Mindset." I have found excellence is all around us if we just open our eyes and look. It is important to stay curious, keep an open mind and be attuned to ideas, processes, or practices we can modify for our specific purposes.

While it is commonplace to search beyond our competition or outside our industry to find excellence, no doubt excellent work is being done within our own team or organization, right under our nose.

I believe there are 4 different, but related places to find best practices—two within and two outside our team/organization.

1. Internal—Individual Best Practices
2. Internal—Team/Organizational Best Practices
3. External—Industry Competitor Best Practices
4. External—Outside of Industry Best Practices

Let's start by looking inward since individual team members are closest to the business and our customers. They provide a rich source of best practices that can be shared with the broader organization. In doing so, we are recognizing and rewarding positive behavior while helping to improve performance in areas of the organization that may be struggling.

1. INTERNAL

—Individual Best Practices

I've seen several situations where merely assessing internal best practices among the most successful individuals and/or teams and institutionalizing them has led to significant performance growth.

Let me give you a relevant example.

When I started at Mimi's Cafe, my very first official day was spent in Columbus, Ohio, with members of my executive team presenting our annual operating plan (AOP) to the CEO and his executive team. Now, that's certainly hitting the ground running.

That AOP stated one of our strategic goals was to increase our dinner business by featuring some exciting new menu items along with our new and improved wine options. Given that Mimi's was known primarily for its unique breakfast, brunch, and lunch experiences, many guests and prospective guests did not consider Mimi's an attractive dinner option.

To get our target audience's attention at dinner time, we knew we had to elevate awareness of our wide array of beers, wines, and spirits. With mimosas, which are basically a brunch drink (sparkling wine and orange juice), representing our number-one-selling alcoholic beverage, we wanted to focus on building awareness of our exciting new white and red wines paired with corresponding dishes on our new dinner menu.

As a creative way to allow guests to sample our different white and red wines, we created wine flights consisting of three, two-ounce glasses at a reasonable price. Our plan was to roll out this wine flights program along with a new dinner menu in the fall.

The team was working hard to finalize our rollout and training materials when I found myself once again in Columbus for a board meeting prep session. I was sitting in one of our restaurants debriefing with the Mimi's general manager just before I was about to leave to catch a flight back to California, when he said "Joe" (one of his bartenders) wanted to speak to me. I nervously checked my watch, and seeing that I still had a few minutes, I said sure.

Building on the success of our mimosas, Joe had created a unique twist on the wine flight concept by creating "Sparkling Wine Flights." This featured three distinctive, colorful, and incredibly flavorful options combining a split (single-serving bottle) of sparkling wine with different juices. They were artfully served in champagne flutes delivered in a wire rack—like our wine flights—which allowed our servers to parade them through the dining room past the wide-eyed and jealous guests. As part of the experience, servers opened the split of sparkling wine and poured it in even portions in each of the three champagne flutes while explaining the different flavor profiles.

Brilliant!

I thanked Joe for his tremendous initiative in developing this idea to complement our soon-to-launch wine flights program. The only question was whether we could add this new element to our rollout and training materials. I quickly called Herbert Billinger, Jr., our executive vice president of operations, integration, and productivity, to see if we could squeeze this potentially big idea into our fall menu rollout. Fortunately, he said yes.

Fast forward to a few months later and the results were very encouraging. While the original wine flight program was off to a solid start in helping us build our dinner business, the new sparkling wine flight options were a huge hit. In fact, even though they were sold primarily at breakfast or brunch, they represented 58 percent of *all* flights sold. Keep in mind this program built sales by driving up guest check averages, and it did so quite profitably since alcoholic beverage sales have great margins. Now we had an idea that could help build *all* dayparts.

Just think, if the bartender did not take it upon himself to go above and beyond his job description, if the general manager did not support him, if I did not take time to listen to the idea, if my operations leader did not find a way to make it work, we would not have had the tremendous success we had with this unique wine/sparkling wine flights program.

Of course, we touted the success as a relevant example of accountability and honored Joe appropriately with accolades and awards.

By internally recognizing and rewarding his behavior, we thought we could cultivate more "Joes," and we could begin to tackle some of our bigger challenges. And we did.

I'm sure you can think of your own list of one-off ideas that may have generated similar results. But the key to sustained excellence is not merely to perform heroic, Houdini-like efforts on a one-off basis—you must go beyond developing a best practice mindset to instituting a best practice process.

Do you have a process for eliciting best practices from within your organization? What can you learn from them to stimulate growth for your team or organization?

2. INTERNAL

—Team/Organizational Best Practices

An example of harnessing the "best and brightest" within an organization also came from my time at Mimi's Cafe when it was owned by Bob Evans Farms, Inc. Our CEO, Steve Davis, had a mantra of "five big changes to five big things," which represented both our responses to the critical challenges and significant growth opportunities within each of the three divisions of the (then) integrated and diversified growth firm. This included Bob Evans restaurants, Bob Evans food products, and Mimi's Cafe restaurants.

Even though Bob Evans restaurants were in the family dining category and Mimi's Cafe was considered casual dining, there were some obvious overlaps in menu optimization, product procurement/distribution, and labor productivity. Given that both restaurant brands sourced some items from the Bob Evans food products division, there were also potential growth opportunities within our cost of goods based upon quality and buying efficiencies.

Quality management pioneer Dr. Joseph Juran coined the phrase, "The vital few and the trivial many" back in the 1940s to emphasize the importance of prioritizing a few big ideas as opposed to chasing many smaller ones. This is a corollary of the "80/20 Rule" or Pareto Principle whereby, for many outcomes, 80 percent of consequences come from 20 percent of causes.

Working with an outside consultancy, the executive team representing all three divisions got together to hammer out our "vital few"—the "five big things" we agreed to focus on to achieve our explosive growth objectives. Once the five growth opportunities were identified, two executive sponsors were assigned to lead each team along with a coach from the consulting firm we employed.

Just like the NFL draft, the executive sponsors "drafted" team members to work on their respective projects. The pool of resources consisted of the top forty team members across the organization (director-level and above) who provided subject matter expertise in a variety of important disciplines (e.g., marketing, finance, research and development, operations, training, legal, human resources, supply chain, etc.). As the project teams were formed, they were told: 1) given its importance and visibility, it was an honor to be selected for this special growth project, and 2) they would have to find a way to accomplish the project's objectives while still handling their daily responsibilities. Given the tremendous growth potential for not only the organization but each team member, everyone was fired up and ready to get started.

The project teams met to begin the process of identifying the size of the growth opportunity in their respective areas. By establishing the "size of the prize" *per se*, the CEO and the executive team could better plan capital investments, human resource needs, and budget allocations to achieve each goal in a reasonable timeframe.

A friendly competition emerged between the teams as we feverishly prepared for our many check-in meetings where the CEO and the executive team got to ask us a litany of probing questions. While each team certainly wanted to "win," we knew the fruits of this project would be good for us all in many tangible and intangible ways.

Finally, it was presentation day and the five teams presented the "big change(s)" they recommended. At the end of the day, we celebrated this tremendous accomplishment together.

This broad-based, organizational "crowdsourcing" approach helped us prioritize, fund, and staff growth opportunities in mid- and long-term strategic planning and annual operating planning processes. In addition, every team member learned some great lessons. In fact, the benefits of our disciplined, collaborative, strategic planning approach and the learning opportunities for our mid-level team members all the way up to the executive team were priceless.

Do you know who your key players are? What can you learn from them to stimulate growth for your team or organization?

3. EXTERNAL

—Industry Competitor Best Practices

Now, let's look at some examples of a more traditional way of learning from best practices—from both direct and indirect competitors we admire within our industry. Let's stay with Bob Evans restaurants for a look at how they viewed a specific direct competitor.

Direct Competitors—During our monthly business review meetings, topics often came up that our CEO, Steve Davis, wanted to learn more about. Often this curiosity was inspired by something he felt a competitor did well and helped them grow their business and/or take business away from us. In one such case, the CMO and her team presented a comprehensive review of one of Bob Evans restaurants' biggest direct competitors.

The presentation included a review of key growth strategies related to a competitor's menu, pricing, merchandising, marketing, messaging, and media approaches. To take it a step farther, the CMO put together a strengths, weaknesses, opportunities, and threats (SWOT) analysis of that competitor to compare and contrast with the Bob Evans restaurants' SWOT Analysis. The purpose was to identify potential growth opportunities for Bob Evans restaurants *vis-a-vis* its biggest competitor. Finally, they worked to put themselves in the "mind" of their competitor in an attempt to anticipate what they might do next—either proactively or reactively. Several ideas came out of this review of a direct competitor that bore fruit almost immediately.

Do you know who your direct competitors are? What can you learn from them to stimulate growth in your team or organization?

Here is an example from a totally different industry that learns from indirect competitors.

Indirect Competitors—All across the country, collegiate alumni associations are facing flat to declining membership. Millennials are not big on joining associations unless they are work- or personal interest-related. As long-time alumni association members age out, it leaves a gap that must be filled. As you can imagine, this has created a budget shortfall, causing many alumni associations to be absorbed into their respective school administrations or major fundraising foundations.

The Kansas University Alumni Association (KU Alumni Association or KUAA) is strong and remains committed to its independent status. However, the members realized a few years back that, instead of just a typical marketing plan, they needed to develop a much broader and more systemic strategic growth plan to ensure their vitality for years to come. I was brought in as a consultant to lead the organization through this change that included a new strategic planning process.

On a KU Alumni Association survey of its membership, one vitally important word kept coming up again and again—*relevance*. Simply put, older alumni have a much different definition of relevance than younger alumni. This should come as no shock as this phenomenon is present in many industries and product segments. From a brand marketing perspective, it's "Lifetime Value 101."

A follow-up survey was designed to ask both KU alumni, non-members, current alumni association members, and current students what was "most relevant" to them based on their respective life stages (demographics) and lifestyles (psychographics).

Results from the survey spawned a host of actionable items, including highly relevant programming, events, and activities to boost the value of a KU Alumni Association membership. This included the launch of the Jayhawk Career Network—a multi-faceted digital network founded on the KU mentoring platform and includes a wide variety of career building features—that now has more than 10,000 alumni and student participants.

But something was still missing from KUAA's membership model, which was based on an annual membership fee payment traditionally due during the holidays, which meant competing with many other appeals.

Collegiate alumni associations are tight-knit groups with no problem sharing information. They all face pretty much the same issues, so KUAA looked at possible *indirect competitors* to identify a psychological approach to membership that worked. They found the monthly subscription model.

Studying the dynamics of highly successful monthly subscription models such as Netflix, ESPN+, Spotify, and others provided the inspiration for the KU Alumni Association to revise its traditional annual membership model to reach younger alumni who are already predisposed to participate in monthly subscription services.

Do you have indirect competitors with a similar business model you can learn from to stimulate growth?

Finally, some of the most intriguing ways to learn from others' best practices is to study various elements of products or services outside our industry.

4. EXTERNAL

—Outside of Industry Best Practices

When I was leading marketing and sales at Universal Studios Hollywood, our president, Larry Kurzweil, instilled a best practice process mindset to stimulate growth. We had our sister park

(Universal Orlando Resort) to share ideas with. And we had our direct competitors such as Disneyland/Disney World, Knott's Berry Farm, Six Flags Magic Mountain, and SeaWorld to mine for ideas. However, I was most captivated by a story I heard about Southwest Airlines' approach to incorporating others' best practices.

From its inception, Southwest was a regional, short-haul airline. Sometimes, that meant flying travelers from point A to point B to point C with a plane change (or two) involved. Based on this unique "hub 'n spoke" business model, Southwest didn't necessarily stand to benefit much by studying their key competitors (American, United, Delta, etc.) who did not share the same short-haul strategy.

Given the importance of getting its airplanes in and out of airport gates as quickly, safely, and productively as possible, Southwest decided to "go to school" and study an outside organization. They selected an organization with a similar need to get vehicles in and out as quickly, safely, and productively as possible. Have you guessed who that might be?

NASCAR. Zoom! Zoom!

That example blew my mind and inspired our team to study a brand outside the theme park industry to help us sharpen our approach in key growth areas.

- ✓ **Brand Positioning/Brand Equity Building:** We were in the process of launching a bold integrated marketing campaign touting Universal Studios Hollywood as "The Entertainment Capital of LA." I elected to study Target given how much I admired their landmark red bullseye campaign and the disciplined way they integrated their unique brand—both internally and externally—with a consistent branding look, tone, and feel.

- ✓ **Website/Online Ticket Sales:** As ecommerce began to grow rapidly, we wanted to learn from the best. We knew creating a "sales funnel" to encourage prospective guests to buy tickets and other products online was an efficient, productive, and profitable approach. Thus, a colleague chose to study Amazon's optimized user experience, which was designed to help guests find what they were looking for with ease and just a few clicks.

- ✓ **Database/Loyalty Marketing:** When "Big Data" accessibility became more truth than fiction, we sent someone to Las Vegas to study Harrah's Casino. At the time, Harrah's had just rolled out a massive database-driven loyalty marketing approach using customer data from previous visits—along with other relevant demographic and psychographic information—to build customized messages, experiences, and promotional opportunities. That information was relevant in building our successful "Buy a Day, Get a Year!" annual pass promotion into a more comprehensive, integrated guest engagement program.

I also heard stories about David Overton, chairman and CEO of The Cheesecake Factory, looking outside the restaurant industry for inspiration. Specifically, David was looking to raise the bar on The Cheesecake Factory's guest experience over and above the unique building design and legendary food, beverage, and dessert menu. David was always striving for excellence and trying to live up to the mission of delivering "absolute guest satisfaction."

Quite candidly, no other restaurant concepts really come close to replicating the depth, complexity, and uniqueness of The Cheesecake Factory, so instead of researching other restaurants, David decided to study the best practices of the undisputed leader in hospitality, Ritz-Carlton—"Ladies and gentlemen serving ladies and gentlemen."

Perfect!

Do some *external brands* have a business model or philosophy similar to your own you can learn from to stimulate growth?

When you incorporate a best practice mindset (individually) and a best practice process (collectively) to leverage the successes of outliers within your team or organization—or outside of it—you can progress from *adaptability* to *excellence*. Once we achieve and sustain excellence, we can move along a parallel path to account for innovation that keeps us from obsolescence—leading us to developing future growth opportunities.

CHAPTER 26

ACCOUNTING FOR OBSOLESCENCE FROM EXCELLENCE TO INNOVATION

"We must invent the future while we manage the present."

— Steve Jobs

If studying the best practices of outliers leads to *excellence* within our current business model, that is obviously a major plus. However, it is not enough to improve efficiency, productivity, and profitability for *today*. We must guard against the very real threat of obsolescence by developing opportunities for *future* growth through *innovation*.

In researching evolutionary biology, I learned that organisms are in perpetual competition with one another. One will have the upper hand until, eventually, the competitor becomes equal. This natural process repeats over time. This is called "key innovation," but in what I call "revolutionary biology," I believe we can speed up, or in some cases, improve the evolutionary process.

A great example is the progress being made in plant science where engineers are creating mutant forms of grain that are more resilient against the elements and insects, resulting in higher yields per acre. In human science, we are seeing tremendous breakthroughs in stem cell research and genetic engineering. In both cases, scientists are revolutionizing their thinking to obtain step function change growth as opposed to waiting around for evolutionary growth to occur naturally.

In business, those who let their brands merely "evolve" can become extinct. In fact, there is a Product Life Cycle model that features six stages: Development, Introduction, Growth, Maturity, Saturation, and Decline. These brands serve as a cautionary tale of what can happen if we don't balance the needs of our business today while sowing seeds of innovation for tomorrow.

- ✓ **Circuit City**
- ✓ **Blockbuster Video**
- ✓ **Toys R Us**
- ✓ **Nokia**
- ✓ **Blackberry**
- ✓ **Oldsmobile**
- ✓ **Kodak**

You see, in today's global marketplace, a host of headwinds conspire to thwart business growth such as macro-/micro-economic factors, government regulations, trade policies, demographic shifts, inventions, industry/brand performance trends, competitive intrusion, supply chain disruption, customer acquisition/retention costs and labor cost/scarcity. Oh, and let's not forget the impacts from a global pandemic. Often, this results in the trimming of capital budgets and innovation development opportunities. But strong leaders understand the investment that must be made to support growth by creating a "spirit of continuous improvement."

In fact, legendary PepsiCo CEO, the late Wayne Calloway had a famous saying that speaks to the importance of innovation, "If it ain't broke, fix it anyway because if you aren't fixing it, the competition is and they will pass you by."

Like mice running on a wheel in their cage, we can exert a lot of time, energy, and resources without really getting anywhere (but tired!). And if your organization is publicly traded, the cadence of quarterly board meetings, earnings calls, analyst reviews, and investor presentations can be all-consuming. That is, *if* you fail to properly invest in creating a culture of innovation.

Michael Eisner, former Chairman and CEO of the Walt Disney Company, talked about the importance of innovation in its 1996 Annual Report, "it is about creating change before it creates you." He went on to say, "nearly half of Disney's growth over the past 10 years has been generated by business that did not exist in 1985."

And the pace of change has sped up several-fold since then, creating even greater emphasis on innovation moving forward. Think back to the last ten years—look at all the products and services that are popular today but weren't even around then. Wow!

Unfortunately, a concept called "innovator's bias" can easily creep in and take hold of our ability to do what is necessary to take our business to the next level. Simply put, we tend to fall in love with our own ideas. Either as a sense of ego or pride (e.g., "We are clearly the best in class!") or possibly job/career protection (e.g., "I can't admit that Brand XYZ has some advantages over us, right?"). But in a rapidly changing world that is spinning seemingly faster (and faster) each day, we simply *must* challenge the status quo and pursue ways to innovate, or run the very real risk of obsolescence. Before it becomes too late.

So, what do we mean by *innovation?*

It has been said the definition of creativity is the melding of two unrelated ideas together into one *new* idea. And we know that creative thinking or problem solving is a key element of innovation. In fact, innovation's fundamental goal is to disrupt the status quo to provide new growth opportunities.

I remember an off-site strategic planning session when author and consultant Bob Johansen was invited to speak to our executive team at The Cheesecake Factory. As cited in his book *Leaders Make the Future,* he spoke about what it is going to be like living in a VUCA world. VUCA stands for Volatile, Uncertain, Complex, and Ambiguous. I believe many events in the last several years—including the far-reaching impacts of COVID-19—suggest that is, indeed, our current environment.

Now, to compete and win in a VUCA world, Johansen provided us with 4 counter measures that would lead to the possibility of creating disruptive innovation in driving growth—Vision, Understanding, Clarity, and Agility.

Again, I think his thesis is correct on many levels because a good leader must adopt a broad-based worldview with a curiosity to understand how different variables can work together to spark innovation. That said, there are two different, but related characteristics I have found to be quite powerful in driving innovation—*convenience* and *scalability*.

Here are a few examples of brands who have combined *convenience* with *scalability* to provide innovation for future growth that should be familiar to you:

- **FedEx:** Created a new concept (overnight delivery), which disrupted the mail and package shipping industry. Geez, how many times have they saved my hide?

- **Gatorade:** Created a new concept (sports drinks), which disrupted the beverage category and spawned a new multi-billion-dollar industry. In addition to performance benefits, the ubiquitous "Gatorade Shower" is now virtually synonymous with victory celebrations.

- **Red Bull:** Created a new concept (energy drinks), which also disrupted the beverage category (both soft drinks and coffee) and grew an entirely new category. More than an energy drink, Red Bull has become a lifestyle brand among its target audience—linked to stretching the boundaries of the human experience beyond what was previously thought possible.

- **Apple:** Created a new concept (iPhone), which disrupted three different industries—cell phones, cameras, and film development. I wonder how much Nokia and Kodak are worth today?

- **Amazon:** Created a new concept (home shopping), which disrupted not only bookstores, but the entire brick-and-mortar retail industry. Leaving venerable 100-year-old retail brands (e.g., Sears, JCPenney, Macy's) clinging to dear life on a respirator.

- **Airbnb:** Created a new concept (home-based inns), which disrupted the hotel industry. This—along with the next example—ushered in the advent of the gig or sharing economy.

- ✓ **Uber:** Created a new concept (ride sharing), which disrupted the taxicab industry. This also created a flexible schedule along with a "moonlighting" revenue opportunity for its drivers.

- ✓ **Disney/ESPN+:** Created a new concept (transportable TV Entertainment/Sports viewing), which disrupted the over-the-air broadcasting industry with live-streaming capability from virtually any digital device.

And, of course, there have emerged a host of digital-based brands such as Canva, Fiverr, and Upwork that have created a whole new gig economy where individuals can provide products or services from their home computer that can be accessed through a centralized brand portal anywhere in the world.

I'm sure you can think of several more examples, but I highlighted these brands because they all share a common thread—the combination of both *convenience* and *scalability* in the development of a relevant and valuable *new* concept. One that not only has disrupted the status quo of a given industry, but in many cases has created a whole new growth industry.

When you go back to Ram Charan's growth model focusing on *velocity* and *yield*, you can see there is a direct correlation between the importance of *convenience* (drives velocity) and *scalability* (improves yield). I do not believe this is a coincidence. We love products and services that solve problems to help make our lives easier. So, convenience is a major component of a brand's value proposition, driving velocity. Given the dynamics of smarter, more powerful and readily accessible technologies, we can offer convenience in a more scalable and profitable manner, improving yield.

Ninety-five percent of all McDonald's restaurants have a drive-thru and that channel provides approximately 65 percent of its business. This speaks to the power of convenience/velocity, so innovation focused on improving drive-thru speed is of great importance to helping increase its scalability/yield. Again, this is where sales and profit growth come from. How to improve drive-thru volume without sacrificing food quality, friendliness, and order accuracy is where the magic lies. That is certainly a difficult combination of benefits to achieve, but it can be done!

Pal's Sudden Service (or Pal's for short) is a quick-service restaurant concept with twenty-nine locations in Northeast Tennessee and Virginia. As the name implies, it is known for its speed of service, but that's not all. Restaurant operators have long studied what makes Pal's so effective in serving its drive-thru guests high quality food made to order within a very short time *and* with an extra helping of Southern hospitality. In 2001, Pal's won the prestigious *Malcolm Baldridge National Quality Award*—the only restaurant to have ever received this honor.

To be clear, Pal's does not possess any better restaurant equipment, nor does it employ more technology enhancements than the (much) bigger concepts have. For Pal's, it's all about the *people*. The amount of time, energy, and resources focused on training its people is Pal's secret sauce innovation platform.

For other restaurant concepts, the use of technology or external resources in helping to optimize the windows of time when guests want to dine is of paramount importance. For example, mobile ordering and delivery—along with beacon technology—are providing convenience/velocity and scalability/yield to their businesses.

Helping them deliver greater sales and profit growth for today while building new business channels for tomorrow.

How can you apply the innovation principles of both convenience/velocity and scalability/yield to your business?

In addition to this model, several other ways certainly exist to combine different, but related, elements together to create an innovative and totally fresh, new approach. Harking back to my days at Pizza Hut, our marketing and menu development teams were always hard at work in driving innovation with the variables they had to work with:

- ✓ Sizes
- ✓ Shapes
- ✓ Forms
- ✓ Varieties
- ✓ Crust Types
- ✓ Ingredients
- ✓ Flavors
- ✓ Packaging
- ✓ Promotions
- ✓ Partnerships

The fruits of their labor helped create some of the most innovative products in the pizza category that led to step function change growth for Pizza Hut in an extremely competitive environment. Those products included:

- ✓ Original Pan® Pizza
- ✓ Personal Pan Pizza
- ✓ Kid's Pizza Pack
- ✓ Lover's Line (e.g., Pepperoni Lover's, Meat Lover's, etc.)
- ✓ Stuffed Crust Pizza
- ✓ Wing Street Chicken
- ✓ Cheesy Bites Pizza
- ✓ P'ZONE®
- ✓ Hot Delivery Pouches
- ✓ Stuffed Cheez-it Pizza™
- ✓ Triple Treat Holiday Box

Not to be outdone, YUM! Brands sister company Taco Bell has emerged as arguably the *most* innovative (and successful) restaurant brand over the past several years. And its pantry of ingredient options may be even more limited than those at Pizza Hut.

Here are just a few examples to jog your memory (and make you very hungry!).

- ✓ Doritos Locos and Cool Ranch Tacos
- ✓ Gordita
- ✓ Chalupa
- ✓ Quesalupa
- ✓ Crunch Wrap
- ✓ Breakfast Crunch Wrap

- ✓ Naked Crispy Chicken Chalupa
- ✓ Toasted Cheddar Chalupa
- ✓ Nacho Fries

Finally, a wide variety of one-off success stories in the foodservice universe demonstrate the awesome power of innovation in establishing new growth opportunities. Many of you may remember the "Cronut" from a few years back that combined the essence of a croissant with a doughnut.

Brilliant!

While all very inspiring, I assure you these several examples of innovation did not happen by luck or chance. Rather, each one likely invested in a disciplined, process-driven approach including hours and hours of research, development, testing, and tweaking to ensure the "big idea" could make as big an impact in the marketplace as it did in the test lab. We'll put a focus on the importance of process within the next section of this book.

What other examples of innovation can you think of that provided step function change growth opportunities for a product or service?

What areas within your business could you positively impact based upon learning from these—or other—examples?

As I said earlier, you can learn best practices from many places—your internal team/organization or competitors in your category or even players in totally different industries (remember the Southwest Airlines/NASCAR example). Innovation is all around you—you just need to know where to look. And you must also invest appropriate resources for team members to be on the lookout for innovation when and wherever it presents itself.

> "Inspiration exists, but it must find you working."
>
> — Pablo Picasso

Through successfully navigating the Purposeful Accountability Revolution, we've learned the 4 interwoven sub-processes—Outcomes, Obstacles, Outliers, and Obsolescence—will lead to *Achievement* of our shared business growth goals.

THE PURPOSEFUL ACCOUNTABILITY REVOLUTION

Outcomes

Obstacles

Outliers

Obsolescence

=

ACHIEVEMENT

THE PURPOSEFUL FULFILLMENT REVOLUTION

A SEASON FOR NURTURING GROWTH

Nurturing:
The process of caring for and encouraging the growth or development of someone or something. "Nurturing ideas."

CHAPTER 27

FULFILLMENT REVOLVES AROUND *GROWTH* ECOSYSTEMS

*"The glory of gardening: hands in the dirt,
head in the sun, heart with nature.
To nurture a garden is to feed not just on the body,
but the soul."*

— Alfred Austin

Depending on where you live and your tolerance for inclement weather, winter can take on many forms. This season can conjure up a variety of thoughts, emotions, and memories, both good and let's just say…not so good. I grew up in Kansas and have lived in Dallas, Chicago, Atlanta, Austin, and Los Angeles, so I can personally attest to the differences in both intensity and duration of the season. But there's a time in early winter that, regardless of geography, conjures up very positive memories for most of us—the holidays. In fact, just thinking about the smell of a freshly cut pine tree, warming up with a steaming mug of cocoa, a roaring fire, and gingerbread cookies baking in the oven brings a smile to my face.

Regardless of religious beliefs, the holidays are "the season of joy." According to the dictionary, "joy" is a noun defined as: a feeling of great pleasure and happiness. I'm sure we can all understand and relate to the power of joy and happiness in many ways.

In addition to sharing the joys of the holiday season with family and friends, I use this time to both reflect on and celebrate the past year's accomplishments while getting rejuvenated to embrace the challenges and opportunities of the new year ahead. This is the same process we find in nature as winter plays a significant role in plant rejuvenation. While it may appear most plants are dormant since their leaves have fallen and we see no outward signs of growth, a lot of activity is actually going on in the soil.

In fact, winter is a season of care and feeding for plants and trees as leaves compost into mulch and enhance root systems, building a strong foundation for rebirth in spring. Mulch from fallen leaves serves as a natural fertilizer.

According to Dennis Patton, a horticulture agent with Kansas State University Research and Extension within one of his weekly columns written for the *Kansas City Star*:

> Leaves are a rich source of organic matter. Once decomposed, they can transform our heavy clay soils. As leaves naturally break down, they feed the living soil mass of fungi, bacteria, and other life important for building our food web. Leaves raked, bagged, and hauled away rob the soil profile of this benefit. Resources such as fuel are used, contributing to greenhouse gases and potentially harming the environment. The key is to keep the leaves at home.
>
> Leaf litter is essential for a healthy ecosystem. Many of

our native pollinators and beneficial insects use leaves that collect at the bases of trees, shrubs, and corners of the yard as protection over the winter. Removing fallen leaves removes habitat and reduces the population of these much-needed insects.

A leaf can fulfill its purpose by "leaving" behind a living legacy through nourishing its ecosystem to help future plants flourish and creating a virtuous cycle of reciprocity for the benefit of others' growth.

Coincidentally, I recently came across an article written by David Brooks published in *The New York Times* highlighting the difference between happiness and joy. I thought it was both thought-provoking and highly relevant to this section. Brooks states:

> Happiness usually involves a victory for self. Joy tends to involve the transcendence of self. Happiness comes from accomplishments. Joy comes from when your heart is in another. The core point is that happiness is good, but joy is better.

While I don't disagree with Brooks' thesis, it got me thinking there might be an even deeper, more meaningful, and longer-lasting feeling than fun, happiness, or joy—fulfillment.

- **Fun takes place in our body**
  - Momentary outer-level feeling
  - Connected to context
  - "I had fun at the concert last night!"

- **Happiness takes place in our mind**
  - Short-term, surface-level feeling
  - Connected to self
  - "I'm very happy at the moment."
- **Joy takes place in our heart**
  - Longer-term, deeper-level feeling
  - Connected to others
  - "It gives me great joy to serve others."
- **Fulfillment takes place in our soul**
  - Eternal, spiritual-level feeling
  - Connected to purpose
  - "I feel a deep sense of fulfillment."

All these feelings are vitally important for growth; however, I believe fun is an important respite while happiness on certain levels can lead to a deeper sense of lasting joy. But I believe the concept of the Purposeful Fulfillment Revolution is even more important—encompassing all of one's life journey and the living legacy paid backward for the benefit of others.

Fulfillment: 1. To bring into actuality; effect or make real: fulfilled their promises; fulfilled their dream. 2. To do, perform, or obey; carry out. 3. To meet; satisfy.

I believe we attain fulfillment naturally when we "grow into" our purpose and in communion with our creator. But given we are human organisms who thrive in community, we need to be nurtured along our growth journey to fulfill our unique purpose while helping others do likewise.

For me, it's not "nature versus nurture" as the old debate poses. I believe it is vitally important to have an interrelationship between both elements in cultivating full growth potential. We must establish a growth environment to attain Purposeful Fulfillment.

According to *National Geographic*, an ecosystem is a geographic area where plants, animals, and other organisms, along with weather and landscape, work together to form a bubble of life. There are 4 conditions that must be correct for seeds to germinate: temperature, moisture, air, and light. It is important to note that each seed type has individual needs.

Consider the delicate balance of key variables that enable a tree to fulfill its purpose. While it's true some plants can adapt to new surroundings, most tend to thrive in the ecosystem in which they evolved, which best fits their unique growth traits. This means the best combination of soil, sunlight, rain, and protection, and a balance of oxygen and carbon dioxide.

As you've read throughout this book, I believe the word "nature" is a metaphor for growth—linking key aspects of a plant or tree to represent the revolutionary 4 LEAF *GROWTH* processes found in successful individuals, teams, and organizations. I further believe the way to optimize growth is using a nurture-based approach representing the entire ecosystem, including the care, feeding, and safety of the plant, which can also be said of the cultural environment of a team or organization.

The word "nurture" is both a verb and a noun. According to Vocabulary.com, "If you plant a seed, water it daily, and give it lots of light, you can *nurture* it until it is ready to be transplanted outside. When you *nurture* a person or thing, you care for it and help it to grow."

As we apply this metaphor to the growth of an individual within the context of a team or organization, we call it a "culture." It stands to reason then that Nature + Nurture = Culture.

And, in the immortal words of the great marketing guru Peter Drucker, we learn, "Culture eats strategy for breakfast."

Stay with me because this is a vitally important concept in helping us work toward Purposeful Fulfillment. Without a nurturing culture to provide an environment for purposeful growth to occur, the prior three processes will not be as effective in fulfilling an organism's true growth potential.

THE PURPOSEFUL FULFILLMENT REVOLUTION

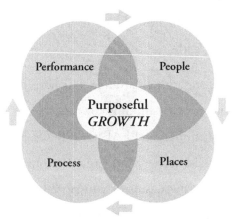

Four integrated elements comprise the Purposeful Fulfillment Revolution—*People, Places, Process,* and *Performance*—the final revolutionary process within the 4 LEAF *GROWTH* model. Let's examine each one individually and then collectively because, together, these 4 holistic elements represent the ecosystem or culture that will allow you, your teammates, and the entire organization to thrive in every season.

CHAPTER 28

CULTIVATING FULFILLING PEOPLE FROM PURPOSE TO PRINCIPLES

"Nothing we do is more important than hiring and developing people. At the end of the day, you bet on people, not strategies."

— Lawrence Bossidy, former COO of GE

Almost every organization I've worked for has focused on the importance of its people ("Our people make the difference," "Our people are our most valuable asset," "Our people…"). Organizations refer to their people as employees, team members, associates, partners, or even cast members. The common denominator in any organization, regardless of its output, is *people*.

News flash—we are *all* in the people business!

Based on the dynamic and highly competitive labor market most industries face today, in addition to finding talent that fits the specific organizational culture, we absolutely must get the people part right. Given the time, money, and resources it takes to find, recruit, hire, train, compensate, and retain people, we can't afford not to. We must move from *purpose* to *principles* through the growth and development of our people.

As I mentioned, we hear a lot about becoming the best version of ourselves. It is obviously a worthwhile goal. Unfortunately, it is easier said than done. For us to fulfill our unique purpose and thrive as individuals, we must find the right culture fit (Think ecosystem) to nurture us along our growth journey. In doing so, we can work collectively as a team or organization to create a work environment in which we can fulfill our purposeful vision, mission, shared values, and, of course, our related growth objectives.

To nurture our people, we must develop a Revolutionary 4 Rs Culture:

1. **Recruit:** Find, attract, and hire diverse talents

2. **Ripen:** Train and develop talent to full potential

3. **Recognize:** Provide both intrinsic and extrinsic rewards

4. **Retain:** Create a growth path for long-term success

Let's review each of these 4 Rs individually as well as collectively to help us understand how to cultivate a nurturing growth environment to maximize our human resources.

1. RECRUIT:

—Find, attract, and hire diverse talents.
Instead of simply matching incoming resumes with job descriptions, today's hiring managers have more sophisticated resources to draw on to ensure a successful search. Some organizations employ in-house or regional recruiters. Outside talent search firms have proliferated, going beyond the large, multi-national executive search firms to smaller, regional, boutique firms providing a spectrum of services to accommodate any industry, position, or budget.

Online talent search services also abound from stalwarts like LinkedIn, Zip Recruiter, and Indeed to more specialized firms. Given the advent of social media, organizations can vet potential candidates by searching their public personas. Finally, several firms specialize in diagnostic testing to ensure prospective candidates meet selection criteria that helps predict their ultimate success.

According to Gary Burnison, CEO of Korn Ferry and author of *Lose the Resume, Land the Job*, interviewers are looking for ten things in searching for the right candidate for a given job.

The Top 10 Things Interviewers Are Looking For

1. **Culture fit:** The sense that you would work well with others in the company, department, or team.

2. **Motivation:** What drives you to succeed.

3. **Skills:** Mostly technical skills for junior positions and management and leadership skills for more experienced executives.

4. **Leadership potential:** How you lead yourself and others; your ability to be groomed for a leadership position.

5. **Communication skills:** Your speaking and listening ability.

6. **Poise and appearance:** How you present yourself; how customers or clients will perceive you.

7. **Problem-solving skills:** How adept you are at finding a solution by looking beyond the obvious or what's already being done.

8. **Interpersonal skills:** How you interact with others; how you make them feel.

9. **Willingness to accept responsibility:** How you respond when you're tasked with trying to create the "new and different" and when "failing fast" is to be expected.

10. **Working well under pressure:** Being able to handle workplace stress without losing your cool.

How do you stack up in each area? What can you do to improve in areas where you may have a growth opportunity (or two)?

We've covered many of these areas already; however, I would like to address the first, culture fit—the sense that you would work well with others in the company, department, or team.

Obviously, working well as a team is important; however, great danger exists in merely thinking as a team. In 1971, Yale psychologist Irving Janis published an article in *Psychology Today* in which he coined the term "groupthink." It refers to a group of people who find comfort and harmony in community at the cost of critical evaluation of ideas, which leads to dysfunction and poor decision-making. The reason focusing too much on cultural fit is dangerous is it suggests working well as a team requires us to agree, which leads to groupthink.

I totally agree with that philosophy since I can't imagine how a team or organization could establish a foundation for driving step function change growth (much less incremental year-over-year growth) if everyone thought the same way.

As Dr. Phil often says, "And how's *that* working for you?"

Of course, we do not want to take on "bad seeds" for all the reasons you would expect. However, for any team or organization to cultivate and nurture a growth culture, we must harness the awesome power of diversity, equity, inclusion, and belonging. But I want to take this opportunity to repurpose the conversation to include what I believe this vitally important concept really means—starting with diversity.

In my mind, outward diversity and inward diversity are different but related. Both are of equal importance because they combine to create a new and even more powerful concept: Total Diversity.

- **OUTWARD DIVERSITY = WHO YOU *ARE***

These are the characteristics that make you who you are. Of course, only some are visible from the outside: your age, gender, race, creed, color, religion, and sexual identity or preference. Where you come from along with your collective life experiences help create a unique perspective of you that your team and/or organization can draw on.

Within the concept of outward diversity, *context* is most important.

I like to think we all represent different sizes, shapes, and colors of thread that, over the course of our lifetimes, are woven together in a grand and glorious tapestry of life reflecting our unique purpose within God's master plan. Everyone has value and a perspective they bring to the team.

Once again, *different is good!*

- **INWARD DIVERSITY = HOW YOU *THINK***

These are the characteristics that demonstrate how you think. Are you more right-brained (visionary, creative, intuitive) or left-brained (analytical, process-driven, fact-based)? Are you considered a strategic or tactical thinker? Do you tend to go with the flow, or are you comfortable challenging the status quo? Do you tend to ask powerful questions, or are you content allowing others to do so?

Within the concept of inward diversity, *content* is most important.

Essentially, your diversity characteristics represent the value you bring to the table. We discussed within the first part of this book the use of personality assessments like DiSC, Myers-Briggs, or StrengthsFinder 2.0 to help determine who we are. Remember, there are no right or wrong answers; it takes people with personality traits mixed within all 4 quadrants to develop a high-performance team.

Think of mustard seeds planted among rows of grapevines. They serve an important purpose in providing cover for the grapevines while aiding in the health and vitality of the roots, ensuring the highest quality fruit. According to SonomaCounty.com, "Whether it's growing wild or planted by thoughtful vineyard managers, mustard is more than just a feast for the eyes; it's a feast for the vines. It thrives just until bud break, when it is turned under to mulch and provide valuable nutrients and phosphorus to the emerging grape plants."

We absolutely need agitators or change agents to challenge our thinking to help us fulfill our shared purpose and achieve our related growth objectives. Author, speaker, and influencer Luvvie Ajayi Jones has a name for these people that I like even better—"professional troublemakers." Perfect! Regardless of nomenclature, it all comes down to ensuring we have the best fit for our team or organizational culture. Otherwise, we get groupthink, tend to maintain the status quo, and will get merely average results. And, according to a pet phrase of David Novak, "Average is awful."

Promoting an environment of *Total Diversity* can unleash the awesome power of human potential in achieving team goals. But it takes more than this to get the very best out of people. Consider the related concepts of diversity, equity, and inclusion (DEI). Incorporating diversity merely grants us a seat at the table; whereas equity and inclusion provide us an opportunity to participate with an equal voice. This is certainly a good start but not enough. We must ensure *all* people feel welcomed, safe, and genuinely valued for their contributions with no fear of judgment or recrimination.

To me, adding a fourth element—*belonging*—to this list makes a huge difference in cultivating a fertile environment for purposeful growth to create maximum value for the enterprise. When every team member feels their vulnerability will not be held against them, their contributions are encouraged and genuinely valued, they will give their best and not hold back.

> *"The role of a creative leader is not to have all the ideas; it's to create a culture where everyone can have ideas and feel that they're valued."*
>
> — Sir Ken Robinson

For teams and organizations to maximize the value of diversity, equity, inclusion, and belonging in aligning the Employee Value Proposition (internal commitments) with their Employer Brand Proposition (external commitments), they must provide a success framework based on 4 vitally important and integrated elements:

1. Recognize and embrace "Total Diversity" as a competitive advantage, not some sort of political correctness box to check.

2. Create a safe environment for facilitating "Discourse" (impersonal, constructive) over "Discord" (personal, destructive) where every voice is welcome and heard.

3. Challenge the status quo by asking powerful questions (Why? Why not? What if?).

4. Value opposing ideas, thoughts, and/or opinions while ensuring that, ultimately, the team supports the decision to move forward. Make sure everyone feels like they belong.

Remember the phrase I shared earlier about PepsiCo's vision of developing high-performance teams: "Eagles who can fly in formation."

Imagine that incredibly powerful image of beauty, alignment, and strength the next time you look toward the sky!

Regardless of which services, assessment tools, and personnel resources are employed, it all comes down to fit. At The Cheesecake Factory, they invariably ask a very simple, but profound question when evaluating a candidate: "Are they cheesecake?"

Based on my thirty-five years working for or with some of the world's most highly respected brands, The Cheesecake Factory has cultivated the most distinguishable and people-focused brand I've ever worked with. I used the word "cultivated" on purpose because it not only ties directly back to my 4 LEAF *GROWTH* model, but it indirectly ties back to the root word "cult." But not based on the negative perception of the word. Just the opposite—The Cheesecake Factory has worked very hard to grow a "cult-like" following among its legions of fans all over the world. In fact, many markets send out surveys asking which restaurants or retail outlets community members would like to see come to their town. The Cheesecake Factory is almost always at the top of the list (including Wichita, Kansas, my hometown…hint, hint).

My use of the word cult should be seen in a positive sense because it serves as the organizational ecosystem in which a highly complex, people-centric brand like The Cheesecake Factory can live up to its sacred mission: "To create an environment where absolute guest satisfaction is our highest priority."

The mission is not open for discussion or debate; however, the *way* in which the team works together to achieve it certainly is.

2. RIPEN:

—Train and develop talent to its full potential.
As you can imagine, team members at The Cheesecake Factory put in long hours setting (and continually resetting) the bar of excellence for a restaurant providing a highly immersive, over-the-top dining experience for its guests. With a food menu featuring more than 300 items, almost all of which are made fresh from scratch in its restaurants every day, and a bar menu boasting a similarly wide array of handcrafted beverage recipes, The Cheesecake Factory is an incredibly complex operation. And, despite the rigorous training and physical and emotional demands, many remain loyal team members for years. Why?

In addition to being part of the amazing vision of its legendary founder, David Overton, an unbreakable bond links the organization together. It includes a loud, raucous, and unifying "Cheesecake Factory Cheer!" at the end of each daily pre-shift meeting that gets the blood pumping and helps set a positive vibe among the team before the restaurant opens.

Over time, this bond strengthens, building *esprit de corps* among team members that motivates them to accomplish any goal they set for themselves and helps The Cheesecake Factory continue its nearly fifty years of growth and prosperity.

es·prit de corps

/eˑsprē də ˈkôr/

noun

1. the *spirit* of a group that makes the members want the group to succeed.

The term is French, and it literally means "the spirit of the body." In this case, the body refers to a team. Originally, *esprit de corps* was used to describe the morale of troops as they prepared for battle.

In fact, those of us with marketing backgrounds use the term "campaign," which also comes from the military. It stands to reason the *spirit* of a team or organization can help it achieve its shared purpose in the form of specific *campaign* objectives. Charge!

A second definition for *esprit de corps* I ran across, which I feel is complementary to the first, is more specific about what *spirit* means:

es·prit de corps

/eˑsprē də ˈkôr/

noun

2. a *feeling* of *pride, fellowship*, and common *loyalty* shared by the members of a particular group.

Let's break this down into 4 different, yet interrelated parts:

1. **Feeling:** When we *feel* at our best, we tend to *do* our best.

2. **Pride:** We take great pride in the things we care about most (family, school, sports teams, work teams).

3. **Fellowship:** As humans, we all crave connection (both emotionally and physically) and want to feel we are part of a team.

4. **Loyalty:** Despite our internal/external obstacles, we must remain loyal to each other—both as individuals and members of a team—to achieve our shared purpose.

I'm sure we've all seen the famous painting by Archibald M. Willard that depicts US soldiers from the Revolutionary War marching behind fife and drum players and a flag bearer titled *The Spirit of '76*, right?

What a perfect example of an unquenchable feeling of optimism and righteous indignation against tyranny, pride in the pursuit of freedom, fellowship, and loyalty to each other and shared goals. The indomitable spirit of the American Revolution's band of ill-trained, poorly equipped, and under-provisioned soldiers fought (and won) a war against a far superior, better-trained foe.

The key takeaway here is that the *ripen* phase must be focused on *who* we serve while providing appropriate training in both the skills required to perform one's job and why and how this mastery fits within the organization's purposeful vision, mission, and shared values.

By valuing a diverse collection of people, backgrounds, and ideas, coupled with the integration of an aligned culture via education and training techniques, we can build high-performance teams and purposeful growth organizations.

3. RECOGNIZE:

—Provide both intrinsic and extrinsic rewards.
Let's fast forward a few hundred years to another great example of how a small, Texas-based airline named Southwest built on a unique spirit-centered culture to become one of the biggest, most profitable, and highest rated airlines in the country. It did this by recognizing the importance of its people.

Consequently, I don't think it's a coincidence Southwest's major hub, located in Dallas, Texas, is called Love Field.

"A company is stronger if it is bound by love rather than fear."

— Herb Kelleher

Since Herb Kelleher founded Southwest in 1967, the company's unique culture has been based on its rare ability to imbue its definition of love across its employees—from the tarmac to the cockpit and everywhere in between.

According to those who worked for him, Kelleher was a very hands-on CEO who led by example. He was known to spend hours hopping on Southwest flights to get a personal feel for the passenger experience so he could develop ways to make it better. This was his form of research. Kelleher also used these opportunities to check on the welfare of his employees, including mechanics, baggage handlers, ticket agents, gate agents, flight attendants, and, of course, pilots.

Kelleher realized early on that to fight and win against the larger, more established airlines, Southwest had to stand out and become special. Southwest couldn't rely solely on its cheaper airfares (originally called "peanut fares") that could be matched in a fare war, but had to win by providing a better overall experience for its passengers from start to finish.

To accomplish that, Kelleher knew he first had to win his employees' hearts before he could win the hearts of his customers. This started a cultural revolution throughout the organization where, despite his passing in 2019, the indomitable "Spirit of Southwest" he inspired remains alive and well today.

Traveling on Southwest is simply different. I've heard flight attendants having fun reciting safety instructions and singing just prior to landing. In between, the service is always warm, courteous, and friendly while never sacrificing professionalism or safety. And they get to wear shorts!

Of course, every airline's mission is to transport passengers to and from their destinations safely, on-time, and at a price comparable to other travel options. Is it asking a lot of passengers to enjoy the travel experience? Southwest doesn't think so, and it shows across all metrics. When you capture the heart of your people, they will love their customers—and superior grades in the key metrics of success will follow.

You see, a difference exists between people who receive purpose-based *intrinsic* rewards and those who earn performance-based *extrinsic* rewards. Studies show people who are happy in their jobs take pride in their work, feel heard, believe they are making a positive difference and growing in their purpose, and are more productive and reliable than those who chase monetary rewards. Of course, we must provide competitive pay and benefits to compete for talent. However, emphasizing intrinsic rewards can, at a minimum, be the tiebreaker in attracting and retaining talent and maximizing a team or organization's performance.

Isn't it as simple as recognizing people as humans instead of as employee ID numbers?

Something as easy as listening to your team is gold without costing the company money. By listening, you often get ideas you may not have thought of otherwise that may lead to process improvements yielding productivity gains, higher sales, greater profitability, and yes, less employee turnover.

When I was at Noodles & Company, we created an organizational listening and feedback program by instituting a specific email address—ideas@noodles.com—to capture ideas from our thousands of restaurant-level team members. The ideas were sent to a central repository and reviewed by executive team members. Based on the nature of the idea or feedback, a response was sent within twenty-four to forty-eight hours from the appropriate executive. For example, brand, marketing, and menu-related emails came to me.

In addition to the benefit the team member got from being heard and responded to promptly, their supervisor was also copied on the response so the team member could be recognized in front of their peers, which enhanced their feeling of wellbeing about their contribution—and it incentivized others to do likewise.

Other tools are available to make it easy to incorporate team feedback regularly to ensure engagement and buy-in in a safe environment. I came across an app called POP*in*, which provides ways to engage team members directly, immediately, and anonymously using a variety of crowdsourcing, surveys, polls, and prioritization techniques. Very cool.

Another example comes from a recent conversation I had with Shanaz Hemmati, the chief operating officer for ZenBusiness, a rapidly growing tech services firm based in Austin, Texas. She told me her company believes in getting employee satisfaction feedback *monthly* as opposed to annually or semi-annually like many companies do. Given ZenBusiness' rapid growth, they want to get real-time feedback to reinforce their special culture as they grow. I love that.

"Customers will never love a company until the employees love it first."

— Simon Sinek

4. RETAIN:

—Create a Purposeful Growth Plan for long-term success.
Once we recruit the right people, ripen them to their full potential, and recognize their tremendous value to the organization via both intrinsic and extrinsic rewards, how do we retain them?

So often, we hear about people who leave a company for another opportunity, and we wonder how it got to that point. They were considered "high potential" talent and very much valued for their contribution to the team/organization. Why did they decide to leave?

To answer these questions, human resources will set up an exit interview. Well, if we can't change their mind, we may as well learn something from the situation. This is a noble and important practice since learning from past experiences helps improve our future. But The Cheesecake Factory has an innovative technique for understanding where team members are before they ever start thinking about bailing.

They call it a "Stay Interview." That's right, human resource representatives set up periodic meetings with team members to check in on them, listening to ensure they are fulfilled in their role and have everything they need to be successful and grow within the organization.

Oh, by the way, The Cheesecake Factory has been on the Fortune 100 Best Places to Work For list for eight consecutive years (and counting). Here is the response of David Overton, founder, chair, and CEO of The Cheesecake Factory Inc. to this honor:

> The Cheesecake Factory is incredibly honored to be named on the Fortune 100 Best Companies to Work For list for the eighth year in a row. 2020 was a particularly challenging year in the restaurant industry, and we couldn't be prouder of our incredibly talented managers and staff members who worked so hard to continue to fulfill our purpose of nurturing bodies, minds, hearts, and spirits during such an unprecedented time.

Notice the power of the last portion of David's quote?

Brilliant!

Within any industry, we must employ a disciplined "success"-ion planning approach designed not only to retain key team members, but to give them a path for knowledge, skill, and career growth while creating the necessary bench strength to fill in the void they left behind.

At the end of the day, success is all about people—carefully nurturing them from purpose to principles to ensure we have the best resources who fit our desired culture. The next step is to cultivate fulfilling places—where we transform our principles into playgrounds to effectively harness the true growth potential of the team or organization.

CHAPTER 29

CULTIVATING FULFILLING PLACES FROM PRINCIPLES TO PLAYGROUNDS

"We don't stop playing because we grow old; we grow old because we stop playing."

— George Bernard Shaw

Now that we've discussed the processes involved in cultivating fulfilling people, let's talk about some ways we can cultivate fulfilling places for them to work—moving from *principles* to *playgrounds*.

Throughout my career, I have been blessed to work with some fantastic people in places such as Dallas, Wichita, Chicago, Atlanta, Los Angeles, Austin, and now Kansas City. I often get asked which of those places I liked best, and my answer is always, "I like certain elements of all those places; however, it is the people I remember most fondly."

What role does place play (hint) in helping us grow into our purpose to fulfill our true potential? As it turns out, quite a bit. In addition to looking at the importance of place from a geographical perspective, I am going to talk about it from a unique, historical perspective—a perspective I believe we can probably all relate to in some way, where both individual and team growth emerged.

THE PLAYGROUND...

Let's unpack what life on the playground—the Great Outdoors—was like for many of us growing up and connect it to how we can improve performance in the workplace.

When I was in elementary school, we had a very popular game called "nationball." How it got that name is a mystery for the ages and part of the lore of those who attended McCollum elementary school (Go Buffaloes!).

Like dodgeball in some ways, yet different in others, nationball was a game that featured two teams lined up opposite each other with a center line, two back lines, and, of course, sidelines to serve as boundaries. The object of the game was for your team to have the last player standing. A member of one team would run up to the center line and throw an inflated rubber ball (or sometimes a soccer ball), trying to hit a member of the other team. If the opposing team member was hit with the ball, they were "out" and had to go to the backline behind your team. However, if that person caught *your* ball, you were out and had to go to the backline behind their team.

While you were out in one sense, you were still part of the game as a member of your team now participating behind the backline. That is an important difference from dodgeball. You weren't out. You could throw balls too and create a crossfire. *That* was where the game got interesting!

We played nationball at recess almost every day because it stoked our competitive fire and gave us a sense of unity and place. As I began writing this section, I got to thinking about the importance of place and how the school playground provided all we really need to know about how to translate that same feeling to a team or organization.

We can learn 4 simple rules from the playground:

1. **Include everyone.**

2. **Play hard, but fair.**

3. **Team works.**

4. **Shake hands after.**

Let's briefly look at each one in more detail.

1. **Include Everyone** (everyone has value and a role to play)

> I'm sure many recall the dreaded process of picking teams when we were kids on the playground. We all pretty much knew who the captains would be, so we just hoped we were not the last one picked.
>
> But once the game started, no one cared in which order we had been chosen; it all came down to results. Did we win or lose, and, even more importantly, did we have fun and grow together as a team in the process? We all tend to settle into our specific roles and contribute. Some were good at throwing the ball while others were good at catching it; others were good at dodging it altogether. Even those who were "out" early played a role in the crossfire volleys throughout the rest of the game.
>
> In the workplace, our teams work similarly to the playground with each team member contributing a unique and interesting perspective to help the team and/or broader organization achieve its purpose and business goals.

Sometimes when we won, we were simply better than our opponent that day. However, when we lost and figured out what we did right and what we could learn from the experience to do better next time true growth occurred.

2. **Play Hard, But Fair** (be honest, open, and candid; no cheating)

To be successful in a game on the playground or in the game of life, we must understand the importance of competing at our best. That's right, "life" is indeed a competition that has evolved over many generations. From competing for food and survival to competing for a job and career path, it is most fulfilling to compete hard but fair.

As in nationball, the boundaries must be respected—you can't go over the line. In the workplace, that means doing your best every single day—your best energy and enthusiasm, your best ideas and solutions, your best quality and quantity of work and, of course, your best version of you as a total team player. To that end, you must be honest, open, and sincere—show your cards. In addition, you must not cheat either the game or its players. For example, in nationball, you cannot throw at someone's head. That's a no-no.

Likewise, if you have a conflict with someone, don't "throw at their head." Set up time to speak with them in person to resolve your differences in a respectful way. Like welding two pieces of metal back together, I believe you will find your relationship will turn out stronger than ever. When that happens, the reunified team gets even better. The point is, we must ensure a safe environment for everyone to play up to their potential.

When you play hard but fair, you win much more than you lose. And in both cases, you will do so with honor and integrity that leads to a higher sense of fulfillment—individually and collectively as a team.

3. **Team Works!** (play your role; serve others first)

We've already talked a lot about the importance of teamwork, so I will only emphasize a few points I have found to be important to success.

First, you must remain humble and serve others first. It doesn't matter if you are clearly the best player on the team. The way to influence the team in its quest to achieve your shared purpose and related goals is to put the needs of others in front of your own.

Simon Sinek's TED Talk and related book titled *Leaders Eat Last* do an excellent job of using historic examples from the military illustrating why this concept is so important. Sinek's thesis is simple, yet extremely powerful: "Leadership is about taking care of people. Leaders aren't responsible for the numbers; leadership is about people. Take care of the people, and the numbers will take care of themselves."

As someone who has had full profit and loss responsibility, I have had to learn this lesson the hard way. You see, on a quarterly earnings call, no analyst ever asks questions about the health and vitality of your culture. They're asking about your numbers so they can plug them into their models to support a decision to buy, sell, or hold your stock—or upgrade or downgrade its rating for their clients. And the share price of your stock obviously affects your market capitalization, which, in turn, dictates your access to capital for pursuing new growth opportunities.

Leaders must balance these two important factors, having the courage to first take care of their people before focusing on the key performance metrics they are expected to attain. As a mentor of mine, Bill Dunlap, once told me, "Mark, you're a pretty smart guy; however, I assure you that before your team cares how much you know, they need to know how much you care."

That's right, Bill…that is absolutely right.

4. **Shake Hands After** (ultimately, we're all on the same team)

After our nationball games concluded, we shook hands and made our way back into the school building; we were all classmates once again, unified by our grade, teacher, and school. Likewise, when a meeting concludes and decisions are made, we must move forward as a unified team, regardless of whether we agree with the outcome.

In fact, I've participated in meetings when emotions ran high and people got a bit personal with one another. While I don't recommend that environment in all cases, sometimes this type of meeting can be cathartic and even purifying for the team.

Think about the sports team going through a slump or individual performance issues. We've all heard about the closed-door, players-only meetings where grievances are aired, individuals are called out, and, ultimately, a new resolve is created. This new bond creates a recommitment to the team's goals, which can change its fortunes—even rescuing a poor season. This happens in business too. And it is okay.

The important thing is once the game is over, we shake hands as team members who must continue to push each other to attain higher levels of excellence in a civil manner. When we hurt someone's feelings, we must have a sense of contrition and the strength to apologize with humility when necessary. Whether we play on a sports team or a work team, we all spend a great deal of time with one another—sometimes more than we spend with our family. To that point, we know that families fight sometimes, but they always have each other's backs.

I'll admit, sometimes the playground can be a rough place to play, but it doesn't have to be. If we follow its rules, we can all come away winners, feeling good about our individual contributions and celebrating our collective successes along the way, while remembering we are ultimately all on the same team.

Now let's look at the notion of how physical space fosters creativity and team bonding. Research studies supporting the importance of physical space on productivity abound.

Even before COVID-19, many organizations had been reimagining their office spaces to be less department-focused and more team-focused. While the agency business has been doing this for some time—organizing individuals representing different areas of the firm within centralized client teams—we're seeing more and more companies doing likewise via "Integrated Brand Teams."

I think this change is smart on many levels because it brings diverse people, thought processes, and job functions together in a much tighter, more focused environment. This makes it easier to communicate, is more efficient from a time-management perspective, and, overall, creates a more positive and productive result.

But sometimes place can be made into something even more exceptional and productive. When I served as group account director for DDB Promotions, a division of Omnicom, I was responsible for leading our largest account: Frito-Lay. Headquartered in Plano, Texas, Frito-Lay was easily among the very best and certainly most innovative consumer packaged goods companies I have ever worked with as they lived the adage, "Everything's *big* in Texas!" Led by President Steve Reinemund and Chief Marketing Officer Brock Leach—along with an incredibly deep and talented team of brand management professionals—Frito-Lay craved "big ideas" as much as I crave Lay's potato chips!

With their blessing (and funding), we created a unique space within the offices of DDB in downtown Dallas dubbed "The Zone." (Thanks, Martin Hennessy.) When athletes achieve peak performance, they often reference a feeling of being in "the zone" to help explain how they accomplished a spectacular feat.

The Zone was designed to be a type of in-house retreat area to get away from our daily distractions and meet with each other, our Frito-Lay client-partners, key suppliers, or sports and entertainment agents. We had couches, bean bag chairs, lava lamps, and a few pinball machines along with foosball and ping-pong. We also had an assortment of toys and bobbles such as Play-Doh, Silly Putty, and colored pipe cleaners to help stimulate creativity. And we had music, soft drinks (Pepsi products, of course), and snacks (yes, lots and lots of Frito-Lay snacks).

More than merely a boondoggle or a place to hide from the real work, The Zone spawned some truly big ideas for Frito-Lay, which helped its leading snack food brands expand, growing its sales and profits. Here are three examples of those ideas:

- ✓ **Holiday Promotion:** The holidays are obviously a huge opportunity for snack sales, as friends and family gather together to share the joy of the season. Instead of the obligatory Santa Claus with red and green merchandising materials, we worked with Disney's Pixar unit to create an integrated, multi-brand promotion featuring a movie you may have heard of—*Toy Story*.

  We created special packaging for each major brand featuring characters from the movie. The products were featured in displays and leveraged the creative assets of *Toy Story* to bring attention to its location in the highly coveted perimeter of the store. The movie—and the integrated, multi-brand Frito-Lay *Toy Story* holiday promotion—were huge hits at both the box office and the grocery store.

- ✓ **NFL Football:** When I was a kid, the NFL broadcast on Sunday afternoons on either CBS (NFL/NFC games) or NBC (AFL/AFC games), with ABC hosting their unique *Monday Night Football* package, felt more like an entertainment event than a football game. But when TV contracts came up in the mid-1990s, it was brash upstart FOX that won the bid to unseat CBS.

  We wanted to capitalize on the excitement and popularity of NFL football and the unique personalities FOX featured in their pre-game show each Sunday—Terry Bradshaw and Howie Long—so we worked with Frito-Lay and FOX to create a massive fall, in-store merchandising program featuring the new "NFL on FOX." This highly successful integrated marketing program was relevant to its football-loving target audience (both males and females) and helped sell tons of Frito-Lay products during the heavy snacking season.

- ✓ **College Football Bowl Season:** The bowl season represents an opportunity to reward the most successful teams with an opportunity to square off against other successful teams from different conferences that normally wouldn't play each other. While many bowls have their unique and long-held traditions, the Fiesta Bowl, held in Tempe, Arizona, has always felt like a party (hence the name "fiesta" I guess). And the Fiesta Bowl had just broken through as one of 4 rotating bowl games that would comprise the new Bowl Championship Series—including the National Championship game in year one.

With Doritos representing a huge share of the tortilla chip market and, at that time, Tostitos languishing far behind, Frito-Lay wanted a way to boost awareness of Tostitos as *the* tortilla chip perfect for dipping and parties—creating a "fiesta" in every bite. To boost top-of-mind awareness for Tostitos—along with its complementary salsa, black bean, and nacho cheese dips—we kicked off a successful relationship with the *Tostitos Fiesta Bowl*. Until its end a few years ago, Tostitos enjoyed an incredible eighteen-year run as title sponsor of the Fiesta Bowl, which makes it one of the longest and most successful college sports sponsorships ever. And Tostitos' market share has been growing ever since. Now, *that* is putting the ball in the (end) zone!

In his landmark book *The Dream Society: How the Coming Shift from Information to Imagination Will Transform Your Business* published in 1999, Rolf Jensen envisioned an era of imagination replacing the information age. He believed there would be a transformation in the workplace with companies evolving into tribes and moving from valuing hard work to valuing hard fun:

> Work will become hard fun: motivating, creative, and engrossing. Success is no longer measured by the size of the paycheck. Success equals meaningful and challenging work. Charles Handy reminds us how Abraham Maslow in later years spoke about an addition to his five-level hierarchy of needs. Maybe there was a sixth need, he said, which we might call idealization, or the search for a purpose beyond oneself. Whoever finds such a purpose in work (in the sense the word is used here: hard fun) has succeeded.

I happen to agree with Mr. Jensen. A big part of the "hard fun" concept is developing and implementing purposeful creativity at work. I've always believed big ideas drive successful brands. And big ideas often come from people who are encouraged to challenge the status quo for the purpose of creating step function change growth within their respective business environments.

Apparently, Monty Python comedian John Cleese agrees with this principle based upon his view of creativity and the importance of play in the workplace:

> I believe that anyone can become more creative. It doesn't mean everybody can become Mozart, but you can become more creative than you are now and that process can continue. You have to get in a frame of mind to be creative, and in order to do that you've got to avoid interruptions. In our modern society it is incredibly difficult to avoid interruptions. You must get rid of that sense of hurry and get very relaxed, a bit like meditation. The essence of creativity is being able to play.

Cleese extolled the benefits of setting up a specific time and place for this activity to avoid distractions, before returning to a more regular environment for work:

> All creativity comes out of the ability to play. It's nothing to do with IQ or anything like that. At school when people say "work hard" it means you have to concentrate and get a bit tight, and that's the opposite of what you do if you play. People in charge don't understand the play process.[1]

---

1 From John Cleese's speech at the "Festival of Marketing: The Year Ahead" as reported by Matthew Valentine in *Marketing Week*, October 22, 2021.

Cleese explained that his new book, *Creativity: A Short and Cheerful Guide*, is the distillation of a long study of the process of creativity.

Amen, John. I was very fortunate enough to work with some leaders who understood the relationship between fun, creativity, and innovation more than twenty-five years ago. And it's even more important today.

Now let's move from the physical place to the digital space because a variety of professional needs and personal circumstances require more flexibility in both communication and project management techniques due to the disruption caused by COVID-19.

While many companies are beginning to welcome employees back to the office full- or part-time now that it is becoming safe to do so, COVID-19 has made many others rethink the need for a centralized, physical location. In fact, Kelly Roddy, the CEO of **WOW**orks, decided to sub-lease its suburban Philadelphia headquarters to allow team members to work remotely wherever they live across the country, while gathering executive leadership at various locales as necessary for project updates, team building, and strategic planning.

A study recently published by Nicholas Bloom, a Stanford University economics professor, suggests, as a result of COVID-19, "Working from home is here to stay, with hybrid arrangements fast becoming the dominant strain." Bloom concludes that companies may see approximately half of their employee base return to work, whereas 10 percent of employees will continue to work remotely and 40 percent will have a hybrid schedule with some days remote and some days in the office.

The genie is simply not going back into the lamp, so we must adapt accordingly.

How do you create a sense of place when not everyone is in daily face-to-face contact?

Given the confluence of technology (hi-tech) with humanity (hi-touch), here are just a few ideas to help cultivate a fertile and productive *place* for remote or hybrid collaboration:

- ✓ **Personal Life Sharing:** One benefit of working remotely is the ability to get to know team members on a more personal level. While navigating the vagaries of COVID-related quarantine via videoconferencing, a nice by-product of working remotely was the opportunity to view our team members through a different lens. Instead of seeing people dressed up in work clothes within a typical office setting, we interacted with our colleagues in their home environments. Those with kids being home-schooled offered both a challenge and an opportunity as we got to know their family and/or pets whom we may not have met otherwise. We used our team Zoom meetings as a way to celebrate birthdays, work anniversaries, hear about vacation experiences and holiday rituals, and learn about hobbies or special interests. Getting to know people on a more human level provides a deeper level of empathy that can help the team grow even stronger together. And I like to insist that everyone participating in the meeting has their video on. This ensures everyone stays engaged throughout the meeting.

- ✓ **Team-Building Exercises:** Countless ways for building team engagement exist in a remote environment if you are creative enough. And you are. For example, you can create opportunities for remote team members to actively lead a team meeting from wherever they are. This allows them to demonstrate their leadership capabilities in a visible way. At **WOW**orks, we scheduled time on the calendar for each departmental team to introduce themselves to the broader organization. Each team worked together to develop informative, yet highly creative ways to introduce their members while highlighting key priorities and accomplishments. This type of forum can also be used for crowdsourcing solutions—unlocking the collective wisdom of the team—to help overcome key challenges that directly or indirectly affect the broader organization. Hey, it is always easier to consult on someone else's business, right?

✓ **Continuous Learning Opportunities:** Create a forum for learning best practices and information sharing in the form of a "Lunch 'n Learn" approach. While I'm sure many have done this in a physical workplace, it works just as well if not better in a remote or hybrid work environment. This provides remote team members an opportunity to showcase their work in ways that can inspire the broader team. In addition, you can have people share key knowledge on relevant topics they gleaned from virtual conferences, webinars, podcasts, blogs, vlogs, etc. to enrich the broader team. Be sure to record these sessions and put them in a central repository or library for future viewing.

✓ **Reward/Recognition:** It can be easy to overlook the accomplishments of a remote team member, so make sure any reward or recognition goes two-way. This allows the remote team member an opportunity to recognize a deserving person at the home office while ensuring they are provided an equal playing field to receive recognition themselves. Tom Cole, the Executive Chairman of Tandem Theory—a data savvy digital agency based in Dallas—told me they set up a Slack channel called "Tandem Slays" in which team members can send special shout-outs to one another. Each one is then read aloud during monthly team meetings. In addition to planned employee of the month-type celebrations, some of the most powerful forms of reward/recognition I've seen are organic and unplanned. They provide a deeper level of authenticity, enriching both the team member and the broader organization.

These are just a few ideas I have heard of or been involved with—some created by our team members. At both Noodles & Company and Saladworks, we created a culture committee that consisted of members from various levels of the organization. They met to come up with fun, new ways to build on our purposeful vision, mission, and shared values through cultural enrichment and team engagement to help make the work experience more fulfilling.

Whether in person, remote, or some form of hybrid, it is vitally important for leaders to cultivate a sense of place—moving people from principles to playgrounds. This will allow all team members a safe, mutually respectful environment to take the next step—instilling disciplined processes to move from playgrounds to productivity—to help fulfill their purpose in alignment with team or organizational goals.

CHAPTER 30

CULTIVATING FULFILLING PROCESSES FROM PLAYGROUNDS TO PRODUCTIVITY

"In a person's career, well, if you're process-oriented and not totally outcome-oriented, then you're more likely to be a success. I often say, 'pursue excellence, ignore success.' Success is a by-product of excellence."

— Deepak Chopra

Okay, playtime is over, and now it's time to ensure our team or organization is as effective as possible at translating ideas into actions—moving us from *playgrounds* to *productivity*. It's not enough to establish a fun, collaborative, collegial team environment—or place; we must incorporate a suite of disciplined processes to remain focused and working together, aligned, and moving toward our stated goals.

Let's shift gears a bit. I want to take a few moments to emphasize the equal importance of *creative inspiration* and *executional excellence* in driving successful innovation that leads to more than just short-term "boom! splat..." success, but long-term, step function change growth opportunities—big ideas focused on fulfilling your unique purpose.

In my experience leading high-performance teams and participating on many others, the best results come from adhering to a disciplined process and using appropriate work-flow management tools. To fulfill our shared purpose and achieve our related growth goals, we must transition from place to productivity via 4 GROW-focused process management techniques.

1. **Goals**

2. **Roles**

3. **Ownership**

4. **Win Together!**

1. GOALS

We start by outlining our goals. This can best be done using a framework known as a project charter, which does an excellent job of outlining the scope of a project, including its key priorities—gate-based performance milestones necessary to achieve the desired outcome.

But before we jump headfirst into our list of priorities, we must develop a solid business case to justify the time, energy, expense, and opportunity cost for a project team to be assembled in the first place.

Let's start by answering these 4 foundational questions:

✓ **How does this project align with our purposeful vision and mission?**

The project must be well-thought-out and offer long-term improvement aligned with your purposeful vision and mission to be considered the right/best use of limited time, money, and resources.

Great teams and organizations know *who* they serve and *why* they do what they do, and every *how* or *what* that follows is disciplined and calculated toward achieving shared goals.

✓ **How does this project fit within our strategic growth plan?**

Assuming you have developed a ten-year vision plan or, at minimum, a three- or five-year strategic growth plan, you and your team should be able to link your proposed project to one of your organization's stated strategic growth pillars—noted previously as "The Vital Few" as opposed to "The Trivial Many." If you cannot, go back to the drawing board.

✓ **What is the potential "size of the prize" of this project?**

Showing how the project aligns with your purposeful vision, mission, and strategic growth plan overall is merely the ante to get into the game. Then you must put a pencil to your project to demonstrate its financial benefits to the organization.

Remember, in any size organization, multiple—and often competing—priorities are present at the same time. And you only have so many resources to go around. Marketing wants more money to spend on advertising to support topline sales growth. Operations wants a new labor management system to maximize efficiencies. Finance wants a new enterprise management solution to enhance information collection and analyses. IT wants an upgraded point-of-sale system to connect all users to real-time data. These are all important and worthwhile projects…but they don't take place in a vacuum.

For C-Suite executives, the key is to use facts to support your respective area's needs while working collegially and collaboratively to support each other. After all, we're *all* on the same team.

- ✓ **What alternatives might we consider if we do not take on this particular project?**

Wait a minute…I thought we were done? Sorry. Despite aligning with the three questions above, the executive team will likely ask you this question for a few reasons.

First, they are likely performing a conviction check. Are you really committed to leading this important project and seeing it through? Do you really understand what's at stake? Are you showing any sign of hesitation or weakness? If so, a ton of work can go down the drain—possibly along with your career. No pressure, though.

Second, they are looking for objectivity and critical analysis. We all tend to fall in love with our own pet projects. But in doing so, we may not be able to see alternatives that could possibly be even better. Are we open to that possibility?

Either way, the stakes are extremely high, and the final go/no-go decision is like making a bet at the horse track. If you bet correctly, you could go home a winner. On the other hand, if you bet poorly, you (and your team or organization) could lose much more than just your shirt.

The scope of work and related business goals must be clearly documented in the body of the project charter to ensure 100 percent alignment among project team members. In addition, there must be clear and definitive "gates" or milestones through which the project must pass before it proceeds to the next phase.

2. ROLES

We must outline the specific roles involved in completing the project in the project charter. The "RACI Model" has been around for several years, and while many other excellent project management tools exist, I have found this one simple and effective, with key roles clearly identified.

RACI is an acronym for:

- ✓ **Responsible**—Project Manager
- ✓ **Accountable**—Executive Sponsor
- ✓ **Consult**—Department Leaders/Subject Matter Experts
- ✓ **Inform**—Executive Management/Board of Directors

When forming a project team, it is important to chart the specific role each member will play up-front to avoid confusion. In many organizations, some team members are asked to play on multiple teams. And, quite often, these projects are on top of a team member's regular workload, so focus, clarity, and alignment are vital.

Many larger organizations incorporate a Project Management Organization (PMO)—individuals specifically trained on the most effective and productive techniques to manage a project team. (Think cat herders.) Smaller organizations do not have that luxury, so project management skills must be imbued at all levels by providing cross-training opportunities so team members can be prepared to step up to lead when called upon.

3. OWNERSHIP

As stated previously, a good team player must take ownership and be accountable for their responsibilities—living up to one's personal commitments made within the project charter and RACI model.

Have you ever been to an Air Force Thunderbirds or Navy Blue Angels air show? The precision with which they fly jets at incredible speeds—including gravity and logic-defying maneuvers—inches apart is simply amazing. If a pilot is out of sync even a little it could be disastrous. To ensure success and a safe landing, everyone must own their role to instill a deep sense of trust and confidence among the team.

With everyone on the project team assigned a well-defined role, let's look at a project management model to provide an example of how this process *should* come together. As I pointed out when talking about the importance of innovation, this model was originally developed for product development. However, this process management approach is intuitive and flexible enough to accommodate multiple uses.

Marketing books and journals are filled with different product or service innovation models. I have found no silver bullet solution; instead I have found many ways to achieve the same end. However, each model has a logical, strategic, process-driven approach. One I've used successfully is the DEDVIM model. If memory serves, I believe it was developed at Pizza Hut and exported to the other YUM! Brands. It was later presented to our executive team at Bob

Evans Farms by a consultant, Larry DeVries, whom I worked with at Pizza Hut.

As you might have guessed, DEDVIM is an acronym that stands for six different, but very interrelated processes:

- ✓ **Define:** What growth opportunity are we specifically attempting to address (project scope)? What "size is the prize" if we're successful (base case, best case, worst case)? How does the project fit our purpose-based mission, vision, values, and alternative priorities (opportunity cost)? The DEDVIM process can be packaged and presented via a document usually called a Business Case. Assuming the project gets approved, we can move to the explore process. Keep in mind that this might not happen after the initial business case presentation because the executive team may have questions or concerns that require further investigation or additional fine-tuning before approval.

- ✓ **Explore:** What broad universe of ideas might we explore to match the definition of success outlined previously? Again, going back to our approach to learning from best practices outlined in the previous chapter, what internal and external resources will we employ to develop this broad list of initial ideas? Once we feel we have exhausted all relevant ideas and receive approval, we can move the project forward to the next gate.

- ✓ **Develop:** This is where we transition from the fun, exciting "What if…" phase to the more analytical, practical, fact-based *develop* process. If we proceed, how will the ideas change our human resources, training, operational, and guest satisfaction metrics? Based on how each idea fits into our stated success criteria, which should we spend time, money, and energy developing? After receiving the answers to these questions, we're left with a short list of approved "finalist" ideas, allowing us to move the project forward to the next gate.

- ✓ **Validate:** Once we have it narrowed down to two or three finalist ideas, we can *validate* the biggest/best one through a series of sequential research methods—featuring both qualitative and quantitative studies. In the restaurant business, this would also include taste panels, "menu studies," and on-site tests. A specific set of criteria must be developed and strictly adhered to so each idea can be compared with integrity and accuracy. Of course, somewhere during the validation process, we may learn something new—either positive (ingredient/recipe change) or negative (supply chain issue)—that may influence the results, affecting which idea gets approval to move on to the next gate.

- ✓ **Implement:** Once we've thoroughly validated our decision, it's time to *implement* our *best* idea in the marketplace. To ensure success, we must employ a similarly disciplined approach to that used during the validation process. This means we must communicate our program throughout the enterprise while providing thorough internal training and clear execution standards. At the same time, we must plan and launch a strategically targeted and optimized external marketing plan to build awareness, engagement, profitable sales, and then repeat while encouraging positive word-of-mouth by delivering guest satisfaction. This leads us to the final gate.

✓ **Measure:** By this time, we should have established a clear dashboard of appropriate people, guest, sales, and profit metrics to *measure* success. This will help us understand how the project is doing in the marketplace, allowing us to make changes along the way that we may not have learned through the more narrowly focused validate process. Regardless of the outcome, there will be tons of key lessons we must share as part of a post-analysis. This information will help us improve all aspects of the DEDVIM innovation process for the next major project.

If you think of innovation as being like placing a bet, the strategic and disciplined DEDVIM process helps you significantly improve your odds of success.

WASH. RINSE. REPEAT.

In addition to a given project management process (strategic growth), it is important to point out the importance of a meeting management process (tactical growth). One of the biggest time sucks any organization faces is "Meeting Madness." We have too many meetings, taking too long, with too many people, and getting too little accomplished. If we believe "people are our greatest asset," then we must act like it and respect their time.

But we need meetings to ensure the team makes progress toward its stated objectives, right? Good news! We have a simple, disciplined, and effective way to make meetings more productive and satisfying for all participants.

Here are my 4 growth tips for *actively* managing successful meetings:

1. **State the Purpose:** When setting up the meeting, the facilitator (leader) should clearly state the purpose in the invitation and attach the agenda and any materials participants will need to review. Don't wait until the last minute to do this. Recipients should review the materials promptly, before the meeting, and be prepared to respond if needed.

2. **Invite the right People:** Once you know the purpose of the meeting and the desired outcome, only invite the people necessary to achieve that end. You'll often see people in the room who don't need to be there and could be doing something more productive. They can be copied on the meeting notes and informed of next steps after.

3. **Manage Performance:** Note that meetings do not need to be an hour or some other arbitrary duration. If the agenda can be accomplished in forty-five minutes, schedule the meeting for forty-five minutes. Regardless of meeting length, start on time with the facilitator establishing ground rules and a safe environment for sharing ideas, thoughts, or opinions in addition to providing a brief recap of the meeting's purpose, agenda, and intended outcome. Agendas should include a specific duration for each item, and this time should be monitored by a designated timekeeper. The facilitator should move participants through the agenda, ensuring each item is covered completely, everyone has an opportunity to contribute, and specific follow-up/action items are noted and assigned an owner. Once all items on the agenda are covered, the facilitator (or preferably a designated notetaker) recaps the key decisions, action items, next steps, agreed timing, and designated owners responsible for each item. This should be done before the meeting ends (on time) to ensure everyone is

on the same page before walking out of the room (or logging off Zoom).

4. **Follow up on key Priorities:** We've had a successful, highly productive meeting, so we're done, right? Nope. The facilitator—or the designated notetaker—must send out a written recap promptly. This should include summarizing key decisions and related action items, deadlines, and specify owners (team members responsible for completing each action item). This must go out to the entire project team established in the RACI model. This will ensure those not present remain in the loop and aware of any action items affecting them.

WASH. RINSE. REPEAT.

4. WIN TOGETHER!

Remember, when used correctly, a process is merely a management tool for achieving a desired result; it does not run all by itself. Of course, it takes the personal alignment, commitment, and accountability of each team member to make a given project successful. Is each team member fully engaged: heart, head, hands, and habits?

To ensure an individual team member's performance is measured objectively, meld it into the ongoing Purposeful Growth process. Notice I didn't say annual performance appraisal process. I believe the entire Annual Performance Appraisal process has become antiquated and ineffective in evaluating team member performance against SMART goals for a variety of reasons. Based on feedback from my peers, no one seems to like it. Why:

✓ The end of the calendar/fiscal year is not magic; business needs are ongoing.

- ✓ Many annual performance appraisal forms are way too long and hard to fill out and/or use productively.
- ✓ Most only provide a look back, lacking the important go-forward perspective.
- ✓ Annual reviews tend to feel like a "gotcha" instead of a growth opportunity.

Instead of a one-way, top-down annual performance appraisal approach that is often prepared by a manager and administered to a team member at the end of the year, I prefer a much more frequent, ongoing approach based on interactive dialogue. In fact, I dislike the word appraisal because it is also used in evaluating property.

Invariably, the next step is for the leader to breathe a sigh of relief (*Whew…I'm so glad that is over!*) and the team member—depending on the review—tends to do likewise. Then, the appraisal goes in their respective desk drawers until they dust it off to prepare a new appraisal the following year.

Can we go to lunch *now*?

> *"Coaching is not doing, and it's not telling people what to do. It's guiding, questioning, prompting, and encouraging forward movement. Most important, it's inspiring people to take ownership of their own careers."*
>
> — Simon Sinek

I call it a Purposeful Growth Plan because it's just that—a dynamic, process-based *plan*, not an annual, one-time *event* that is designed to align individuals, teams and organizations behind purposeful growth outcomes. This process puts equal responsibility on the team member and their leader to collectively manage *both* of their performances throughout the year. Yes, I said both because a good leader shares responsibility for the success of their team members' growth and development. I have found it very productive to ensure these discussions allow for feedback to flow both ways.

Here are the 4 key components of a well-rounded, strategically aligned, highly productive Purposeful Growth Plan.

1. **The *Who*:** Focuses on exactly who we will *serve* based on our plan—both internal and external brand stakeholders.

2. **The *Why*:** Highlights the importance of the team or organization's purposeful vision, mission, and business goals.

3. **The *How*:** Incorporates both personal and professional growth plans within our framework of shared values.

4. **The *What*:** Specifically links to annual plan SMART goals and/or team project strategic growth opportunities.

I have learned that a streamlined format incorporating more frequent, interactive check-ins is a much more productive and mutually satisfying approach to performance management. It places an emphasis on more actionable, forward-facing behaviors. This approach provides the opportunity for questions, feedback, and course corrections in real-time, no waiting.

And the good news is we can fit all this information on just *one* page. Wait…. What? The customizable quarterly check-in approach only takes an hour or so to administer, leaving just a few minutes at the end for questions and/or mutually agreed-upon next steps.

I recently incorporated this multi-faceted approach—featuring the *who*, the *why*, the *how*, and the *what*—with a consulting client who says it is working extremely well. The organization's president said it was far superior to the unwieldy annual performance appraisals they used before. His team was actively using this one-page form and related multiple check-in process to achieve their growth initiatives.

Now that we have our crisply written and mutually agreed-upon Purposeful Growth Plan, it should serve as a living, breathing document from which we gauge our progress throughout the year. For leader/team member interactions, I have found the following cadence works well in building relationships, engaging team members, and ensuring alignment behind our priorities:

- ✓ **Daily**—Personal interactions/observations
- ✓ **Weekly**—One-on-one meetings
- ✓ **Monthly**—Team meetings
- ✓ **Quarterly**—Check-in meetings
- ✓ **Annually**—Goal-setting meeting

Think of these more frequent interactions like the gentle pruning of a plant. We are accentuating the positive aspects of the plant while removing any damaged, diseased, or dead spots. This allows the plant to grow stronger and more resilient, and its flowers or fruit will be more colorful and plentiful.

In any human endeavor, there will likely be conflicts from time to time. That is natural. We learned earlier in this book that we are all *different* and *different* is good! Still, how do we address and resolve conflicts that left alone may disrupt the effectiveness of our project team? If you have established a solid foundation at the beginning of the team's formation, it is possible to resolve conflicts in a healthy, positive, and productive manner. Instead of focusing on what not to do, let's discuss ways we can maximize the tremendous value of teamwork.

- ✓ **Team Together-Team Apart:** Simply stated, the team stays together from start to finish—whether they are working as a team on various phases of the project or working independently. Everyone has value, and everyone has an important role to play if the team is to be successful.

- ✓ **Hug it out:** It is inevitable given our inherent differences that conflicts will arise. And when they do, it is important not to let a situation fester; rather set up a time to talk one-on-one and work together to resolve your differences. Not only will it strengthen your personal relationship with that team member, but it will have a net positive effect on the overall team dynamics. Again, conflict is okay if managed appropriately. In person is best, but if not, pick up the phone and call—resist the urge to go back and forth electronically.

- ✓ **Trust but verify:** While we know that trust is foundational to any team or relationship, we must be comfortable in challenging the assumptions or information provided by our team members. Remember, the stakes are high, and no one should take any challenge personally. It is better to have multiple eyes on an issue.

- ✓ **Celebrate success:** Given the gate-based project management model, we find many opportunities to celebrate the team's success and several more in between. Everyone on the team is working hard and sacrificing for each other to achieve the shared goals set forth in the project charter. Emotions can run high, and fuses can get short, so it is vitally important to blow off steam in a healthy, positive, and productive way. Hey, it's called, happy hour for a reason.

In addition to team celebrations, both the project team leadership and individual team members should take time out to recognize individuals who have gone above and beyond on the team's behalf. Keeping the mood light and the energy high is the way to develop an environment where every team member feels confident in their individual contributions and the team's collective performance.

When we practice our team-building skills, it is more than likely we will be successful in our endeavors. And, in my experience, the sweet taste of victory is best savored together as a *team*—no longer a group of individuals. You become a single unit, one that has fought in the trenches beside each other, had each other's back through difficulty, and encouraged each other to achieve their peak performance at each step along the journey.

And make no mistake, there *will* be setbacks and obstacles along the path (breakdowns). It's how you work collectively as a team to overcome them (breakthroughs) that makes all the difference in your collective success.

I first heard about a can-do attitude from David Novak, and I feel that both words, *can* and *do*, are equally important. We've spent time talking about the importance of the action word *do*. Now let's set that up with an equally important concept, the word *can*. Can is not only positive, uplifting, and aspirational, but it serves as a challenge to *do* what's necessary for the team's success:

- ✓ Can the team stay positive if the plan needs to change along the way?

- ✓ Can the team stay together to manage through conflict when the pressure gauge rises?

- ✓ Can the team be genuinely supportive of those who receive special accolades?

- ✓ Can the team honestly and objectively reflect on its performance for future growth?

Now *that* is how we *can* win together as a *team!*

CHAPTER 31

CULTIVATING FULFILLING PERFORMANCES FROM PRODUCTIVITY TO PROFITABILITY

> *"Live from the inside out. Your mind, body, and spirit are interconnected. Nourish your soul with mental and physical wellness."*
>
> — Janet Taylor Spence

We are close to the end of our journey together, right? Not so fast! This is merely a new beginning, as the concept of the Purposeful Fulfillment Revolution in relation to our personal, team, or organizational performance is—like the annual change in seasons—a never-ending, *revolutionary* cycle.

We are *all* (still) works in progress—ever growing into our purpose.

Cultivating the benefits of relevant executional processes can lead us from playgrounds to productivity. This sets the stage for fulfilling performances—assisting individuals, teams, and organizations in moving from *productivity* to *profitability*.

In essence, moving from productivity to profitability is the bottom line. At Pizza Hut, my friend and mentor Pat Williamson used to say, "Don't confuse effort with results." As a former president and

CEO with full profit and loss accountability, I wholeheartedly agree with that statement. However, I also know no one is perfect. And as I said upfront, chasing results for the sake of results is not very fulfilling, so a corollary I have heard to that saying is, "Pursue progress over perfection" because that is how purposeful growth will lead to performance improvement.

Yes, this is coming from a serial achiever and perfectionist who has now realized how much stress and lost time I have caused myself and others by agonizing over details that—in the long-run—don't really matter. Given that background and a new perspective, I believe making steady progress *toward* perfection is the key to achieving desired results.

It is vitally important to meld together both *focus* and *action*.

If we have focus without action, we are merely stuck in idle. Likewise, if we have action but no focus, we are merely spinning our wheels—getting tired but, unfortunately, no closer to our goals.

Now, if we have a clear focus on the right/best direction for our journey *and* we take the appropriate action, we *will* get to our destination even if we have to course-correct a few times along the way. But it all must start with a clear focus—followed by purposeful action. Let's remember our old friend the small, but powerful word *do*.

In cultivating fulfilling performances the magic really happens. *Ayurveda* is a Hindu term for medicine. It represents the harmonic balance between a person's mind, body, and spirit to nurture one's health. I won't argue with that; however, I feel like there is an important fourth element—the *soul*—to help fulfill one's unique purpose.

> *"Constantly regard the universe as one living being, having one substance and one soul."*
>
> — Marcus Aurelius

As I said, fulfillment represents a more eternal, outer-directed pursuit than fun, happiness, or joy, and it leaves behind a *living* legacy that enriches others on their growth journey.

Only when these 4 elements are in alignment and you are living your life pursuing purposeful growth can you expect to achieve and sustain peak performance.

1. **Mind**—*Do* you cultivate a positive growth mindset?

2. **Body**—*Do* you nurture your body so growth can occur?

3. **Spirit**—*Do* you exhibit a spirit of continuous improvement?

4. **Soul**—*Do* you want to establish a growth legacy?

Is your mind, body, spirit, and soul focused clearly on growing into your unique purpose? It doesn't matter what your specific purpose may be, like a tree, we are all put on this earth to grow and bear fruit. According to Galatians 5:22-23 (ESV), the fruits of the Spirit are love, joy, peace, patience, kindness, goodness, faithfulness, gentleness, and self-control. Regardless of your religious convictions, can we all agree these fruits can be fulfilling on both a personal and interpersonal level?

If so, are you taking intentional actions toward growing into your purpose to help make a positive difference in your life, your family's, your team/organization's, and the lives of others in the world?

Believe it or not—you *do* have a choice.

And what if you played on a team or worked for an organization that cultivated a fertile and nurturing growth environment where you and others could achieve and sustain peak performance? How powerful would that be? Let me ask it in a way geared more to C-Suite executives, boards of directors, and shareholders: How much more *profitable* could that be?

- ✓ New Employee Attraction *Growth*
- ✓ Employee Retention *Growth*
- ✓ Revenue/Profit *Growth*
- ✓ Market Share *Growth*
- ✓ Guest/Customer Satisfaction *Growth*
- ✓ Stock Price *Growth*
- ✓ Market Cap *Growth*

To compete for and retain top talent in The Great Repurposing era, companies are going to have to think radically about how to fully leverage the power of their people. The outdated command and control leadership model is going the way of the dodo. Instead, leaders who provide ways to help team members enrich their mind, body, spirit, and soul to nurture the growth and development of the whole person will be even more important than just financial compensation.

Power to the *people*.... Right on!

As I said, I am a firm believer in cultivating a strengths-based approach to performance management. Likewise, I am equally a believer in a positive, uplifting recognition and rewards-based culture, but only when individual performance is authentically aligned with team and organizational goals. You simply cannot separate the two because that sends the wrong message to the team or organization. One-off, heroic behaviors not aligned with the SMART goals outlined in one's performance management plan can be an unnecessary distraction.

At YUM! Brands, David Novak was legendary for employing recognition and reward techniques that aligned individual performance with team and organization goals. Pictures of David posing with various award recipients covered the walls *and ceiling* of his office. With no more space in his office, he had to nail them up and down the hallways.

What an awesome tribute to the power of recognition—anyone entering David's office would instantly know what he stood for. And the results showed as his team grew YUM! Brands into the leading multi-brand restaurant company in the world. After his retirement, David's passion for developing leaders within recognition-based cultures lives on with his new venture based on his book *O Great One!* Like his previous book, *Taking People with You*, it is a must-read for anyone who wishes to create a growth culture—whether you play on a team or work for any size or type of organization.

But long before there was ever the YUM! Brands "Chattering Teeth," Pizza Hut "Cheesehead," KFC "Rubber Chicken," and Taco Bell "Sauce Packet" awards, David established the "Silver Pan" award—when he served as senior vice president of marketing at Pizza Hut. During every monthly business review meeting, David would stand up-front and extoll the virtues of a team member who accomplished a major achievement tied to our strategic plan while exemplifying the organization's shared values. This was often the highlight of the meeting.

For me, it was one of the highlights of my early career when David selected me to receive this award. I felt the awesome power of this very simple, but meaningful gesture. While the engraved silver pan cost next to nothing, it etched an impression on me that has lasted throughout my career.

When I became chief marketing officer for Schlotzsky's, a fast-casual restaurant division of Focus Brands, I wanted to come up with an award to recognize excellence that was relevant to our Austin, Texas, roots and fun, quirky brand. In Seth Godin's book *The Purple Cow*, which had a core theme of uniqueness, I found my answer:

The Purple Cowbell Award—given to a team member who "shakes things up, makes some noise, and stands out from the herd!"

I found some cowbells with the Schlotzsky's logo in a storage closet, took them home, and spray-painted them purple so each recipient could have their own Purple Cowbell Award to display on their desk. I used our monthly marketing/menu team meeting as the venue for giving out the award—waiting until the end to generate maximum suspense. Once the award recipient was revealed, I had them come to the front of the room to stand next to me while I told the team why the person deserved the award. As the meeting concluded, everyone on the team applauded the recipient and went up to personally congratulate them. Not a bad way to end a meeting, huh?

But the Purple Cowbell Award did not stop there. In addition to serving as a marketing/menu team recognition award, it became a much bigger, broader symbol of performance excellence throughout the organization. In fact, during our monthly all-staff business review meetings, we used the Purple Cowbell, ringing it to punctuate achievements announced by senior leadership.

When it was my turn to represent the marketing/menu team, I used the opportunity to reveal the Purple Cowbell Award winner to the broader organization. This created an important second hit of recognition for the recipient beyond the team meetings. I knew we had something special when people representing different areas of the company started asking me to ring the purple cowbell when they shared their own positive performance stories.

Again, this type of fun, positive, and enthusiastic display of recognition creates a palpable energy that is felt throughout the room and lasts long after the meeting concludes and the swirl of the day-to-day takes over. In fact, I understand the Purple Cowbell Award tradition remained in place well after I departed.

When a team member feels appreciated, loved, and cared for in a safe, nurturing environment, they tend to perform at their best and raise the bar of excellence even higher. When the rest of the team sees others earning this type of recognition, it tends to stimulate their performance, taking them to a higher level, resulting in a deep sense of both satisfaction and, yes, purposeful fulfillment.

Everyone wins!

Hey, we're all human, and we must continue to actively pursue growth—both individually and collectively—to become prosperous and fulfilled. Physiologically (according to Abraham Maslow), we simply *need* to feel loved and appreciated. If we don't, we may decide to look for it elsewhere.

"I've learned that people will forget what you said, people will forget what you did, but people will never forget how you made them feel."

— Maya Angelou

THE PURPOSEFUL FULFILLMENT REVOLUTION

People

Place

Process

Performance

=

ENVIRONMENT

By now, you have learned the integrated nature of the 4 LEAF *GROWTH* processes and how they revolve around the power of purpose in helping individuals, teams, and organizations find their purpose in fulfilling their true growth potential. Similar to the harmonious balance within a plant's internal structure and external ecosystem, there are many interwoven parts that must work together to help each of us along our respective growth journeys.

We have proven that **Purposeful Leadership**—representing the sown seed and root system established by an individual, team, or organization—can, through Clarity, Connection, Communication, and Commitment, result in growth *Alignment*.

We have proven that **Purposeful Engagement**—representing the transformational trunk, branches, and system of nourishment for an individual, team, or organization—can, through a total commitment of one's Heart, Head, Hands, and Habits, result in growth *Empowerment*.

We have proven that **Purposeful Accountability**—representing the leaf and fruit of an individual, team, or organization—can, through the ability to manage Outcomes, Obstacles, Outliers, and Obsolescence, result in growth *Achievement*.

We have proven that **Purposeful Fulfillment**—representing the nurturing ecosystem of an individual, team, or organization—can, through cultivating People, Places, Process, and Performance, result in a growth *Environment*.

But let's all remember, the mighty oak tree did not grow tall, strong, and fruitful overnight. It took years (and years) to fulfill its purpose—with each growth ring representing a new and different season of its lifespan. The same can be said for your personal and professional growth journey.

> *"And let us not grow weary while doing good,*
> *for in due season we shall reap if we do not lose heart."*
>
> — Galatians 6:9, (NKJV)

To ultimately find your unique purpose and fulfill your true growth potential and bear maximum fruit, you must be prepared to persevere through all weather conditions in all seasons, confident that each experience, observation, or lesson adds strength and vitality to you as a human organism just like it does for a plant found in nature. And like the oak tree, your knowledge, experience, and skills will provide bark-like protection from the elements. This will allow you to become resilient—to stand strong when the storms come.

To that point, there is one final reveal I hope you will take to heart. Within each of the 4 LEAF *GROWTH* processes, you will recall there are 4 key sub-processes that all begin with the same letter:

1. **Leadership**

    ✓ Clarity, Connection, Communication, Commitment

2. **Engagement**

    ✓ Heart, Head, Hands, Habits

3. **Accountability**

    ✓ Outcomes, Obstacles, Outliers, Obsolescence

4. **Fulfillment**

    ✓ People, Places, Process, Performance

When we combine the first letters of these definitions, it illuminates an important new word: CHOP, representing the importance of consistency and perseverance in overcoming life's challenges to find your purpose and fulfill your true growth potential and bear much fruit.

As the saying goes, "Keep chopping wood!"

PART IV

SCATTERING YOUR SEEDS FOR PURPOSEFUL LIFE

*"It's not what you gather,
but what you scatter that tells what kind of life you have lived."*

— Helen Walton

CHAPTER 32

MOVING FROM *ME-GO* TO *WE-GROWTH!*

"A tree is known by its fruit, a man by his deeds.
A good deed is never lost; he who sows courtesy reaps friendship,
and he who plants kindness gathers love."

— Saint Basil

Another Bible parable that has had a profound effect on my life is The Parable of the Sower (Matthew 12:3-8). In the story, a sower sows seeds; some fall on the path, some on rocky ground, and some among thorns, and they are lost, but when the seeds fall on good soil, they grow, yielding exponentially.

The same can be said for the seeds we scatter to help cultivate growth in the lives of others. Up to now, this book's purpose has been to help *you* find your purpose in fulfilling your true growth potential. When you do that, you will bear plentiful fruit—from that fruit comes seeds with the potential to sprout new growth opportunities for others.

Let's move the conversation from *me-go* to *we-growth*.

You see, plants, like people, share common biological goals: grow and reproduce. It's called a family tree for a reason.

In addition to enriching our own lives, we are taught in the Bible to love our neighbor as ourselves, so in a broader sense, we are *all* part of the *Tree of Life*. As such, we have a responsibility to extend and enhance this tree by helping others along their growth journey. By bearing much fruit and scattering our seeds, we can create a positive, lasting, and *living* legacy to help make the world a better place because of our presence.

"We make a living by what we get; we make a life by what we give."

— Sir Winston Churchill

Social psychology teaches that reciprocity is the social norm of responding to a positive action with another positive action, rewarding kind actions. It comes from the Latin *reciprocus* "moving backward and forward" (see reciprocate). Reciprocity is the practice of exchanging things with others for mutual benefit. As we learned earlier, this two-way growth process in a plant is the integration of both xylem and phloem based upon the photosynthesis that occurs in each leaf.

Social psychologists call it *the law of reciprocity*. Essentially, this means when someone does something nice for you, you will have a deep-rooted psychological urge to do something nice in return. In fact, research suggests you may feel led to reciprocate with a gesture even more generous than the original good deed. Remember my Starbucks example in "paying it backward"? I'll take this concept one step farther and refer to it as a *virtuous cycle of reciprocity*. This is defined as a recurring succession of uplifting events exchanged for mutual benefit resulting in exponential growth opportunities when multiplied by others.

- Reciprocity of your *self*—nurturing relationships
- Reciprocity of your *team*—supporting team members
- Reciprocity of your *organization*—enriching communities
- Reciprocity of your *world*—sustaining the planet

The *virtuous cycle of reciprocity* is not just a one-to-one, closed-loop, single event; it's a one-to-many, open-loop, recurring dynamic with the potential to revolutionize your world and build a *living* legacy for others—*pay it backward*.

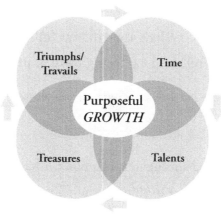

This is where the awesome power of mentorship comes in. I view mentorship through 4 different, but interrelated investments—giving back the gift of one's time, talents, treasures, and triumphs/travails to support others on their growth journey.

1. **Time** = Personal and Professional Mentoring
2. **Talents** = Interests, Skills, and Abilities
3. **Treasures** = Financial and Charitable Contributions
4. **Triumphs/Travails** = Life Experiences (both good and bad)

I have been blessed to have many people profoundly influence my life by investing in me along my growth journey. I know you also likely have a few or maybe several people who have helped you along your journey. And my guess is you have done likewise for others, so I have 4 important questions for *you*:

1. Who has invested in you?
2. Have you told them what they meant to you?
3. Whose lives have you invested in?
4. Are you inspired to add to that list?

The good news: You *still* have time to bear (much) fruit and scatter your seeds to help others along their growth journey!

"It's never too late to be who you might have been."

— George Eliot

As you have noticed throughout this book, I have purposely posed many questions for you to think about. But I feel like all have led up to what Dr. Gregory C. Ellison II cites in his book *Fear+Less Dialogues* as the 5 Hardest Questions you will face in life:

1. Who Am I?
2. Why Am I Here?
3. What Is My Gift?
4. How Does It Feel to Be a Problem?
5. What Must I Do to Die a Good Death?

Dr. Ellison summarizes his perspective, "Both individually and collectively these hard questions constantly cycle through the depths of my soul. They call me and Fearless Dialogues to reckon with identity, purpose, vocation, resilience, and legacy."

"I am what survives me."

— Erik Erikson

Depending on where you live, you may or may not be familiar with the mangrove tree. Mangroves are found in coastal regions and help protect the coastline from erosion. When the tide is in, these trees look like many other trees. However, when the tide goes out, the unique network of roots that connect the trees to each other is visible.

The trees also provide safe harbor for marine life, which live in and among the labyrinth of roots under the waterline that predators cannot penetrate. Mangroves demonstrate how, biologically, we are all interconnected as human organisms. As such, we can come together to enrich not only ourselves and those we love, but we can use our gifts to help support others in need.

In addition to perpetuating a virtuous cycle of reciprocity by generously donating a portion of your time, talents, treasures, and triumphs/travails to support others' growth journeys, you can scatter your seeds in other ways and build a living legacy of growth opportunities.

What seeds have you sewn? What fruit have you bore? What additional seeds have you scattered from your fruit to help leave a living legacy of growth in others?

If you want to change the world, plant a tree!

As reported by Seth Borenstein of the Associated Press, a study conducted by Swiss scientists suggested the most effective way to fight global warming is to plant lots and lots of trees. We need a trillion—maybe more.

Even with existing cities and farmland, there is enough space for new trees to cover 3.5 million square miles (roughly the size of the United States). The study calculated that over the decades, those new trees could suck up nearly 830 billion tons of heat-trapping carbon dioxide from the atmosphere. That's about as much carbon pollution as humans have spewed in the past twenty-five years.

According to Thomas Crowther, a climate change ecologist at the Swiss Federal Institute of Technology in Zurich, "This is by far—by thousands of times—the cheapest climate change solution." And the most effective, he said, in addition to cutting emissions.

Remember, the best time to plant a tree was twenty years ago; the second-best time to plant a tree is today!

You see, we *all* have the ability to help others along their personal and professional growth journey while we are very much alive or even long after we've left this earth. And by doing so, we can fulfill our unique purpose—making the world a better place when we leave than it was when we came.

My sincere hope is that, in whatever season of life you may be, you, too, may experience revolutionary growth that will bear much fruit in your life while sowing seeds of growth inspiration to benefit everyone you touch, including those you may never meet.

What do you want your *living* legacy to be? Or better, how will you fulfill your life's work once you've fully grown into your purpose?

The choice is *yours*.

And only you can answer this question. In fact, I purposely kept this last section to a single chapter because my goal is to inspire you now to go write the chapters of your own life story.

> *"There is not one big cosmic meaning for all;*
> *there is only the meaning we each give to our life,*
> *an individual meaning, an individual plot,*
> *like an individual novel, a book for each person."*
>
> — Anais Nin

While this book may be over, our growth journey together has only just begun....

What are *you* waiting for? What am *I* waiting for? Today is the *best* day to plant our tree.

Let's get *GROWING!*

ACKNOWLEDGMENTS

It's a bit ironic that I profess the importance of starting with *Who* yet my acknowledgment of those who have served me so well is relegated to the end of this book. I assure you that does not diminish their importance to me in any way since it provides yet another example of *paying it backward*.

While I have been blessed to be touched by several caring mentors, I would like to specifically recognize the contributions of a few of the people who have helped nurture me along my purposeful growth journey in 4 important ways.

THOSE WHO HELPED ME CULTIVATE MY FIELD FOR PURPOSEFUL GROWTH

Both of my parents, **Jim and Shirley Mears**, were only children. Maybe that is why they poured so much love into their own family of four children. In different ways, both provided fertile ground in which to establish my growth and development, teaching me values that have served me well throughout my life. In addition to unconditional love and sacrificial giving for my benefit, my parents lived out their faith in the way they treated others—serving as role models for our family. I would also like to acknowledge my sister (aka "Saint" Julie) and brothers David and Terry for their love and support. At the end of the day, it always comes down to the importance of family.

Ms. Barbara Firestone was my fifth-grade teacher at McCollum Elementary School in Wichita, Kansas. In addition to being an exceptional teacher who exuded a unique passion for each of her students, Barbara served as a personal inspiration to me. She instilled in me a deep sense of confidence that a young boy from the west side of Wichita could grow up to experience the world in ways that have inspired me to help make it better. *"Oh, the Places You'll Go!"*

Bruce Swart was my AAU swimming coach with the Wichita Neptunes. He was incredibly passionate about not only the sport of swimming, but the broader concept of competition. Bruce was fascinated by the power of the human spirit—what it took to build a champion's mindset to push past pain, overcome great odds, and achieve peak performance when it mattered most. The discipline I learned under Coach Swart helped me not only become a better athlete in all sports, but they made me better in all aspects of life.

THOSE WHO HELPED ME PLANT MY SEEDS FOR PURPOSEFUL SELF

When I attended Real Life Church in Valencia, California, **Pastor Rusty George** left an indelible impression on me, not only through his faithful vision and talent for bringing his messages "to life" on Sundays, but in demonstrating the essence of humility and servant leadership every day of the week. I will always cherish the time I was fortunate to spend with him and his executive team in supporting the growth of that church, which helped deepen my own spiritual roots.

Being a father is definitely an awesome, life-changing experience. I believe it is God's way of giving us just a tiny glimpse of how much he loves us. To watch my daughters—**McKenna and Brianna**—grow from sweet little girls to strong young women has been an incredible blessing.

Dr. Tim Bengtson was my professor in the William Allen White School of Journalism and Mass Communications at the University of Kansas. I simply would not be where I am today without his teaching, caring, and mentoring. Tim saw something in me that I didn't see in myself, which steered me toward my career path.

Professor Don Schultz, PhD was the head of my graduate program at Northwestern University. Since he was widely considered the "Father of Integrated Marketing Communication," it was truly an honor and a privilege to learn Don's principles of IMC at the feet of the master himself.

THOSE WHO HELPED ME GROW 4-WARD FOR PURPOSEFUL WORK

I was fortunate to have **David Hall** as my supervisor at Bozell in my first ad agency job straight out of grad school. David taught me how to be a leader—exhibiting high integrity, a strong work ethic, strategic thought leadership, and deft interpersonal skills in working with both our internal agency teams and external client partners. David also had a very good sense of humor and kept a calm, cool demeanor even in times of stress, which made a very positive imprint on my life at the very beginning of my career that I have never forgotten.

When I worked for **David Novak** at Pizza Hut, I saw him as a charismatic leader, fierce competitor, and master motivator. He believed in the importance of investing time to coach and engage with others to perform at their highest levels. Even after he became co-founder and CEO of YUM! Brands, David took time out of his busy schedule to personally teach seminars on the importance of leadership, personal growth and development, and teamwork—all within a culture founded upon authentic recognition and reward.

David Overton, the founder, chairman, and chief executive officer of The Cheesecake Factory, is a legend within the restaurant industry for many reasons. During my time working for David, what comes to mind for me are his combination of vision, excellence, hospitality, and hard work. He carried around a stack of yellow legal pads with ideas to help make every single facet of the business better. And he was a master at holding everyone accountable for raising the bar of excellence higher (and higher)—starting with himself.

I worked for **Kelly Roddy** on two different occasions, and both times I saw first-hand what leadership looked like in purposeful action. Kelly created a nurturing environment where diversity of both thought and style were valued within an empowering, team-centric culture. Most importantly, Kelly allowed me to be myself, recognizing both my strengths and growth opportunities while carefully pruning me back when necessary.

THOSE WHO HELPED ME SCATTER MY SEEDS FOR PURPOSEFUL LIFE

In putting this book together to package my own leadership and legacy-building lessons in a unique way, I had the good fortune to work with two distinguished professors at the University of Kansas.

Dr. Joy Ward, an internationally recognized leader in evolutionary biology studying the impact of the environment on plants and ecosystems, and her colleague, **Professor Mark Mort**. Both were enthusiastically supportive of my thesis, and their vast knowledge of this topic helped bring my concepts to life with added credibility.

In addition, I met with **Dennis Patton**, a horticulture agent at the Kansas State University Research and Extension and weekly columnist for *The Kansas City Star*. I found the lawn and garden information he shared with me and his readers to be both insightful and relevant as well.

Christine Gail and her team at *Unleash Your Rising* helped me navigate the book-writing process as well as break through my own FUDD in getting this book across the "finish" line. The love and support I received from the entire *Unleash Your Rising* author community will never be forgotten.

Tyler Tichelaar and **Larry Alexander** at Superior Book Productions helped shape and mold my content into a result far superior than the original manuscript I gave them to work with.

Shiloh Schroeder at Fusion Creative Works provided insights and a creative spark that helped me communicate the essence of my 4 LEAF *GROWTH* concept from the dynamic book cover design throughout the internal layout.

My publisher, **Susan Friedmann** at AVIVA Publishing who helped me navigate the complex world of book publishing, distribution and promotion.

Finally, I want to thank everyone who took time out to meet me for coffee or lunch while patiently listening to my concept at multiple points along my author journey. More than just a sounding board, you served as my **"Garden Club"**—providing growth-affirming advice, counsel, feedback, and support that both inspired and encouraged me when I needed it most.

Stacy Mears, Jerry Carstensen, Nowell Upham, Tom Millweard, Tom Cole, Susan Lintonsmith, Colonel Tom Magness, Lee Stuart, Tim Shanahan, Dr. Matt Tidwell, Jean Boland, John Geyerman, Adam Terranova, Tim Manners, Mark Boyer, Janna Markle, Teri Jordan, David Patrick, Brian Bacica, Jacqui Mueller, David Johnston, Ken Calwell, Sandy Calwell, Reed Wells, Brad Wells, Elizabeth Allen, Gerry Chiaro, Jan Talamo, Kate Talamo, Linda Adams, Stephanie Haubach, Greg Rieke, Mike Willich, Michael Iammorino, Ron Hill, Melissa Doolin-Koehne, Jenifer Kern, Susan Cantrell, John Holt, Joel Goldberg, Harry Campbell, Scott Havens, DeLinda Forsythe, Brandon Hatton, Dr. Kim Townsend, Megan Galloway, Kit Chadick, Kelly Crane, Jennifer Love, Jeff Slutsky, Steve Rottinghaus, Josh Cole, Herbert Billinger, Jr., Bill McClave, Lynn Zimmerman, Beth Clauss, Joseph Heilner, and Arjun Sen.

According to my count, there are approximately 92,782 words found within the text of this book; however, if you will indulge me, I wish to add two final words in heartfelt tribute to all who have helped me along my purposeful growth journey…*"Thank You!"*

ABOUT THE AUTHOR

Mark Mears is a keynote speaker, consultant, and visionary business leader. He has a significant track record of building shareholder value by driving innovation and profitable growth among world-class, high-profile brands such as PepsiCo/Pizza Hut, McDonald's, Frito-Lay, JCPenney, NBC/Universal, and The Cheesecake Factory.

Today, Mark serves as Chief Growth Officer for LEAF Growth Ventures, LLC—a consulting firm he founded that helps individuals, teams, and organizations find purpose in fulfilling their true growth potential while making a positive, lasting difference in the world.

GROW WITH MARK A. MEARS
INSPIRING * EDUCATING * ENGAGING * ENTERTAINING

Are you ready to join The Purposeful Growth Revolution? Would you like to find a deeper sense of purpose and fulfillment in your life and work? Do you want to carry this message to a wider audience and create even more positive impact in the world?

Take the free Purposeful Growth Self-Assessment at www.MarkAMears.com

Whether you are seeking individual coaching and guidance, or are part of a team or organization that can benefit from Mark's revolutionary 4 LEAF Growth principles, Mark is available to help you fulfill your true growth potential.

As a gifted visionary and purposeful author, speaker, consultant, teacher, and mentor with over twenty years as a C-level executive, Mark Mears draws upon his wealth of experiences in helping to build Fortune 500 companies as well as mid-sized growth brands, global marketing agencies, and service providers.

Mark can help you, your team, or your organization find purpose in fulfilling your true growth potential in 4 ways:

- **Reading:** Do you want to share *The Purposeful Growth Revolution* with your team? You can order multiple copies for your entire organization at a discount.

- **Speaking:** Do you want to make any size gathering a success? Your audience will be inspired, educated, and entertained with actionable next steps to get growing.

- **Consulting:** Do you want to build a purposeful growth organization that profits all stakeholders? Mark can help you employ his revolutionary 4 LEAF Growth process across your team, customers, business partners, and the communities you serve.

- **Learning:** Do you want a deeper level of training that is flexible to fit your specific growth needs on a timeline that suits your schedule? Masterclasses for you and your team are available online.

To set up time to discuss with Mark how he may help fulfill your purposeful growth objectives, contact him at:

www.MarkAMears.com

The Purposeful Growth Revolution is on!

Are you in?

Made in the USA
Middletown, DE
07 October 2022